Building and Surveying Series
Series Editor: **Ivor H. Seeley**
Emeritus Professor, The Nottingham Trent University

List continued overleaf

List continued from previous page

Information and Technology Applications in Commercial Property
  Rosemary Feenan and Tim Dixon (*editors*)
Introduction to Building Services, second edition
  Christopher A. Howard and Eric C. Curd
Introduction to Valuation, third edition David Richmond
Marketing and Property People Owen Bevan
Measurement of Building Services G. P. Murray
Principles of Property Investment and Pricing, second edition
  W. D. Fraser
Project Management and Control D. W. J. Day
Property Development: Appraisal and Finance David Isaac
Property Finance David Isaac
Property Management: a Customer-Focused Approach Gordon
  Edington
Property Valuation Techniques David Isaac and Terry Steley
Public Works Engineering Ivor H. Seeley
Quality Assurance in Building Alan Griffith
Quantity Surveying Practice, second edition Ivor H. Seeley
Real Estate in Corporate Strategy Marion Weatherhead
Recreation Planning and Development Neil Ravenscroft
Resource Management for Construction M. R. Canter
Small Building Works Management Alan Griffith
Structural Detailing, second edition P. Newton
*Sub-Contracting under the JCT Standard Forms of Building
  Contract* Jennie Price
Urban Land Economics and Public Policy, fifth edition
  Paul Balchin, Jeffrey Kieve and Gregory Bull
Urban Renewal: Theory and Practice Chris Couch
1980 JCT Standard Form of Building Contract, second edition
  R. F. Fellows
Value Management in Construction B. Norton and W. McElligott

Building and Surveying Series
Series Standing Order
ISBN 0–333–71692–2 hardcover
ISBN 0–333–69333–7 paperback
(*outside North America only*)

You can receive future titles in this series as they are published by placing a standing order. Please contact your bookseller or, in the case of difficulty, write to us at the address below with your name and address, the title of the series and the ISBN quoted above.

Customer Services Department, Macmillan Distribution Ltd
Houndmills, Basingstoke, Hampshire RG21 6XS, England

Property Development

Appraisal and Finance

David Isaac

Professor of Real Estate Management
Head of Property and Land Management
University of Greenwich

Published by
PALGRAVE
Houndmills, Basingstoke, Hampshire RG21 6XS and
175 Fifth Avenue, New York, N. Y. 10010
Companies and representatives throughout the world

PALGRAVE is the new global academic imprint of
St. Martin's Press LLC Scholarly and Reference Division and
Palgrave Publishers Ltd (formerly Macmillan Press Ltd).

ISBN 0–333–64690–8

This book is printed on paper suitable for recycling and made from fully managed and sustained forest sources.

A catalogue record for this book is available from the British Library.

10   9   8   7   6
06   05   04   03   02   01

Copy-edited and typset by Povey-Edmondson
Tavistock and Rochdale, England

Printed and bound in Great Britain by
Antony Rowe Ltd, Chippenham, Wiltshire

For Louis

By the same author

The Valuation of Property Investments (with N. Enever)
Property Companies: Share Price and Net Asset Value (with N. Woodroffe)

Contents

Preface

This book is intended to reveal the property development process from conception (almost) to completion and to look at the process as the development passes through the various stages. It is intended to give an overview but also, more realisticly, to concentrate on the 'core' areas of the process. I have taken these core areas as financial appraisal and finance of the project but as part of the process of development I have also examined other areas, whilst recognising these may be in the domain of other professionals. The approach taken is to look at the property development process as a project manager, providing a sufficient overview for the role of project management without falling into the trap of dealing with specialist areas too lightly. That is the intention, an overview of the process comprising an introduction, a specification of the role of the project manager, details of the appraisal process, the financial appraisal, project and corporate finance, design and construction and finally the process of marketing and disposal. The core areas are contained in Chapters 4–6 for the financial appraisal and Chapters 7–10 for property development finance.

The book will be useful for both students and practitioners. For students it will provide a text at intermediate level (2nd–3rd year undergraduates) in estate management, property, surveying, planning, design and construction disciplines. Those in adjacent areas of study such as housing and economics will find this a useful introduction to the area of commercial property development. Practitioners involved with property development – and this includes a wide area of professionals, including surveyors, builders, construction managers, architects, engineers, estate managers and agents – will find this a useful overview, perhaps enlightening them as to the range of activities involved in the development process and updating them on some basic techniques in the process. Professional advisers such as bankers, financial advisers, accountants, investors, analysts and lawyers should also find this text useful as an aid to their dealings in the property development sector.

Where possible I have obtained data and statistics to place the property development process appropriately in the wider economic context of the property and construction sectors. I have aimed to reference the material as well as possible but apologise for any omissions. There are relatively few texts in the area of property compared to most other investment sectors and I have tried to reference existing ones as fully as possible to provide additional views and perspectives for the reader in a very complex and potentially risk-laden area of activity. The art of property development in the decades following the second world war was relatively sure-fire, but three property slumps later we should be more conservative and much wiser – or are we? Perhaps property development requires individuals to throw caution to the wind and strike out imaginatively in the way many entrepreneurs have successfully completed complex and enormously expensive schemes with confidence and alacrity in difficult circumstances? Anyway, that will be the content of another book!

Finally, I would like to thank those who have assisted me in writing this book, Professor Ivor Seeley, the series editor, who has provided ongoing advice for my writing and encouraged many authors in the property and construction area and Malcolm Stewart, my publisher, who is ever patient and supportive. I would also like to thank Mike Riley and Chesterton International for practical support in my researches. Many colleagues and external organisations have provided me with information and assistance and these are listed in the Acknowledgements below. I would also like to thank Terry Steley, John O'Leary and Simon Birchall of the University of Greenwich and Keith McKinnell from the University of Hong Kong for their help and observations on the book. Finally, as ever, I am reliant on the continued support of Professor David Wills, Lewis Anderson and the staff of the School of Land and Construction Management at the University of Greenwich to develop my research and studies, and I am grateful for their help.

School of Land and Construction Management   David Isaac
University of Greenwich

Acknowledgements

The author and publishers wish to thank the following for the use of copyright material:

Journal of Property Finance and *Journal of Property Valuation and Investment*; S. G. Warburg Securities; UBS; Paribas Capital Markets; Chesterton Financial; Savills Research; DTZ DebenhamThorpe Research; IPD; *Estates Gazette*; Kogan Page Limited; Butterworths.

Every effort has been made to trace all the copyright-holders, but if any have been inadvertently overlooked, the publishers will be pleased to make the necessary arrangement at the earliest opportunity.

List of Statutes, Cases and Regulations

List of Abbreviations

BCIS	Building Cost Information Service
BPF	British Property Federation
CAT	City Action Trust
CIOB	Chartered Institute of Building
DCF	Discounted cash flow
DoE	Department of the Environment
DTI	Department of Trade and Industry
EPs	English Partnerships
ERDF	European Regional Development Fund
EU	European Union
EZ	Enterprise Zone
GDO	General Development Order
GDP	Gross Domestic Product
GDV	Gross Development Value
GNP	Gross National Product
HAT	Housing Action Trust
IRR	Internal Rate of Return
JCT	Joint Contracts Tribunal
LIBOR	London Interbank Offered Rate
MAFF	Ministry of Agriculture, Fisheries and Food
MBS	Mortgage Backed Securities
MoF	Multi-option facility
NEC	New Engineering Contract
NPV	Net Present Value
PINCS	Property Income Certificates
PUTS	Property Unit Trusts
REITS	Real Estate Investment Trusts
RICS	Royal Institution of Chartered Surveyors
SAPCOS	Single Asset Property Companies
SEAQ	Stock Exchange Automated Quotation System
SMM	Standard Method of Measurement
SPOTS	Single Property Ownership Trusts
SPZ	Simplified Planning Zone
UDC	Urban Development Corporation
USM	Unlisted Stock Market
YP	Years Purchase

1 The Property Development Process

1.1 INTRODUCTION

Property development is the process by which buildings are erected for occupation or for sale/investment. Owners may build premises for their own occupation, for example major retailers may erect supermarkets; alternatively, property developers may construct the same type of buildings for lease or sale. The process may be the same although some aspects of the financial appraisal may be different. A building offered for sale or investment is driven by a profit motive, a building for owner-occupation may be related to the profitability of the enterprise within the building and thus profit motivation may be redirected or constrained.

The owner-occupier sector has tended to be overlooked in property development texts except those of a macro economic nature. The problem lies with the fact that there is a substantial investment market in the UK where properties are developed for lease and sale, and it is this activity that is the most traditional approach for property developers in the property markets. This is unlike the situation in the European markets, where development is more likely to be for the purpose of owner occupation.

Property development is much like any other economic activity, satisfying wants with the application of scarce resources. In the case of property development, the wants are for space to work in, sell from, live in and enjoy recreational activities in. The process by which buildings are erected to provide space employs the key factors of production: land for the site, capital for purchase of the land and materials, labour to erect a building and manage the process and the entrepreneurial talent of the property developer to initiate the process and bring the pieces together.

A simplified approach to property development from inception to completion would involve a number of stages. In the first case there would have to be a need for the space, either a direct demand from a potential owner-occupier or indirect demand as assessed in market conditions (demand outstripping supply and driving the price of space upwards). If a developer intends to develop a site then there would need to be a situation where the sale price or completed value exceeded the costs of development involved for the process to be initiated. This surplus profit arising from the profit in the development and also the size of the profit will need to reflect the efforts and risk of the developer as entrepreneur. If market research carried out on a proposed development shows sufficient demand exists, then the developer can produce

1

sketch plans for the proposals as these will need to be discussed with the planning authority. In the UK as in most countries, development of land is subject to restriction under the planning regulations and this is the first hurdle in the development process. Generally an informed consultant will be invaluable at this stage by knowing the type and scale of development which may be acceptable to the local authority, and the consultant may be able to negotiate the most advantageous bargaining position. In parallel with these sketch plans, an initial development appraisal is drawn up. On the basis of the scale and type of development, a value can be assessed and rough costs calculated; this will indicate a level of profit and whether it is worth continuing further.

This calculation is called a residual valuation and is covered in detail in Chapter 4. The costs of construction are usually assessed by comparison. There are databases and source-books which analyse recent building contracts in different locations for different types of buildings. A cost per square metre can thus be calculated and applied to the gross internal floor area of the building (measured between the internal faces of external walls).

Further informal discussion with the planning authority will lead to a formal application to the planning authority. This application may be for outline permission (a permission indicating the type and density of the development) and subsequently for detailed permission. Once the detail of the scheme is known, then a detailed appraisal can be carried out. The planning application would require detailed drawings and these will now be complemented by additional drawings from the architect. In a traditional approach the drawings are costed in a bill of quantities by the quantity surveyor. In the early stages of the design process, the quantity surveyor will prepare a preliminary estimate, probably using one of the methods described by Seeley (1995) (these methods include unit, floor area, cube, approximate quantities, elemental comparative or interpolation). The valuer will provide updated values and rents and funds will be raised to purchase the site (if not in ownership) and also for the costs of construction and ancillary costs.

With the finance, a building contract can be entered into and the building erected. At the same time, the valuer or agent will be advising on a marketing strategy and seeking possible purchasers or occupiers so that once the building is completed there will be a minimal period when the property is empty and not providing a return. The return will be an income if the property is let and retained as an investment or as a capital sum if the building is sold. If the building is built and occupied by the owner as developer then a notional rent can be assumed to be passing.

Development value

Development value exists where land or buildings can increase in value by the application of capital. It may be that this arises from a change of use of the land permitted by planning permission but the property development process usually implies the application of capital in the form of works to the land. The residual valuation, one of a number of techniques of property appraisal which assesses the profitability of the proposals, calculates the increased capital value of the land because of the proposals and deducts the costs of works and the original value of the land and buildings. In an economic sense, costs should include a 'normal' profit which reflects the risk and commitment of the developer; however, depending on the price paid for the land, an 'abnormal' profit may arise because of the particular circumstances.

The analysis can be summarised thus:

$$\text{Value} - \text{Cost} = \text{Profit}$$

However, the residual valuation differentiates between the cost of construction and the cost of the existing land/building: the existing use value (EUV). The value of the completed development is termed the gross development value (GDV).
Thus:

$$\text{GDV} - (\text{Building costs} + \text{EUV}) = \text{Profit}$$

If the land value is known because it has been agreed as a purchase price then this equation provides the calculation of the profit. However the general case is that the land cost is not known and thus the equation is rearranged:

$$\text{GDV} - (\text{Building costs} + \text{Profit}) = \text{EUV}$$

The EUV, being the existing value of land and buildings on the site, will thus determine whether or not a normal profit is earned. For instance, if the actual land cost negotiated is lower than the EUV determined by the above calculation, then the profit increases assuming the other costs to be static and an abnormal profit is achieved.

The need to use a residual valuation approach arises because of the uniqueness of land and property as an asset class. This is reinforced by the uniqueness, in most situations, of development proposals for each site. If equal sized plots were being sold in the same location with the same density and type of development then a form of comparative analysis could be applied, a price per hectare for instance. In these cases adjustments would need to be made in the comparison and these adjustments, depending on their scale and complexity, could easily undermine the use of comparable valuation. The residual method has been criticised by the Lands Tribunal (the highest court for dealing with property valuation and compensation issues in the UK) because of the number of variables in the calculation and the assumptions and variances underlying the calculations used as inputs to the valuation. The residual valuation needs to be used in practice in most cases because the components of the development value and the profitability of each project will differ dramatically depending on the type and scale of the development proposals. The main variables in the calculation are:

Value of the site:

depends on location, use (under planning law), topography, legal constraints, ground conditions, services and access (for example).

Value of the proposed development:

depends on demand, use, density, design, layout and infrastructure.

Cost of construction:

depends on size, shape and height, design, type of buildings, planning con-straints on buildings and landscaping, site conditions, provision of services and access.

The extent of the variation in these factors means that each site may be unique and thus the calculation for the site value is a residual based on what can be achieved as development on the site. To summarise, there are two approaches to valuing the development potential of a site:

(i)   *A comparative approach*
        This is useful if there are direct comparables of sales but this is unlikely in a complex development situation where each develop-ment, and thus the potential of each site, will be unique.
(ii)   *A residual valuation*
        Here the gross development value is assessed either by a capital comparison approach or by the investment method (the capital-isation of an estimated future income flow using an appropriate multiplier). The net value from the site is calculated by deducting the costs of building and a profit figure from the gross development value, this is thus a residual.

To clarify the valuation approach, it is important to distinguish between property appraisal, property valuation and property analysis. Recent debates have combined with criticism of traditional approaches of property valuation over the last 20 years or so to demand that, in what has previously been termed property valuation, more extensive property analysis be provided. Generally the approach that should be taken (Baum and Crosby 1988) is that the overall property appraisal should be clearly divided between property valuation for purchase (valuation for market price) and the subsequent analysis of performance. In the first case, this is defined as *valuation* and in the second case it is defined as *analysis*; the overall process is termed *property appraisal*. Thus the valuation of a property (the calculation of the exchange value of property) is different from the subsequent analysis of the performance of the property as an investment (the appraisal of its actual worth). Calculations before and after purchase will not agree because of the lack of perfect knowledge in the market at the time of the transaction and the inability to predict future changes in the cash flow and the risk profile of the investment accurately. Thus the techniques discussed later on in this book can be used to anticipate the market value or else to record and analyse the progress of the investment subsequent to purchase. It is critical to understand the difference between these two approaches in the property appraisal process.

Having considered the above, the traditional methods used in valuation are traditionally called the 'five methods;' these are:

- the investment method;
- the comparative method;
- the contractor's test (a cost-based method)
- the profits method; and
- the residual valuation.

The residual valuation, as we have already seen, is used in development situations but, in fact, the residual valuation may rely heavily on the other methods. It may use the investment method to determine the gross development value of the proposed development. It may use the comparative method to compare capital values or site values calculated with examples from the market. The costs calculated for building works are a form of the contractor's test approach. Depending on the type of property, the profits method may also be used to determine the gross development value.

A final point to be made about the valuation of the site is that the value of land is determined by its use and intensity of use. Land may have development potential but it will require planning permission for any form of development except for some minor works and some changes of use. The Town and Country Planning Acts determine this process of granting permission to develop. The Town and Country Planning Act 1990 defines development as:

the carrying out of building and other operations on, under or over land.

Investment in property

Property plays an important part in investment and commerce both as an investment in its own right and as a security for various forms of lending. For the individual investor, shares in a quoted property company are usually the most attractive way of investing in commercial property. The traditional property investment company has a number of characteristics which differentiate it from firms in the manufacturing or service sectors. Usually, it shows a relatively low current yield and the shares are bought mainly for long-term capital and income growth. The property company may finance itself to a greater extent on borrowed money than most manufacturing concerns and it is likely to pay out a higher proportion of its earnings by way of dividend (O'Shea 1986).

Though the property companies' shares will be valued partly according to their yield, the asset backing is also important; thus it is not just profitability but the asset base on which the profits are generated (from rents or disposals) which is important. If the liabilities of the company are deducted from the value of the properties and any other assets it owns, the resultant sum is what belongs to the shareholders. This sum, divided by the number of shares, gives a figure for the net asset value per share. The market value of the shares will normally stand somewhat below this figure, and this is referred to as a discount to net asset value. Shares in a property company are described as giving a yield of so much per cent and standing at a discount of, say, 30 per cent to net assets. This does not mean that the company necessarily has any intention of selling its properties, or that the shareholders would necessarily receive as much as the net asset value for the shares if it did, as capital gains tax on disposal of the properties might have to be paid. Rather, this approach is more of a yardstick for comparing the assets of one company with another and can also serve as indicator of income growth in the future (which is presumed to be based on the income-generating ability of the assets). The relationship between share price and net asset value can fluctuate within wide limits and in the analysis it is important to distinguish between property investment and trading companies. Property investment companies get their income from rents, trading companies get their income from sale of completed developments. The idea of a *development* company on the other hand is not a useful concept as it does not help in distinguishing the two principal objectives of the company to develop either for investment or for trade. The major developers, in terms of the scale of development activity, will tend to be the investment companies rather than the trading companies, in terms of the scale of development activity, although development activity may be carried out in a separate subsidiary.

The majority of quoted property companies invest mainly in commercial and industrial property, in other words, in office buildings, shops, warehouses and factories. Residential property has become increasingly unpopular as an income yielding investment because of rent controls and other restrictions imposed by successive governments. Most property companies will have a fair mix of different types of commercial property though some will tend to specialise in one type: shops as the name implies in the case of Capital Shopping, or factory and warehouse buildings in the case of Slough Estates. Companies may also specialise by geographical area. The biggest of them all, Land Securities Investment Trust, has a spread of different types of top quality commercial and industrial property throughout the UK, but is probably best known for its portfolio of office properties in Central London. (O'Shea 1986)

Some companies hold a fair proportion of their properties overseas particularly in Continental Europe with some investment in North America. Often, however, these overseas ventures have met with disappointing returns and the US market is a particularly specialist and difficult area to operate in. Property companies differ, not only by geographical location and by the type of property they own. The nature of the operation they undertake will also differ. The commercial property investment company, to which we have referred earlier on, does much of what its name suggests: it owns properties and sees its income and the value of its assets rise as inflation and shortages of space force rent upwards in a good market. Many reaped, during the 1980s, the rewards from properties constructed 20 years before. If the income of the property company comes entirely from rents from well-located companies, this income is of very high quality. Up to the end of the 1980s, the rental income could be predicted to a degree but since then rental values have fallen, the incidence of over-renting is now very apparent and it is far more difficult to assess the expectations of rental income at the next rent review. The forecasting of the cash flow stream to the investment has thus become very difficult.

The parties in the development process

The six main parties involved in the development process are:

The professional advisers

The architect, quantity surveyor, valuer, planning consultant and possibly consulting engineer, construction manager and project manager.

The clients

The developer and the landowner, who could be an occupier or an investor/ trader in development property. The client could be a private or public sector client. The client could be the owner of extensive estates such as a statutory undertaker or the heir to historic landed estates, it could be a major investor like a financial institution such as a pension fund or insurance company.

The planning authority

The planning authority would deal with planning and highway matters and may have policies to encourage development for employment purposes, for instance.

The contractor

The contractor is employed on the construction of the building and may in turn employ subcontractors. The nature of the building contract or method of building procurement, as it is now more commonly termed, will determine the relationship of the contractor with the client.

The community

Local residents may have views on the proposed development in addition to the planning authority as may pressure groups or specific interest groups affected by the development proposals.

The funders

These are the providers of short-term funds for the development and the providers of long-term funds in the event of a buyout or partnership arrangement at the end of the development. The development may be initially funded by the client who may also be an owner-occupier or financial institution.

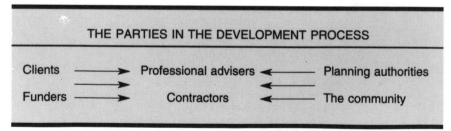

Box 1.1   *The parties in the development process*

1.2   THE ECONOMIC CONTEXT OF PROPERTY DEVELOPMENT

Introduction

The activity of property development in a macroeconomic sense can be considered to assist in:

(i)   regenerating the local economy;
(ii) using assets available in the production process more efficiently to obtain greater economic growth;
(iii) achieving profitability, from an investor/developer point of view.

Government policies in the post-war UK, creating the environment for property development, are examined in box 1.2. There is a need to see the development process in the context of an economic and financial framework. The basic role of property development from a macro-economic point of view is the need to revitalise the economy, to use assets which are available in the production process to obtain greater economic growth.

The role of property development in the economy

1 To revitalise the economy by encouraging investment
2 To use the assets available in the production process to obtain greater
   · economic growth and added value

The need for efficient property relates to government policy

The post-war policy of demand management led to:

- Adjustments in government spending and taxation
- Deflation and reflation of the economy
- Problems of inflation

To solve inflation:

- Economists looked at the supply side of the economy
- Saw the need to encourage efficiency and competitiveness in world markets
- Hence saw the need for efficient space, and
- Hence the need for effective property development.

Box 1.2   *Property development in the economy: role and need*

Government policies until the 1970s relied on a Keynesian approach to 'demand management' which made adjustments of government spending and the amount collected in taxes to deflate or reflate the economy. Some economists rejected this simple approach and suggested that the subsequent rise in unemployment could not be countered by reflation and that this would lead only to inflation in the economy. Reflation has two main effects, the increased consumption causes prices to rise and imports to increase and thus leads to subsequent wage demands and an adverse position on the balance of payments. Limitations on the use of reflationary strategies have encouraged economists to look at the 'supply side' of macroeconomics rather

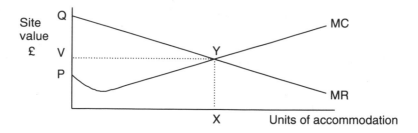

Figure 1.1   *The optimal size of a building*

MC = the additional costs of each extra unit of accommodation. Initially this falls (i.e. in building a second storey) but then it increases (extra lifts, more expensive foundations and the need for a structural frame, project period lengthens).
PQY = the profit the developer will make from the site (the difference between the total revenue and cost) (Fraser 1993, p. 234).

Cyclical trends in development activity

Changes in the level of private sector development activity are caused by changes in the availability of viable development opportunities and the expected profitability and risk of development. Thus the opportunity and the motive for development need to be apparent.

Rental values of commercial property vary according to changes in economic activity. In a reflationary phase of the economic cycle, rental and capital values will tend to rise with occupational demand, whilst supply will be relatively low and construction and finance costs relatively stable. As values rise so there are more opportunities for development, and competition between developers falls. Thus profit should rise at the same time that risk is falling (i.e. risk of rent voids). The opposite will happen in a deflationary period.

The property companies

Property companies have had a significant influence on the property market for most of the post-war period. The development 'boom' of the late 1940s and early 1950s, based on rental growth, low building costs relative to value and low interest rates enabled property companies to increase their own internal funds. Thus the original growth in property companies was financed almost entirely by borrowed monies. A ready source of funding was to be found through insurance companies and pension funds as the financial institutions began increasingly to dominate the savings market. Initially, the funds provided fixed interest finance through mortgages and debentures. Subsequently, as the funds recognised the benefits of participation in the rental growth of property, they began to engage in sale and leaseback arrangements, partnerships and direct development. These developments meant that by the late 1970s the financial institutions came to be the dominant influence on the commercial property markets through their financial control. The tax status of the funds gave them a considerable advantage in direct development over the property companies.

In recent years there has been a decline in institutional interest in property investment and in direct development as the returns from other investments such as equities have risen and the rate of inflation has abated. This has led to increased opportunities for property companies to become more innovative in raising funds and attention being focused on corporate funding as a key source of property finance. Fixed interest securities and discounted bond issues are recent examples of these developments. The problem of raising finance on the Stock Market is that the property valuation of the assets is discounted by the market. The share prices of property investment companies tend to stand at an average discount of approximately 20 per cent to the net asset values of the companies when examined over the longer period.

The share price discount to net asset value dissuades property companies from raising money in the form of equity, and thus encourages them to borrow money and increase their gearing. This is because if the company buys £100 of assets in the market at that property valuation, the Stock Market will only finance them to the value of, say, £80. High gearing, which means a high percentage of borrowed funds in relation to equity capital, is advantageous during periods of rapid rental growth as rental profits can outstrip interest payments to shareholders. However, high debt payments encourage the chances of insolvency during periods of declining profitability. Thus high gearing encourages investors to regard property companies as more risky investments.

Property development for owner-occupiers

Fothergill *et al.* (1987) offer insights into the wider economic context of property development. Fothergill's book *Property and Industrial Development* provides a different approach to the one taken in this book, concentrating on the economic aspects of location and use of buildings. The main argument of Fothergill *et al*'s book is that property is an important asset in the national economy. It maintains that if there is to be growth of the economy and further industrialisation, then premises or space must be available to cater for this expansion. The book sets out to examine the roles of industrial property in revitalising the economy. In terms of the significance of property, however, Fothergill *et al.* maintain that the most important contributor to economic growth is demand management, that is reflation or deflation in the UK and world economies. The authors consider the lack of skills and training of manpower, combined with the reluctance of financial institutions, to provide long-term industrial finance, are important aspects affecting the supply of property. Fothergill *et al.* state that there is considerable ignorance about the role that land and property play in the overall process and how these elements affect location of a firm's activities. It postulates the question: 'does manufacturing activity get buildings in locations where it needs them?' The approach of the book is accepted as being different from that of the approach of general practice surveyors, property developers and financial analysts, the latter grouping of professionals being more concerned with new-build speculative or investment space rather than the total stock of property.

> for purely commercial reasons, the property world needs to know about yields and rates of return . . . our concern is with the industrial buildings as an input to production and a tool of economic development. (Fothergill *et al.* 1987, p. 10)

The trouble is that commercial reasons are often those which underpin the . problems of providing space, and factors relating to return and investment need to be considered to adequately develop an effective strategy for space provision.

Property represents a substantial financial involvement in terms of assets held by commercial firms but there are significant problems of obsolescence in buildings, the existence of a stock of large, old buildings, often multi-storey which are available for sale rather than for rent and have been made available by closure or relocation of businesses. These premises may never find an occupier and thus the only alternative would be to demolish, subdivide or convert them. There exist problems of mismatch where premises, once suitable for occupants, become inappropriate. The problems of mismatch relate to the quantity of space and to problems of design and layout which constrain output and efficiency respectively. Property and locational decision-making are critical to the firm, the supply of land and buildings exerts an important influence on location, but the influence operates not so much through the price mechanism as through physical constraints and availability. There is a role for the public sector in the provision of industrial space, because although private developers would move in once the price is right, this could involve substantial problems in delays. The prejudices of private financial institutic against certain investments and the fact that private enterprise is not always quick to identify gaps in the property market exacerbates the problem.

Fothergill *et al.* suggest that an appropriate strategy for the supply of industrial property space to facilitate the reindustrialisation of the economy requires that:

- no firm should find expansion delayed through lack of space;
- efficiency should be improved by promoting transfers between premises;
- the industrial property market should promote a more equitable distribution of job opportunities.

Fothergill *et al.* calculated that to achieve a growth rate in output of 3.5 per cent per annum, new space is required nationally at a rate of 12.5 million square metres per annum compared to 5 million square metres per annum built between 1974 and 1985 in England and Wales, and that market forces alone are unlikely to be to cope with this level of supply.

1.3 DEVELOPMENT ACTIVITY

Over the last decade there has been a government relaxation in the area of property development reflecting the general laissez-faire attitude in the economy. Funding of projects has been restricted, institutional funding has reduced and has been superseded by international funds, from Europe and the Far East especially, but recently these funds have also dried up.

Changes in the nature of property development because of the scale of building already carried out, because of demands for conservation of areas and single buildings and because of existing constraints of infrastructure and neighbouring buildings have led to a change in emphasis from new-build to rehabilitation. Local authority and government funded intervention has encouraged some urban regeneration and the overhauling of obsolete infrastructure. Local authority partnerships of the most imaginative kind have been developed, although by the early 1990s financial restrictions had limited activity.

Slowdown in the growth of the economy has limited the need for planning intervention at a high level, although problems with national infrastructure and NIMBYism (the tendency to protest at developments which have an effect on the protestors' locality, usually of residence, rather than relating to an ideal or political/social view point, hence the term: *Not In My Back Yard*) has affected strategic planing. New planning legislation puts more reliance on local plans and there has been a call for the reestablishment of a strategic authority for London, following the closure of the Greater London Council.

Trends in the property market include attempts to obtain relaxation of green belt policies to encourage new residential settlements and the private provision of social infrastructure. In the commercial sectors of the property market all sectors are now depressed with industrial looking the most promising in terms of possible expansion. Lack of retail sales and a glut of office space have hit these sectors. Retail warehouses are also less in demand. The provision of large banking floors in the City following deregularisation of the Stock Exchange (Big Bang) has led to a significant over-supply and demand is for smaller cellular office space for professional firms. B1 class property (arising from a change in the Use Classes Order and reflecting a mixed office/industrial use) has led to high-tech industrial development on new estates and again to an over-supply of this type of property.

The development process: a summary

Cadman and Austin-Crowe in an earlier edition of *Property Development* (1978, p. 3) suggested that there were four key phases in the development process: evaluation; preparation; implementation and disposal. The most important phase was evaluation. They state:

> Evaluation encompasses both the analysis of the marketplace in general and in particular – market research – and the financial assessment of the project. It should be carried out before any commitment is undertaken and while the developer retains flexibility. . . Evaluation involves the combined advice of the development team but in the end the responsibility for interpreting that advice rests with the developer who has to decide whether or not to bear the risk of the project.

The development process is looked at in some detail in Chapter 2. This process can be introduced here as a summary of the 12 main stages:

- choosing a location
- identifying a site and carrying out a detailed site survey
- providing an outline scheme and appraisal
- negotiating for site acquisition
- design
- planning consent
- finance
- site acquisition
- detailed plans
- tender documents for construction
- construction
- occupation or marketing and management.

One of the major problems facing property development is the supply of land and building in appropriate locations for development. By providing urban land, rather than looking for greenfield sites with the associated environmental consequences, problems of development would be lessened. There is, however, a shortage of available urban land, Balchin and Bull (1987, p. 193) identify four causes of urban land shortage. These causes are:

(i)   The slowness of planning procedures; the development process is hamstrung by delays at the planning application stage; however, these may be necessary if the local community is to be given adequate time for consultation.

(ii)   In recent decades the government has attempted to contain urban growth by metropolitan and provincial green belts. At the same time, outer suburban local authorities have been reluctant to release land to accommodate the housing and employment needs of the inner city population.

(iii) During the boom periods, commercial development has squeezed out housing development from central and inner urban areas and at these times housing development has been unable to compete for sites.

(iv) A large amount of urban land has been withheld from the market and much is in a derelict state.

Property development

In practice, many property investment companies started out as property development companies in the higher risk, higher reward side of the property business; some still undertake developments as well as their investment activities. In the development boom of the 1950s and early 1960s the approach was to raise long-term finance in the form of a mortgage of two thirds of the value of a completed development at a fixed interest rate from the insurance companies who were far less conscious in those days of the effects of inflation. Provided the development was valued at 50 per cent or more above the costs of acquisition and development, then the whole outlay could be recouped and the profit surplus and any subsequent rise in the capital value of the building was added to the wealth of the developer. Many property companies still have cheap borrowings dating back to those days. Nowadays, rates for fixed interest money are too high; inflation conscious insurance companies want a share in any growth from the building and current developments are more likely to be financed by some form of partnership arrangement between the property company and financial institution.

Some property companies develop buildings to sell at a capital profit on completion rather than to retain them for their rents, and still others make a trade of buying and selling properties without undertaking development. Profit from these sources is not as stable or as certain as income from rents and thus may be a less valuable contribution to the company's cash flow, although a useful addition. Thus the analysis of property companies should be undertaken with a view to where the income comes from and of what quality it is. Investment in the property sector requires expert advice: it is a specialist sector of the market in which very few firms of stockbrokers, for instance, have particular expertise. Bricks and mortar are a sound investment but not in any condition at any price. The virtue of commercial properties, in the past, was that financial institutions invested directly in them on a large scale and there were thus ready buyers for a property company's assets, but this has become less likely and will not be so in the future. The market in property has had a number of ups and downs, the market in investment properties almost dried up in the financial crash of 1974–5 and values slumped dramatically. Property companies which had undertaken too many developments on the back of borrowed short-term money found themselves unable to borrow more to pay the interest and unable to sell the properties to pay the debt. A number went bust, others had to cut their development programmes. In the early 1980s most property shares were relatively indifferent investments and comparatively few new developments took place. There was a revival in the mid-1980s when there was evidence of shortages. During this period, companies with good existing properties and good developments did well in a period before inflation began to decrease. By the end of the 1980s property development companies were viewed in a much poorer light by investors and, although there was a resurgence at the beginning of the 1990s, there is still generally a sceptical view of property investment in property company shares.

Property development is part of the property market which includes a user market, an investment market and a development market. A simple model of the overall property market is suggested by Keogh (1994) and shown in Figure 1.2.

1.4   THE UK CONSTRUCTION INDUSTRY

The UK construction industry is inextricably linked to the property development process. As well as controlling the construction phase of development, construction firms may act as property developers in their own right and also project managers and financiers of property development projects. There are a number of specialist texts on the construction industry in the UK, and this section will provide a brief overview.

The construction industry is characterised by the nature of the product, the structure of the industry and the organisation of the construction process, the determinants of demand and the method of price determination; these aspects set the construction industry apart from other sectors. The nature of demand in the construction industry is for investment goods for which the ultimate use is as:

(i)   a means to further production, e.g. factory building;
(ii)   an addition or an improvement to the infrastructure of the economy, e.g. roads:
(iii)   a social investment, e.g. hospitals;
(iv)   an investment good for direct enjoyment, e.g. housing (Hillebrandt 1985, pp. 7–8).

The demand is influenced directly by central or local government, and even where there is no direct influence the public sector will have indirect influence. The extent of government influence and the investment nature of the demand mentioned earlier means that demand fluctuates in the sector,

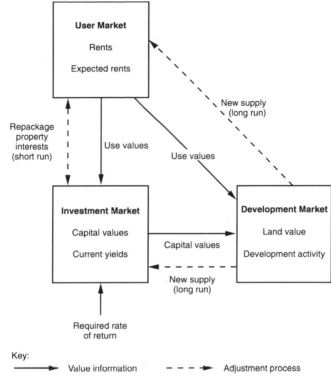

Figure 1.2   *A simple model of the property market*
Source: Keogh (1994), p. 59.

driven by the state of the economy and the government's socio economic policies. Fluctuations are marked and rapid, a situation shared with the corresponding construction sectors in most West European countries. Large variations in output lead to fluctuations in turnover and, because profit margins tend to be low in the sector, the profitability of firms is unstable (Briscoe 1988, p.10). Company insolvency statistics show a rise in insolvency in the construction industry from 15.8 per cent of total insolvencies in 1981 to 23.4 per cent in 1993 (Wright 1994, p. 249). The importance of construction in the economy is related to the size of the sector, the fact that the sector is producing mainly investment goods and finally the fact that the government is the client for a large part of the output (Hillebrandt, 1985 pp. 8, 10), although this role of government has steadily reduced since 1985.

Variations in the gross national product of the UK will influence the demand for construction work and thus the associated level of employment. The output from the construction sector is a response to a demand for buildings, which in turn is a derived demand for other products and services. The construction industry will, however, determine the demand in other areas, for instance the building materials sector (Briscoe 1988, p. 6).

Figures 1.3–1.5 give some indication of the value of construction output in the UK. Figure 1.3 shows the value of non-housing work, excluding infrastructure over the period 1980–93 at 1990 prices, it can be seen that private commercial work peaked in 1990 and has rapidly decreased since then. Figure 1.4 provides a comparison of the types of new work in 1980 and 1993, again measured at 1990 prices. The two areas of particular growth are infrastructure and private commercial work. Figure 1.5 shows how new work is shared between the various sectors as at 1993 at current prices. The statistics generally appear to show, in the wider economic context, a decline in the importance of the construction sector. Briscoe mentions that, measured in terms of gross output, where the value of the material used is also included, construction in 1974 accounted for 18.3 per cent of all industrial output but by 1984 this had fallen to only 12.6 per cent (Briscoe 1988, p. 3).

The construction sector in the UK economic system

In any economy, construction is a key activity; it has effect on the goods and services available in the economy by providing the space in which the extractive, manufacturing and service industries are active. The flow of goods and services in the economy is thus directly driven by the construction process, and determines the size of the Gross national product (GNP). The contribution of the construction industry to the economy is thus vital. It is clear from the statistics that the construction industry remains an important sector in the UK economy despite a decline in recent years (Briscoe 1988).

Construction output derives from a number of distinct types of work. The recent decline in new work of the public sector is manifest in the downward trend in new housing and other work in this sector, which incorporates civil engineering and the construction of public buildings. Since the early 1970s, decline has also occurred in two categories of new private sector work: new housing and industrial and commercial new work. Generally, the reduction in new work in the private sector has been less pronounced than that experienced in the public sector. The reduced activity levels in new output were mirrored in repair and maintenance output in the early 1990s.

It is not only in terms of output that construction makes a significant impact on the UK economy, for the industry also exerts associated influence on national employment. Throughout the 1970s the construction sector was responsible for about 6.8 per cent of the jobs in the economy. Since 1980 this proportion has fallen but construction remains a major provider of employment opportunities. In particular, by the mid-1980s almost one fifth of all self-employed workers were active in the construction industry (Briscoe 1988). By the early 1990s this proportion had been reduced significantly by a spate of insolvencies.

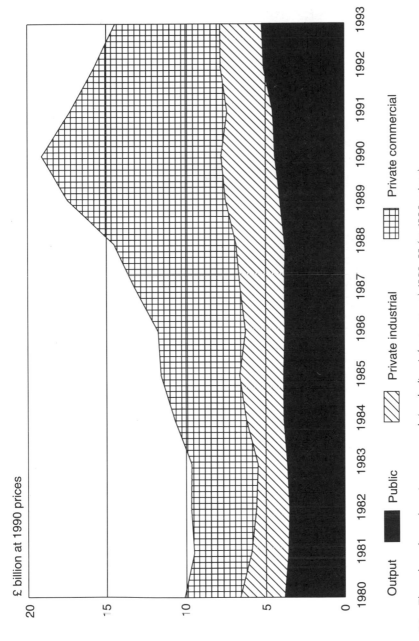

Figure 1.3 *The value of non-housing new work (excluding infrastructure) 1980–93 (at 1990 prices)*
Source: DoE (1994a), p. 19.

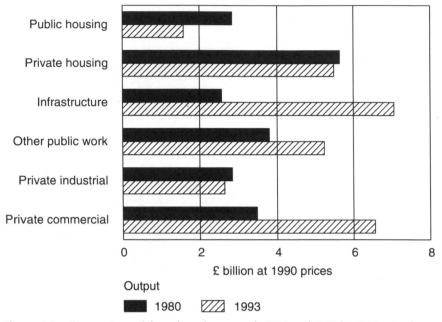

Figure 1.4   *Comparison of the value of new work, 1980 and 1993 (at 1990 prices)*
Source: DoE (1994a), p. 19.

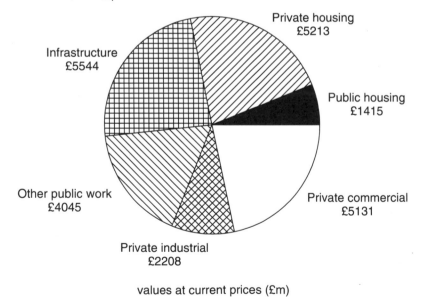

values at current prices (£m)

Figure 1.5   *The value of output of new work , 1993 (at current prices)*
Source: DoE (1994b), p. 3.

The construction sector is greatly dependent on changes in the UK economy, in particular on those which are the direct result of government policy. Construction output is a response to the demand for buildings and this is a derived demand for other products and services. Variations in the gross national product will in this way influence the demand for construction work and the associated level of employment. However, the construction sector itself will determine the demand for products from other parts of the economy, especially the material supplies sector.

REFERENCES

Balchin, P. and Bull, G. (1987) *Regional and Urban Economics*, Harper & Row, London.

Baum, A. and Crosby, N. (1988) *Property Investment Appraisal*, Routledge, London.

Briscoe, G. (1988) *The Economics of the Construction Industry*, Mitchell, London.

Cadman, D. and Austin-Crowe, L. (1978) *Property Development*, E. & F. N. Spon, London.

Cadman, D. and Austin-Crowe, L. (1991) *Property Development*, E. & F. N. Spon, London.

Central Statistical Office (1994) *Economic Trends*, HMSO, London.

Central Statistical Office (1995) *UK Economic Accounts*, no. 8, HMSO, London, January.

Department of the Environment (DoE) (1994a) *Housing and Construction Statistics 1982 1993 (Great Britain)*, HMSO, London.

Department of the Environment (DoE) (1994b) *Housing and Construction Statistics (Great Britain)*, June quarter 1994, part 2, HMSO, London.

Fothergill, S., Monk, S. and Perry, M. (1987) *Property and Industrial Development*, Hutchinson, London.

Fraser, W. D. (1993) *Principles of Property Investment and Pricing*, 2nd edition, Macmillan Press, London.

Guy, G. (1994), *The Retail Development Process: Location, Property and Planning*, Routledge, London.

Harvey, R. C. and Ashworth, A. (1993) *The Construction Industry of Great Britain*, Newnes, Oxford.

Hillebrandt, P. M. (1985) *Economic Theory and the Construction Industry*, Macmillan Press, London.

Hillebrandt, P. M. and Cannon, J. (1990) *The Modern Construction Firm*, Macmillan Press, London.

Isaac, D. (1988) 'Property and Industrial Development', a review of *Property and Industrial Development* by S. Fothergill, S. Monk and M. Perry, *Journal of Local Economy*, vol. 3, no. 1, pp. 56–8.

Keogh, G. (1994) 'Use and Investment Markets in UK Real Estate', *Journal of Property Valuation and Investment*, vol. 12, no. 4.

O'Shea, D. (1986) *Investment for Beginners*, *Financial Times* Business Information, London.

Raftery, J. (1991) *Principles of Building Economics*, BSP Professional Books, Oxford.

Seeley, I. H. (1995) *Building Economics*, 4th edition, Macmillan Press, London.

Wright, K. (1994) 'Company profitability and finance', *Bank of England: Quarterly Bulletin*, vol. 34, no. 3, August.

2 Project Managing the Property Development Process

2.1 TOTAL PROJECT MANAGEMENT

> The history of large projects is often referred back as far as the construction of the Egyptian pyramids or the Great Wall of China. They were certainly large and complex structures, built to high standards, which must have liquidated vast amounts of resources. Unfortunately, there is no documentary evidence of any project management systems. (Burke 1993, pp. 1–2)

Early examples of the project manager might well be the examples of the master masons who controlled the building of the English cathedrals in medieval times (Day 1994); these were clear examples of the project manager's role in managing the total development process from inception to completion. Often, however, in construction management texts, 'project management' is a term used more in relation to the design and construction phases of property development. The Chartered Institute of Building (CIOB) (1982) state that the intention of the appointment of a project manager is to relieve the client of responsibility of providing an organisation to deal with the design and construction of the project. The suggestion is that the client will retain a degree of control necessary to make key decisions and thus the project manager's role will vary according to the project and the client's specific requirements. The detailed responsibilities suggested by the CIOB are very similar to the suggested roles of the project manager set out in section 2.2 of this chapter. One of the key areas of involvement is the initial briefing and discussion with the client. The sorts of issues that will need to be resolved at this stage include the project manager's brief, including terms of appointment, a clear agreement of the level of responsibility of the project manager and the involvement of the client, the project's initial viability and clear indication of possible funding arrangements. Lines of communication and reporting to the client will need to be clarified at this stage.

The CIOB's view of project management is the overall planning, control and co-ordination of a project from inception to completion aimed at meeting a client's requirements and ensuring completion on time within cost and to required quality standards. A number of definitions are quoted by Ratcliffe (1985, p.620) but he finds them unhelpful as, in particular, they fail to recognise the important stages in the development process of funding and marketing. Ratcliffe finds that the definition of the type and characteristics of the client is important and he distinguishes between public and private clients, individuals and corporate clients, the construction experience of clients, clients develop- ing for occupation or speculation, the hierarchical nature of the client's organisation and, finally, whether the clients are based overseas.

Ratcliffe postulates two approaches to the project management process of property development. First he describes a cyclical process suggested by Burgess and White (1979) which explores the stages of the process as:

- *Analysis* – the determination of objectives or goals, identification of problems and exploration of the relationships between constituent parts of the problems, so as to produce order from random informa- tion.
- *Synthesis* – the procedure of creating solutions for the various parts of the problems identified and then grouping these into feasible overall solutions while generating original ideas.
- *Evaluation* – the testing of alternative solutions against appropriate selected criteria to establish those which meet the requirements most adequately.

This approach is similar to that considered in Chapter 1. A second way involves a systems approach suggested by Walker (1989); this summarises the system of the project management process as:

(i)   identifying, communicating and adapting the system's objectives;
(ii)   ensuring that the parts of the system are working effectively;
(iii) ensuring that appropriate connections are established between the system's parts;
(iv)   activating the system so that the connections that have been established work effectively;
(v)   relating the total system to its environment and adapting the system as required in response to changes in its environment. (Ratcliffe 1985, p. 622)

Burke (1993, p. 16) describes a project as a group of activities that have to be performed in a logical sequence to meet the present objectives outlined by the client.

The objectives within project management can be defined in terms of three parameters; these are time, cost and quality. A triangle of forces is often used to depict graphically the trade-off between these factors; this triangle is shown in Figure 2.1.

A summary of the development process and the stages are shown in Figure 2.2.

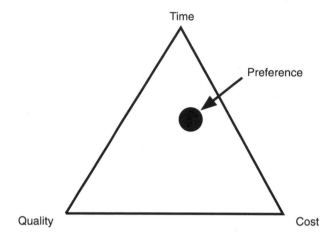

Figure 2.1   *Triangle of objectives in a project*

2.2   THE ROLE OF THE PROJECT MANAGER

The role of the project manager in the development process is outlined in some detail in Box 2.1. The status of the project manager has risen quite dramatically; a survey in 1990 found that the project manager was now second only to the architect in terms of status (*New Builder*, 1990, p. 18). The same article also looked at the background training of project managers and found that they could come from any professional background but that to be successful they would need to have undertaken further training, especially in communication and interpersonal skills. The survey also found that the project manager should ideally be independent of the rest of the building team and that the use of project management was generally client-inspired and used on projects of more than £10 million in value. The CIOB suggested that the role of the project manager demanded a person with considerable understanding of technology, the process of building, design requirements and the complex inter-relationships of law, finance and human relationships involved in the total project (CIOB 1982, p. 18); the CIOB also identified the fact that the project manager must have the ability to develop a strong team spirit on the project and that the key skills were the ability to organise and lead.

The quality of leadership is a basic function of management and the ability to lead and motivate participants in a project are key skills. The CIOB suggested that the 12 key qualities of leadership were:

- ability to lead, motivate, command respect;
- wisdom, knowledge, experience, self-confidence;
- powers of delegation;

Initial consideration
▼
Client's requirements[1]
▼
(3 factors: time, cost, quality)
Assess viability[2]
(depends on funding, planning, professional
team, site appraisal)
▼
Planning
▼
Funding
▼
Establish the project team
▼
Prepare brief (architect's design and costs from
the quantity surveyor) and planning application
▼
Construction
▼
Marketing and disposal

Notes:
1. The key areas of client concern are viability,
    construction and marketing.
2. Appraisal investigates: market demand,
    planning restrictions, land and building
    requirements, location, development cost,
    capital value and rent, user requirements,
    funding, marketing, management of
    completed scheme.

Figure 2.2   *The development process*

- ability to prepare for a task;
- enthusiasm;
- clarity of purpose;
- ability to create opportunities to contribute and develop;
- example and personality;
- responsibility and authority;
- ability to create an atmosphere of compatibility;
- communication and co-operation;
- fairness and impartiality.

THE ROLE OF THE PROJECT MANAGER

Stage 1: Initial consideration of project

- establish terms of reference
- establish authority, if project manager is to be appointed, whether it is overall authority
- establish reporting procedures: who do you report to and when?

Stage 2: Early involvement in scheme

- prior to preparation of the project brief
- establish position as single point of reference for the project team
- agree the form of report with the client

Stage 3: Assess client's requirements

- assess form of development, location, availability of funding and time constraints

Stage 4: Assess viability of project taking into account market trends

Stage 5: Negotiate planning

- assess effects on other parties of the development

Stage 6: Establish variety of funds

Stage 7: Appoint professional team

Stage 8: Prepare brief – basic proposals for design and budgets

- define functions and management activities
- the design team submits preliminary drawings
- submit planning application and make necessary changes

Stage 9: Construction period

- establish preferred pre-contract procedures for building procurement (building contract)
- set up a post-contract appraisal system (to find out if you are on target and performing well) (This is a simplified summary for this stage; for more detail see Day 1994)

Stage 10: Marketing and disposal

- marketing campaign
- draft leases
- check on operation of plant, etc. within development.

Box 2.1   *The property development process: the role of the project manager*

There is a reason for appointing the project manager; it is to relieve the client of the need to become intimately involved with the management of the project and to have to communicate with a number of professional consultants. It follows that the process of project management should be directly related to the needs of the particular client and the project. This suggests that there can be no definitive specification for the project manager's role: not only will the project itself dictate the description and the level of sophistication of the service to be provided, but the degree to which the client wishes to retain an involvement will dictate the authority available to the project manager. Within this need to retain sufficient flexibility in role definition, it is possible to generalise about the characteristics of the project management service, and to extend such a description to embrace project management as the concept, without specific application to the construction industry. We may take as a starting point some of the related activities which are commonly seen as the process of management (Rougvie 1987, p. 208):

- Planning
- Organising
- Motivating
- Communicating
- Controlling.

Although these are useful headings for defining some of the essential features of a management service, they cannot in the project management context be considered as self-contained entities; each overlaps with the others and is supported by others, and in some cases a strong cause and effect relationship exists. Rougvie (1987) details the activities in each of these areas.

Planning

Planning must also embrace the concept of forecasting, in order to establish a client's needs in the context of what is available and desirable in the future, given the constraints which may be predicted within the planning horizons of the project. The planning horizons to be employed must also be a function of the project's needs, and may be subject to change or at least redefinition as a result of the planning process itself. Within this stage, the project manager must be concerned with establishing the project objectives and redefining these so that they may be expressed as operating objectives which can guide the other participants. These objectives may be framed in terms of cost, time, method and quality so that they are communicable to others, and also able to be monitored.

Organising

This stage is concerned with establishing whatever form of organisational framework is necessary to implement the objectives derived at the planning stage. Probably the most important issue here is the identification of the resources required for the project and, in particular, the identification and appointment of the leading participants. As part of the appointment process, the boundaries of responsibility allocated to participants will need to be defined, together with the lines and methods of communication necessary for monitoring and reporting.

Motivating

It is crucial to the operational success of the project that each participant, whether an individual or organisation, is committed to achieving the performance level set out at the planning and organising stages. There must be a will to succeed, to overcome difficulties and to co-operate with others; for this to be accomplished there should be a good match between the project objectives and the individual participants' objectives. In theory, if the planning and organising stages have been thoroughly explored, there should be little problem in achieving the high level of match required. In practice, changes in the operation briefs and in the project environment will mean that constant attention to motivational issues will be required throughout the project.

Communicating

This is probably the one aspect of managing projects which pervades all the others and without a well conceived and effective basis for communication, it is unlikely that the project can succeed. One of the primary tasks of the planning and organising stages will be the creation of the communication system, covering methods, timing and levels of communication to be employed at each stage of the project's lifetime. Communications between human beings have considerable potential for breakdown and misunderstanding, and the level of morale within the project system between the inter-dependent parts will be closely related to the effectiveness of the communication system and the manner in which it is interpreted and implemented.

Controlling

Control is concerned with the overall direction of the project, the identification of deviations from planned targets for time, cost and quality, and the actions necessary to correct or minimise the effect of such deviations. Control is ineffective unless the other processes listed above are effective. Without proper planning and organising, there will be no targets against which performance deviation can be measured; without motivation there will be little incentive for the participants to consent to a regime in which control may take place; and without an effective communication system, there will be no reliable means of ascertaining whether deviations are taking place, or whether corrective action is successful.

2.3   THE FUTURE

Project management of the development process involves management skills which integrate the various stages of the project. Project management requires a wide range of management skills which need to be applied to the particular process of property development. These skills require specialist education and training and the future engagement of professionals in this area will demand people who are more effectively skilled in the tasks outlined below. The skills required by the project manager include:

(i)   Special skills such as problem solving, professional skills and ethics, a management background showing a wide range of experience and commitment.

(ii)   Effective communication.

(iii) The ability to lead through the chairing or leading of the development team. The ability through this leadership to identify problems and to solve them effectively. The ability to deal with the professionals involved in the project team.

(iv)   The understanding of the skills of personnel management, the ability to select through the appropriate interview and selection process the key members of the project team.

(v)   The ability to 'sell' the project through the available public relations channels. The ability to use publicity for the benefit of the developer and the development.

(vi)   Negotiating skills: the ability to bring a working group together, to develop ideas and focus on problems as they arise. To extend the options available, the capacity to bring together the disparate views of the group into a working solution, and ability to solve the problems experienced, is needed.

In 1994 a joint government–industry review of procurement and contractual arrangements was set up under the chairmanship of Sir Michael Latham; the review generated a report entitled *Constructing the Team* (Latham 1994). The role of the project manager could change in the light of the Latham Report; the Report recommends that the terms of appointment and duties of the project manager should be clearly defined and a list of duties for project managers be devised. The Report suggested that the improvements in the role of the project manager should be geared toward benefiting the client rather than the industry. Other recent regulations, the Construction (Design and Management) Regulations implemented in 1995, require a named person to be responsible for health and safety on site. The Latham Report said that improvements were needed in the construction industry in efficiency and training and that the industry should reduce its real construction costs by 30 per cent by the year 2000. The Association of Project Managers in their feedback to the Latham review made the following key suggestions, amongst others, about the role of the project manager in the building production process:

- At the start of any project the promoter should define how he/she intends the project to be managed. The choice should depend upon the objectives, complexity, urgency and importance of each project.
- One manager should represent all the promoter's interests, whether or not the project requires the appointment of a full-time project manager. That person must lead and direct all parties, anticipating and resolving problems amongst them in the interests of the project. (*Project 1994, p. 22*)

In the light of these changes it will be interesting to look forward to the future role of the project manager. In 1984 Ratcliffe predicted that management function within the property development process would become better structured and more sharply defined. With the decline in development activity from the end of the 1980s there was perhaps less inclination to develop this role; however, companies in all sectors have been squeezed by the economic conditions and lack of inflation to conceal errors of financial judgement. The need for the clear structures and a defined role for the project manager is now more evident than ever. It may be useful to investigate the other predictions of Ratcliffe in this area, and these are set out in Box 2.2.

How will the nature of projects and therefore the management of projects change in the future? Turner *et al.* (1994) are clear that the future of project management lies with projects of unclear objectives and goals. Even the functionality of the product required to meet the user's requirements will be uncertain. The only thing that will be reasonably well defined will be the expected benefit from the project. The future of project management is in opportunities which are flexible or even chaotic, and the role will be to maximise the range of potential solutions based on dynamic networks of decision-making rather than rigid hierarchies (Turner *et al.* 1994, p. 31).

The development of project management functions is closely allied to improvements in the management of information technology; a recent article in *Project* (*Project* 1995) provides a case study as an example of these improvements. The case study involves the huge project management problem facing the Hong Kong government over the next few years when it is estimated that over 1500 projects worth more than £9 billion will be implemented before 1997. The need for a software system to handle the projects, control budgets, plan resources and manage corporate cash flows was thus imperative.

MANAGEMENT FUNCTIONS

- Project management as a separate professional function will gain increasing acceptance.
- Overall or total project management, embracing the dimensions of marketing and funding as well as design and construction, will be offered on a wider basis.
- Members of the professional team will recognise the value of being able to pursue their own disciplines within a more effective management structure.
- Professional investment companies and other private and public sector development agencies will increasingly look to set up their own project management divisions, and exercise more direct and continual control over schemes of development.
- There will be a growth in the level of instructions from funding agencies regarding the function of monitoring the progress and performance of projects they have financed, notwithstanding the criticism that this kind of management smacks of authority without responsibility.
- The old chestnut of which profession is best equipped to undertake the role of project manager will disappear as awareness of the true management function grows.

Box 2.2   *Management functions in the property development process: predictions of Ratcliffe (1984b)*

Fortunately, IT systems are now available which can integrate the planning of individual projects into a multi-project environment so that corporate planning is possible. The integration of the financial control of individual projects with the corporate entity will become essential in the future.

REFERENCES

Building Engineer (1994), 'Sir Michael's Cure for Construction Conflict', *Building Engineer*, October, pp. 10–11.

Burgess, R. and White, G (1979) *Building Production and Project Management*, The Construction Press, London.

Burke, R. (1993) *Project Management: Planning and Control*, John Wiley, Chichester.

Chartered Institute of Building (1982) *Project Management in Building*, Occasional Paper, no. 20, CIOB, London.

Day, D.W. J (1994) *Project Management and Control*, Macmillan Press, London.

Isaac, D. and Dalton, P. (1994) 'Education in the Built Environment: Experiences of a Modular Scheme', *Project*, July, pp. 8–9.

Latham, M. (1994) *Constructing the Team*, HMSO, London.

Lock, D. (ed.) (1987) *Project Management Handbook*, Gower, Aldershot.

New Builder (1990) 'Growing Status of Project Managers', *New Builder,* 6 December, pp. 18–19.

Project (1994) 'The Association of Project Managers' feedback to the Latham Review', *Project,* July, p. 22.

Project (1995) 'Case Study: Keeping Hong Kong on Target', *Project,* March, pp. 7–8.

Ratcliffe, J. (1984b) 'Project Management for Property Development', Occasional Paper, Polytechnic of the South Bank, Department of Estate Management, London.

Ratcliffe, J. (1985) '"Total" Project Management', *Estates Gazette,* 17 August.

Rougvie, A. (1987). *Project Evaluation and Development,* Mitchell, London

Turner, R., McLauchin, J. J., Thomas, R. D. and Hastings, C. (1994) 'A Vision of Project Management in 2020', *Project Management Yearbook,* Association of Project Managers, London pp. 30–1.

Walker, A. (1989) *Project Management in Construction,* BSP Professional Books, Oxford.

3 The Development Appraisal

3.1 INTRODUCTION

The assessment of value and cost are dependent on a number of initial surveys and investigations; these include planning policy, planning history, statutory undertakers and the site itself.

Planning policy

Reference in the appraisal should be made to any approved:

- statutory development plans
- relevant planning and development briefs
- design guides
- Planning Policy Guidance Notes (PPGs, from the DoE)
- zoning designations
- density standards
- conservation policies
- highway proposals
- attitudes toward planning agreements.

Planning history

Inquiries into past and present planning decisions relating to the site in question and to the surrounding properties should be made, including any constraints on use and user. You need to be aware of the politics of local planning issues and the councillors, personalities, pressure groups and other third party objectors involved.

Statutory undertakers

In addition to discussion with the local planning authority, it will usually be necessary to consult with statutory undertakers to ensure the availability of gas, water, sewerage, surface drainage, electricity, telephones and transport infrastructure (including road connection).

The site

A thorough and comprehensive survey of the site is essential and will cover aspects such as:

- ownership
- acquisition
- boundaries
- area
- topography
- landscape
- stability
- access
- layout
- buildings
- services
- archaeological remains
- contamination
- physical factors which may affect development value.

3.2 SITE FINDING

Site selection and identification

The selection of a site fundamentally affects the nature and success of a development. No amount of careful design or promotion can totally overcome the disadvantage of poor location or a lack of demand for the accommodation at an economic price irrespective of location (Cadman and Austin-Crowe 1991, p. 19).

In site identification there needs to be a strategy defining the aims, nature and area of the search. The property company may have a business strategy which restricts the company to a geographic location or restricts their activity to particular types of development, for instance, office development in provincial locations. The overall strategy and aims of a development company will be the basis for the identification of the sites and development opportunities. Within this general strategy, a more specific strategy will encompass the size, nature and location of sites. Distance to development sites may be a problem in effectively managing the site where the distance from the development company's centre of operations is great. The development company will wish to spread its risk by spreading development activity over a number of different locations. Previously, in the property development market when there was keen interest from financial institutions, the financial institutions drove the developers to search in prime locations for prime sites. However, with the broadening of funding opportunities, the site-finding approach can be more flexible. The developer's skill and knowledge is important in identifying areas of potential growth where market forces will provide demand for accommodation which will exceed supply by the time a development project is on stream. Whilst recognising the risks, a developer will always seek opportunities to be ahead of the market. Market research will seek to identify the current and projected levels of supply and demand of various types of accommodation in a particular area. The developer should also examine trends in rental and capital values, and the infrastructure can also affect demand. In seeking to identify potential development sites, it is likely that there will be more land available during the time when land values are rising rapidly. The release of local authority land will have regard to market conditions but will also be influenced by the provisions of their development plans, the allocation of land within the local plan and the perceived chances of obtaining planning permission in unallocated areas or land allocated for other uses.

The developer should use an in-house team, agent or planning consultant to actively find development sites based on the acquisition strategy (Cadman and Austin-Crowe 1991, p. 22). Site finding requires a good knowledge of the subject area and also requires some research into the current planning policies. Site finding will need to identify sites allocated in local plans which are not developed, or sites which could be included for development in draft plans by way of the local inquiry process. A report could be drawn up on each site describing its characteristics, planning history and details of ownership. Studies may also identify sites which have not been allocated for development but where there is a good chance of permission by negotiation or on appeal; it should be borne in mind, however, that local authorities and planning authorities use the development plan as a starting point for their decisions. They may then go on to all other material considerations.

The developer may employ agents to find sites in a particular area. If agents are retained by the developer a fee will be payable if the latter is successful in acquiring a site identified by the agent. This is normally 1 per cent of the land price, but could be subject to negotiation. The local agent provides good local knowledge and may be able to negotiate the purchase of sites before they go on to the open market. In may also be necessary for the developer to search the area and identify possible opportunities. When sites are identified, it is necessary to discover their ownership and this can be done by examining the planning register, asking local agents or talking to the actual occupiers. The Land Registry can also now be used to identify landowners. Other means of finding sites which are fairly obvious include obtaining agents' particulars and also through advertisements of properties for sale. Sites are also purchased through company takeover and merger. Where sites are rare this could be a good approach to acquisition; one reason for Sainsbury's purchase of B & Q DIY stores was the latter's portfolio of out-of-town sites.

Site disposals

Site disposals may take place through informal tender and invitations to offer or formal tenders, competitions and auctions. Informal tenders or invitations to offer invite interested parties to submit their highest and best bids within a certain agreed timescale. In these situations, the important point from the developer's point of view is that the bid is made subject to conditions, so that after a bid has been accepted by the landowner, the developer will have the ability to renegotiate the price before exchange of contracts and the developer can thus attach conditions to the bid made. In the case of formal tenders, the formal tender binds both the parties to the terms and conditions set out in the tender documentation; this is subject only to contract. Developers do not like formal tenders as it reduces their flexibility and increases their risk.

Competitions are used when financial considerations are not the only criteria for the disposal of the site. They may be used, for instance, by local authorities or other public bodies in choosing a developer to implement a major scheme. In a major scheme, developers are usually invited to express their interest and are asked to provide details of their financial status and track record. Developers find competitions the least attractive method to acquire development sites; the competition between the bids involves unnecessary time and expense spent on the preparation of models and drawings. Finally, some sites are sold at auction because they are unusual sites which may be difficult to sell by conventional means. At auction, the highest bid secures the site, provided the reserve price has been exceeded. The landowner will instruct the auctioneer of the result of the reserve price which is effectively the lowest price acceptable. If the reserve price is not reached through the bidding, then that particular lot is withdrawn.

Legal problems

Problems may exist in getting possession in order to develop the site; there may be existing tenants on the site or legal encumbrances over it. Business tenants may be served a notice to obtain possession under the provisions of the Landlord and Tenant Act 1954, Part II, but will be compensated. Legal encumbrances may include problems relating to party walls, rights of light, easements across the land and rights of access. These may involve costly legal proceedings and payment of sums to remove the encumbrance. Restrictive covenants can be removed or modified under the provisions of the Law of Property Act 1925, s. 84.

The boundaries are an important element in the demarcation of the land, and the title to the land will need to be properly investigated.

3.3   SITE APPRAISAL

Site factors are physical characteristics affecting the development potential of a site in contrast to planning or legal factors which might act as less obvious constraints. Access, ground conditions, landscape and boundaries, services, referencing documentation, contamination and government/EU funding are all important considerations.

Access

Access is important from a legal point of view. It must be determined whether access is provided from a site to a public right of way such as a road or highway adopted by the local authority. If the road has been adopted, then research into the deeds to discover the extent of rights over access roads will need to be carried out.

Access may be vehicle access and/or pedestrian access. Vehicle access is required for service vehicles and in some commercial situations this access needs to be separated from the access provided to customers and staff. Vehicle access could especially be difficult in older congested town centres where, because of restraints on development coupled with the nature of the surrounding buildings and finally the possibility of pedestrianisation of adjoining roads, conventional access may not be possible. Two solutions spring to mind in situations like this, first, a different form of transport, perhaps a trolley as an alternative means of carrying the goods. Alternative forms of transport can be useful in these situations in the same way that Venice uses its lagoon and canal system because of lack of road access and difficult pedestrian routes. The second solution relates to the use of alternative times for delivery out of conventional shopping hours. In situations where there is pedestrian access only, there may need to be some form of collection point for heavy goods which customers would use, which may be part of the service access.

If a site for development adjoins a roadway, then as well as providing an appropriate crossover into the site from the road, there must be appropriate visibility, termed 'sightlines' for traffic entering and leaving the site and the highway engineers for the local authority will insist on this provision before planning permission can be obtained.

Ground conditions

The ground conditions of a site will be extremely important, whether the site has been an agricultural site, wasteland or a previously used site. The investigation that needs to go into ground conditions will include a check on the subsoil to recognise its type. The type of subsoil will indicate the permissible bearing load of the soil which in turn will determine the nature of the foundation, the use to which the land is put and may also determine the layout of buildings on the site. It may be necessary to pile foundations if a firmer base is required. A ground survey will include the digging of trial pits to determine the nature of the subsoil and the sinking of boreholes in key positions to determine its nature. Some important examples of difficult ground conditions would be:

(i)   The erection of building, particularly two-storey housing, on a clay subsoil, particularly in the vicinity of tree growth. In this situation more expensive foundations and/or protection against tree root damage and removal or lopping of the trees, may be necessary to restrict movement to the foundation caused by the shrinkage of the clay or heave (expansion due to excess moisture in the clay).

(ii)   There could be underground cavities, where land is infilled, which have not been compacted properly. There may also be under-ground cavities where there are underground voids caused by mining or caverns in the rock formations below.

(iii)   There could be landslip in areas of coastal erosion or on steep embankments where surface water may accentuate the problem.

(iv)   There could be underground structures, particularly in industrial areas, including storage tanks, foundations, wells, etc. These pro-blems may link to those of contamination mentioned later.

Surface landscape and boundaries

The existing surface landscape may be treasured on a local or national level. These aspects may relate to planning law and these are discussed elsewhere; at a local level, the loss of amenity land for development, whether there are public rights to it or not, might engender local protest. The nature of tree growth and landscaping on the site may determine the surface water run-off and drainage, as well as providing an attractive setting for the development. In the case of science and business parks (B1 uses) the landscape setting may be critical for successful letting or sale. Trees may protected by Tree Preservation Orders made under the Town and Country Planning Act 1990; protected trees may not be cut or lopped and if anyone is convicted of doing so they may be liable to a fine or imprisonment. You should note that the law only protects specimens in good condition and any necessary application to fell or lop will need to made to the local planning authority or to the Forestry Commission in some cases.

The development of the site will have an effect on the water table and drainage. The run-off for surface water can be provided in the development in a number of different ways depending on the ground conditions and the extent of the water run-off involved. It could, for instance, run off to soak-aways, run into a drainage system connected to surface ditches or water-courses or be linked to a surface water drain, the cost increases, of course, depending on the choice. An interesting example of the need to provide surface water drainage was shown in the Beckton development of London Docklands. The land lying north of the Royal Docks in the Beckton area was left as surplus to the original dock development. It was envisaged that this land would be developed for subsequent docks at a later time. The need never arose because of the movement of docks to the mouth of the Thames due to the increased size of ships and containerisation. This land was left vacant and was generally waste land with some grazing. The land was drained by surface water ditches and because of the nature of the surface water run-off and the topography of the site which was very low lying relative to the potential drainage outlets to the River Thames, a complex system of surface water drainage needed to be installed with a pumping station to achieve the out-flow into the Thames. The provision of this drainage work was very expensive.

A further aspect of the surface landscape of the site relates to the extent of the boundaries. The boundaries should be clearly indicated from the deeds, but these can often be misleading because of the way plans are drawn. Ownership of the boundaries should also be noted from the deeds but there can be disagreement where boundaries have been replaced or where one party has maintained the fence as opposed to another. Where properties are erected against common walls, then work to those walls may require permission under the party wall legislation contained in the Building Regulations. In these situations, surveyors for the adjoining owners could inspect proposals for works before agreement for the development or re-development of the site. Schedules of condition may need to be agreed and there may be the possibility of party wall awards to the adjoining owner. There may thus be costs here which will affect the financial appraisal of the site and which may not be immediately apparent.

There is also the question of rights of support where demolition is involved or rights of light where windows are being obstructed by new development.

Services

Services may go over or under the land. Those running overground are usually cables, probably electricity or telephone cables. Those running below the ground may be cables, drain runs or water or gas services.

The drain runs underground include both foul and surface water. A foul water sewer crossing a site will normally have a width of 3 metres to each side in which building is prohibited to ensure access to the sewer. Thus the only alternative to the loss of this land may be to divert the sewer. Cables and pipelines below ground consist of gas pipes, water supply pipes and electricity cables. Local authorities should have details of where surface water and foul water sewers are running. For the other services it would be necessary to contact the relevant statutory undertaker. In the case of electric cables, the electricity board will have maps of these and, likewise, British Gas and British Telecom. The recent major works of installing television cable which, with the exception of the Channel Tunnel, is regarded as the biggest civil engineering exercise in the UK's history, has provided an interesting case study on the effect of development work on amenity and the subsequent ramifications in respect of planning controls. (Estates Gazette, 1994).

Overhead cables, although unsightly, may provide less restraint on development. There is, apparently, no reason why buildings cannot be erected underneath provided an appropriate gap is provided. However, house-owners and property owners generally do not like the prospect of this and there has been much discussion of the evidence of possible health effects to people living too close to electricity pylons. The effects of pylons are debatable, but it does prove difficult to sell or let property under or close to pylons. Major pylons carry 132kv or 400kv lines and these may cost over a million pounds per pylon to divert (Taylor 1991, p. 63) although smaller power lines, for instance 11kv or 33kv can be moved for much less. Telephone cables do not provide the same level of problem but can also be expensive because of the loss of revenue to the owners during diversion of the cables.

Referencing the site

The RICS draft consultation paper on valuing development land (Royal Institution of Chartered Surveyors 1995, p. 4) suggests that in the case of development properties referencing should include:

(i)   measurement of site and buildings to ascertain frontage, width, depth and built measurements;

(ii)   shape of site and ground contours;

(iii)   plot ratio and site density evaluation;

(iv)   existing building height and that of adjoining properties;

(v)   efficiency of existing building (if to be retained);

(vi)   access arrangements

(vii)   party wall, boundary and rights of light issues;

(viii) a site/soil survey to establish ground conditions and existence of contaminates;

(ix)   availability and assessment of services: main drainage, water, gas, electricity and telephone;

(x)   any evidence of the existence of rights of way, easements, encumbrances, mineral workings, open water courses, filling, tipping etc.;

(xi)   any matters which will affect the cost or practicality of the construction process (e.g. poor access, cramped site conditions).

Contamination

Contamination is a key problem and can render land valueless. The main problem areas are those sites where the land has been subject to chemical waste, for instance from gasworks, factories producing noxious outputs or by-products and rubbish tips. A specialist engineer will be required to test sites which are contaminated before development. Developers of contaminated land will have to satisfy the local authority that they can deal with the contamination. Filled land, for instance land which has been used a waste tip, can also be troublesome in terms of the methane gas which is produced and this will again need to be dealt with, and shown that it can be dealt with, to the local authority's satisfaction. There can also be problems of the migration of gas and leaching of contaminants from adjoining sites. Coal mining areas and other areas of extraction may provide particular difficulties where, beside problems of voids and subsidence there will be the additional difficulties encountered with the waste materials arising from the extraction. Because of the effect on the value of the land, property valuers need to be very clear of the conditions under which they are instructed in such cases. Property valuers, in the same way as developers, will need to make 'reasonable' enquiries of the site conditions. Possible sources of information may include maps and regulatory bodies such as the National Rivers Authority or HM Inspectorate of Pollution (Freedman and Ward 1993, p. 132).

Government assistance

Government assistance is available to developers to assist in developing sites in certain locations under certain criteria. The loans available include money for City Grants and allowances in Enterprise Zones and Urban Development Corporation (UDC) areas. Assistance is also provided through the Simplified Planning Zones (SPZs).

The City Grant came into operation on 3 May 1988. This replaced the Urban Development Grant and the Urban Regeneration Grant. To quality for a City Grant, it is necessary for the developer to prove that the development project will not proceed without such a grant and that the project will benefit a rundown city area. Development projects must be worth over £200 000 when completed to quality for grant aid. City Grant can be applied in the Urban Development Corporation areas and also in the 57 inner city regions which have been designated as target areas. In addition, to obtain a funding, there should be some private sector funding for the development. The amount of grant obtainable depends upon the difference between costs and value. Cost must exceed value in order to qualify.

There are a number of Enterprise Zones in the UK. Enterprise Zone status lasts for 10 years and some zones have already expired; the valuer will need to check on the current status of the zone. The government have indicated they might not be extending the Enterprise Zone experiment as other measures are thought to stimulate development more effectively. However, where zone status still exists, the benefits which are available for 10 years from the date of designation are of relevance to the property developers and include:

(i)   exemption from rates on industrial commercial property;
(ii)   100 per cent allowances for Corporation Tax purposes for capital expenditure on industrial and commercial buildings;

(iii)   a simplified planning system, where schemes conforming to the published scheme in the zone do not require planning permission;

(iv)   rapid processing of other statutory consents required.

The effect of these benefits has been to increase the development activity in the Enterprise Zones, even during recessionary periods, and the money for such development has come mainly from individuals or corporate investors sheltering from tax liabilities, either directly or through enterprise zone trusts (Oxley 1995, p. 120).

There are 11 Urban Development Corporations in the UK. They are similar to New Town Development Corporations and their objective is to regenerate designated areas. They act as the local planning authority and can sometimes offer financial assistance to developers.

In March 1993 it was announced that the Urban Programme of government funding would be phased out; this formed a major part of the government's urban renewal expenditure along with City Grants, Derelict Land Grants, Urban Development Corporations, City Action Teams and City Challenge (see Balchin *et al.* 1995, p. 272). Under the Leasehold Reform, Housing and Urban Development Act 1993 the government established English Partnerships (EPs) to take over policy decision making to complement regional policy, administer the English Industrial Estates Corporation, buy and develop inner city sites, assume the responsibility of the Urban Programme to award City Grants and Derelict Land Grants and administer City Challenge. A Single Regeneration Budget was created in 1994 to include expenditure on Urban Development Corporations, English Partnerships' activities, Housing Action Trusts (HATs) and other programmes. The total planned expenditure for 1995/6 was £1332m and for 1996/7 £1324m (Balchin *et al.* 1995, p. 273).

Simplified Planning Zones were other measures designed to speed up the rate of development in areas where this is required. Local authorities use Simplified Planning Zones to give advanced planning permission for certain types of development within clearly defined zones. The advantage to developers is that they know what schemes will be permitted in advance and do not need to make a planning application or pay planning fees.

Land Registers were set up in 1981 by the DoE. Their purpose is to provide details of unused and under-used land owned by public authorities. The Register is available for inspection and contains information on ownership and planning history. This Register can assist developers in obtaining the release of plots of land for private development.

European funding

European structural funds have been established by the EU to encourage economic convergence of wealth in the different regions of the union. They also assist in the restructuring of traditional heavy industry such as coal and steel as well as fishing and agriculture. Key criteria have to be met before assistance is given, usually that the area in which the assistance is being provided should have a gross domestic product (GDP) well below the EU average and additionally must be facing significant unemployment because of the loss of traditional industries. Applications for such funding are not made by individual property developers operating in the area but are put forward by national governments to the European Commission; the Commission then allocates funds set up under the various grant systems. The monitoring committees under government agencies such as the DTI, DoE and MAFF will then decide how much money each scheme is then awarded (Howarth 1995, pp. 94–5). Community initiatives by the European Union using the European Regional Development Fund (ERDF) are shown in Box 3.1.

COMMUNITY INITIATIVES USING EDRF

INTERREG: To prepare cross-border areas (in England, only Kent and East Sussex are eligible) for a community without national borders

KONVER: To assist regions weakened by the contraction of the defence industry

PESCA: To help the fishing industry adapt to structural changes

RECHAR: To help areas hit by the contraction of the coal industry

RESIDER: For economic conversion of steel-producing areas

RETEX: For areas dependent on clothing and textile industries

URBAN: For areas suffering from urban blight.

Source: Howarth (1995), p. 94.

Box 3.1   *Community initiatives using ERDF*

3.4   PLANNING CONSIDERATIONS

The planning system

It is necessary to obtain planning permission for most development in the UK. Exceptions are covered by the General Development Orders (GDOs). The planning process adds value to the development process but also adds uncertainty because of the time delays and cost increases which may be involved. The planning system is overseen by the Secretary of State for Environment. The Secretary of State issues statements of policy and guidance, usually ministerial Circulars and Planning Policy Guidance notes to planning authorities on relevant planning matters including approaches to planning applications. The Secretary of State monitors matters of strategic policy in county structure plans and through the appointed Planning Inspectorate. The Inspectorate considers all planning appeals against the decisions of planning authorities. The Secretary of State has the power to determine any application or planning appeal if it is of national or regional significance.

Anyone wishing to carry out development for which planning consent is required must apply to the local planning authority, which is normally the local district or borough council. In some cases it is not immediately clear whether planning consent is required, and therefore the planning authority should be approached for initial advice. In these cases, it may be necessary to apply to the local planning authority for determination as to whether the proposals would constitute development under the Town and Country Planning Acts. The local planning authority must give a formal decision on an application within eight weeks and there is a right of appeal against this decision. You can make an application for planning consent in respect of any property and you do not need, in these circumstances, to have any legal or financial interest in the property but, if this is done, then the applicant must serve on the freeholder or any lessee of the property with an unexpired term of at least seven years and on any occupied agricultural property, a note advising them of the application for planning permission.

An initial application for outline planning permission can establish the principle of what type of development can be carried out. This may save a good deal of time and trouble in the subsequent detailed application. There are fees which are payable to the local planning authority in respect of applications, and these must be paid at the time the application is submitted. The eight-week statutory period within which the planning authority should give a decision runs from the date when the application is deposited with the local authority together with the fee; the date of application is the date the application is received by the local planning authority. When application is made to the local authority, the planning authority will consult other appropriate authorities before giving planning permission. The highway authority will be consulted on new roads and access to roads, and other officers, for instance the environmental health officer or the safety executive, might be consulted on other aspects. It is important to consult the relevant planning officer of the district council or appropriate authority at the outset before a formal planning application is submitted. As has been said, the planning authority should give a formal decision within eight weeks of the receipt of the application or such longer period as the applicant may agree. If consent is then refused or granted subject to conditions to which the applicant has objections, an appeal may be made to the Secretary of State for Environment. If no decision is made by the local or planning authority within the agreed time limit, the applicant may assume that planning consent has been refused and appeal to the Secretary of State accordingly. If the development proposals entail the demolition or alteration of the character of the buildings which are on the list of buildings of specified architectural or historic interest prepared by the government, then additional procedures are necessary. A listed building consent is necessary for the demolition or alteration of a listed building. Any trees on site may be protected by a tree preservation order and it is necessary then to obtain consent before felling or lopping them. In addition, large controversial schemes now require environmental assessment to assess predicted impacts and to consider ways of mitigating the effects.

The planning permission which is granted by the local planning authority may be qualified in a number of different ways. Conditions may be imposed on the permission for a duration of time or for the benefit of certain external agencies. Planning permissions will lapse unless the development is commenced within five years from the date permission is granted, or such other time as a planning authority may stipulate. Conditions may be imposed on the property limiting the use of the property. This may be limited to somebody in a particular trade or vocation. A condition which limits occupation to a particular occupier may also be imposed. The powers of planning authorities to impose conditions are governed by DoE advice which sets out the conditions in this respect.

Planning agreements may be set up by planning authorities who impose conditions on developers for the benefit of the community. Such agreements may be related to the phasing of the development of the land or financial contributions by the developer to the infrastructure of the locality. Planning agreements were previously made under the Town and Country Planning Act 1971, s. 52, but now are made under the provisions of the Town and Country Planning Act 1990, s. 106.

The local planning authority must ensure that the application is publicised, most applications require a notice on the site or property and notification of the adjoining owners; major developments will also require local advertising of the proposals and letters will normally be sent to neighbouring occupiers and owners.

In the event of the local authority refusing planning permission or in the event of the authority taking longer than eight weeks to determine the planning application or granting planning permission subject to a condition to which the applicant does not agree, there is a right of appeal to the Secretary of State for the Environment. The appeal must be lodged within six months of the date of refusal. Once a planning appeal has been lodged, the case passes to the DoE Inspectorate. These inspectors make recommendations to the Secretary of State to enable determination of the appeal. The appeal can be pursued by a written representations, by informal inquiry or by formal public inquiry. The local planning authority holds a register of applications and permissions so that interested parties may research the planning history of a particular site and also determine the present position regarding existing permissions. To summarise, the decision of the local planning authority may be:

- to grant permission unconditionally
- to grant permission subject to one or more conditions, or
- to refuse permission.

A standard condition is that development will need to begin within 5 years unless an alternative period has been fixed by the local planning authority.

Planning constraints

There are a number of strategic planning policy constraints which will affect redevelopment proposals. These can be summarised as green belts, national parks, areas of outstanding natural beauty (AONBs), areas of great landscape value, strategic gaps, metropolitan open land, scheduled ancient monuments and high quality agricultural land. These are examples of where the local authority may constrain development (Taylor 1991). Strategic gaps, for instance, are gaps crucial to evaluating greenfield development proposals and are important in dividing existing settlements by providing greenfield gaps between them. Most of the other constraints are obvious from their titles, but in the granting of planning applications there may also well be constraints on car parking and constraints driven by environmental standards. These environmental standards may relate to the density of acceptable development, the amount of daylight, etc.

Development plans

The development plans under which planning permission is approved are set down under of the Town and Country Planning Act 1990, Part 2. The development plans are the prime consideration by which local authorities make planning decisions. The plans differ according to the area to which they apply. In non-metropolitan areas there is a Structure Plan providing the broad framework for planning and a Local Plan for the district. In metropolitan areas there is a Unitary Development Plan which embodies strategic as well as detailed policies.

Structure plans set the broad framework for planning at the local level and they provide the strategic policy framework for planning and ensure that the development coincides with national policy. Local plans set out detailed policies and specific proposals for the development and use of land. Unitary development plans combine the structure plan and the local plan.

Development Control

Development control can include zoning, the flexibility and mix of which may be negotiated. The mass of a proposed development may be based on plot ratio or floor space index. The residential density may be based on dwellings per hectare, houses per hectare or habitable rooms per hectare and there are visual environmental and amenity considerations to be taken into account in the density calculation. User constraints may be imposed limiting the use of a property to a user class, a local user or a named user. Conservation can also affect development control. There may be a conservation area or conservation orders affecting a particular building or tree. Discussions with local authorities on development control matters will be affected by a number of criteria and the progress of negotiations will depend on council officers involved, their level, department and authority. Members of the local council may also be involved and it is important to note their position, their party, the locality they represent and their status on the council committees upon which they serve. The status of the developer's meetings with the local authority is also important: for instance, whether they are formal, informal or working parties. Other bodies which need to be consulted include the statutory highway authority, statutory undertakers, transport authorities, education, environmental health, health and safety and the emergency services. There may also be influential third party organisations to consult with regards to conservation or design matters.

Summary: planning and other statutory requirements to be taken into account in the development appraisal

The RICS suggest that the development appraisal of land should take into account the following in respect of planning and statutory matters (RICS 1995, p. 5):

(i)   Current planning policies affecting the subject site and surrounding area – normally found in the Structure Plan and Local Plan (or the Unitary Development Plan) and supplementary guidance prepared by the local authority. A discussion with the local planning officer may be appropriate and prudent.

(ii)   Emerging or consultative planning policies, including national or regional guidance. These may be taken into account when deciding planning applications and , in the longer term, may influence the supply of competing space.

(iii)   Any existing valid permission whether outline or detailed. The valuer should consider the explicit or statutory expiry date and the likelihood of renewal, unless the valuation assumes immediate implementation.

(iv)   Conditions and reserved matters attached to existing permissions and the requirements of any s. 106 or other agreements.

(v)   Any rights to carry out development under the General Development Order.

(vi)   Any special controls that may apply, e.g. listing of buildings, con-
        servation area designation, tree preservation orders.
(vii) Permitted use of existing buildings (if to be retained).
(viii) Environmental protection legislation (e.g. noise abatement, con-
        trol of emissions).
(ix)   Building Regulation requirements (e.g. requirements for sprinklers,
        fire escape arrangements, etc.).
(x)   Special/specific statutes and regulations affecting the particular
        type of development proposed.

3.5   ECONOMIC AND MARKET ANALYSIS

Market research

Some of this analysis is covered in section 12.2 on marketing; this section
provides an overview rather than a comprehensive research framework. The
increasing fragmentation of the property market means that a higher level of
skill is required in discovering and exploiting the profitable location. Research
is necessary into the likely scale, design, layout, occupancy, tenure and service
requirements of prospective purchasers. Market research is an important area
which would aim to establish the current demand and supply of property
within the area to ensure that the property could be sold or let. The estimation
of current demand may include the estimation of the current total market
potential, which is the maximum amount of sales that might be available to all
competing firms during a given period in a given market segment under a
given level of marketing.
    Estimating current demand in market research will involve the estimation of:

(i)   The total market potential.
(ii)   The territorial potential.

Having established the market potential, the management decision will be to
decide how much of that market a product can gain and how much effort is
needed to gain it. The seller wants to know if the market is large enough to
justify his company's participation. The formula for the estimate is

$$m = n \times q \times p$$

where m is the total market potential, n is the number of buyers in the specific
market, q is the quantity purchased by an average buyer and p is the price of
the average product. For instance, if there are 200 hi-tech companies who
wish to buy a new production facility every five years and the average price of
the facility is, say, £200 000 for an average floor space of 500 square metres,

then the total market potential is approximately £40 000 000 over a five-year period. The difficult component to calculate is the number of buyers in the market in a given time period (Cleaveley 1984, p. 36).

A variation of the formula above is called the 'chain method', based on the premise that it is easier to look at each component of magnitude rather than at the magnitude itself. So, for instance, the current demand for high-tech buildings can be built up as being equal to the number of high-tech companies in the UK times the average percentage of those without spare capacity on site, times the average percentage of those companies who need specialised premises, times the average percentage of those companies who would pay the current market rent for high-tech buildings.

Economic analysis

Property traditionally operates in a demand led market where, because of the inadequacies in the market and restrictions on supply caused by controls and procedures of obtaining planning permission, property developers, except in periods of slump, have managed eventually to dispose of their properties. Since the late 1960s, owner-occupiers have been much more explicit about their requirements, thus market research, economic analysis and proper marketing of the product is more than ever necessary.

There are three steps that can be used, for instance, in the market research of a shopping centre. This retail analysis will include first background analysis, secondly market analysis and thirdly an estimation of the appropriate size of the project:

- The *background analysis* will include the geographical extent of the urban area, the road pattern, the population and growth areas, the level of employment and key employers, retail sales patterns and *per capita* income by sector.
- The *market analysis* will look at the site, its suitability, size and location, its access by roads and transport facilities, its trade or catchment area. This catchment area is defined by natural boundaries, access times, competition and size. The market analysis also includes details of population growth and income and buying power *per capita* and per family. The analysis involves the consideration of competition from other sites, and an estimation of the sales potential, which is the potential population times expenditure for each store type. The residual sales for the site to be developed is this level of potential less an allowance for the competing sites.
- The *recommended size* of the project can be estimated by taking the level of population and multiplying it by the *per capita* expenditure within that type of shopping centre. Assuming a share for the location, this total expenditure can be reduced by a share for competing shop-

ping facilities. This then gives a figure for the potential within that town centre location which is unsatisfied. The judgement them has to be made as to what proportion the project will take of this unsatisfied potential.

The approach to the analysis for a retail development is summarised in Box 3.2.

ECONOMIC ANALYSIS: RETAIL DEVELOPMENT

1. Background
    - geographical extent of the urban area
    - road pattern
    - population and growth areas
    - employment and employers
    - retail sales pattern
    - *per capita* income by sector

2. Market analysis
    - site – size, suitability, location
    - access – roads and transport
    - trade (or catchment) area – natural boundaries, access times, competition, impact zone
    - population growth
    - income and buying power *per capita*, family expenditure
    - competition
    - sales potential – population × expenditure for each store type (population based on total less that attracted by competition or assumed share of total market)

3. Recommendations
    - recommend size of project based on sales potential, provide brief to designer, detailed financial analysis of potential
    - calculation – population × *per capita* store expenditure × percentage captured by town centre store minus effective competition = town centre potential, the project share taken as a percentage of this
    - recommended area schedule will divide up total space into percentages for each user depending on expenditure, i.e. food, chemist, department store, furniture, eating, etc.

Box 3.2   *An approach to a retail economic analysis*

The economic analysis concerns three factors:

- Supply and demand
- Changes in the environment
- Changes in technology.

Supply and demand

Price rises in a market are generally an indication of a shortage of supply of a type of space, for instance, but this conclusion may require further analysis. An estimate of the supply of space will involve the calculation of the existing stock on the market and an analysis of the type of space. There is a need to assess the existing vacant space and the rate of take-up; finally a calculation will be required of the space to be released onto the market by new development or the release of existing premises.

The calculation is:

$$\frac{EV + ND_t + NV_t}{TU_t}$$

where: EV is existing stock

ND_t is new development for the coming year (say)

NV_t is existing space becoming available over the year

TU_t is the take-up rate assessed on an historic analysis and projected forward.

If TU_t is less than $EV + ND_t + NV_t$, then the calculation represents so many years' supply of property on the market; the equilibrium position is 1 year in this case.

Changes in the environment

The strength of the local economy, planning proposals for the development of existing open space or undeveloped land and general economic conditions are of relevance here.

Changes in technology

Technology changes may lead to changes in the demand for space, changes in user requirements and redundant space. Homeworking or teleworking, where employees work full time or for part of the week at home will affect demands for space, as will desk-sharing or desk-renting where exclusive work space is not allocated on a regular basis to employees.

The RICS has summarised the influences on occupier demand as:

(a)   location of property;
(b)   access;
(c)   availability of transport routes;
(d)   car parking facilities;
(e)   amenities attractive to tenant and/or purchasers;
(f)   size of development in terms of lettable packages;

(g)   form and specification of development;
(h)   market supply, including actual or proposed competing developments. (RICS 1995, p. 7)

Potential users of space

In order to assess demand, the key element will be to analyse the potential
users of space. These will essentially be of four types:

- Companies moving into an area either:
  - to open new facilities, branch offices, etc.,
  - or because of a complete relocation of the business operation.
- Expansion of an existing requirement by established firms in the area.
- Small space requirements by business start-ups.
- Companies moving into an area to:
  - rationalise space
  - change location
  - move to updated premises.

Market research procedure

Cleaveley (1984, p. 87) suggests that there are five steps in the setting up of a
market research project, and these are applicable to the property industry.
The first step is the defining of objectives. Here the research objectives or the
subject to be investigated is defined. A clear direction of research activities is
required to ensure that the results come from a right target market, and that
sufficient valid data is obtained. The five steps are:

(i)   *Designing the research methodology*: decisions must be taken
about the appropriate method of obtaining data. These may be,
for instance, desk research, the study of published information or
inhouse information from appropriate agents. It may come from
observation or finally from survey research which may consist of
face-to-face interviews, self-completing questionnaires, interviewing by telephone, or group discussion where opinion leaders are
drawn together to discuss markets under the direction of a trained
group leader. This latter approach can be very effective in finding
out a general consensus of view points.

(ii)   *Sampling*: because of the costs of analysing the total target market,
most research programmes will focus upon samples of that market.
Larger samples obviously give more reliable data, but the degree of
accuracy must be related to the amount being spent on the
research project. Most research projects begin with a pilot survey
which will evaluate the procedure which is intended to be carried

out and also provide feedback on the design of the research method and the level of response to the method carried out. Random sampling is effective and easy to administer but structured sampling or non-random methods have also been designed to achieve maximum statistical reliability from the results.

(iii) *Fieldwork*: trained interviewers or executives can be employed to carry out the fieldwork to provide the information on the research project. The supervisor to the project will need to monitor closely what is happening in terms of the fieldwork and to ensure that it is completed accurately without bias and on time.

(iv) *Data analysis*: the analytical techniques used in the data analysis can vary from simple statistical techniques to a very complex regression analysis. The extent of the analysis should be agreed with the client before the research is entered into.

(v) *Presentation of report*: the results of research and any conclusions are shown in a comprehensive report which should have clear recommendations so that the findings of the research can be translated into action by the client.

REFERENCES

Balchin, P. N., Bull, G. H. and Kieve, J. L. (1995) *Urban Land Economics and Public Policy*, 5th edn., Macmillan Press, London

Cadman, D. and Austin-Crowe, L. (1991) *Property Development*, E. & F. N. Spon, London.

Cleaveley, E. S. (1984) *The Marketing of Industrial and Commercial Property, Estates Gazette*, London.

Estates Gazette (1994), 'Street Trees Threatened by Cable TV — Call for Review of Utility Rights', *Estates Gazette*, 24 September, p. 82.

Freedman, P. and Ward, H. (1993), 'The Environmental Factor', *Estates Gazette*, 27 November, pp. 132–3.

Guy, G. (1994), *The Retail Development Process: Location, Property and Planning*, Routledge, London.

Howarth, A. (1995), 'EU Funding: learning how to play the game', *Estates Gazette*, 4 March, pp. 53–5.

Mackmin, D. (1994) *The Valuation and Sale of Residential Property*, Routledge, London.

Morgan, P. and Walker, A. (1988) *Retail Development*, Estates Gazette, London.

Oxley, J. (1995) 'Enterprise Zones: The Way Forward', *Estates Gazette*, 11 March, pp. 120–1.

Rougvie, A. (1987) *Project Evaluation and Development*, Mitchell, London.

Royal Institution of Chartered Surveyors (RICS) (1995) *Valuation of Development Land*, Draft Consultation Paper, RICS, London, January.

Taylor, N. P. (1991), *Development Site Evaluation*, Macmillan Press, London.

4 The Residual Valuation

4.1 INTRODUCTION: RESIDUAL VALUATION

A residual valuation is very sensitive to slight variations in its different elements such as rent, initial yield, construction costs, finance rate and building period. Because of this, the Lands Tribunal has regarded this method as one of the last resort (as in *First Garden City Ltd* v *Letchworth Garden City Group* (1966); see Butler and Richmond 1990, p. 111).

The distinction between valuation and analysis

The property crash in the early 1970s focused attention on valuation methods used by the property profession. In the period since, there have been a number of pressures on valuation professionals to improve the quality and standard of the valuations produced. This has arisen for a number of reasons. Large-scale investment, for instance, has taken place in recent years by the financial institutions, and the investment advisers acting for the institutions and other large investors are looking for more explicit market evidence and analytical techniques to be used in the valuations which have been carried out. Because of situations which have occurred involving institutional investors, where actual returns on property investments have not reflected target returns predicted by the price paid, there has been much debate about the validity of the methods used. There is also much more awareness in the market now of the responsibilities of the professional to clients' demands, that property professionals should not just act as agents but provide, during the buying and selling process, some idea to the client of the forecast of income arising from the investment in the future.

This added awareness and monitoring of valuation procedures has been a subject of debate in the professional institutions as well as in the market place. Recent suggestions by leading members of the Royal Institution of Chartered Surveyors are that valuations should try to reflect a view of the future movement of prices and forecast potential supply and demand situations which may affect price levels. This has been especially the view of a recent RICS President, Clive Lewis. The findings of the Mallinson Report suggested that the valuer should get clearer instructions from the client and should more clearly explain the valuation of property in company accounts. In addition, the Report suggested that there should be more comment on valuation risk factors, price trends and economic factors and use of more refined discounted cash flow (DCF) techniques. The recent debate and the earlier debate have combined to demand that, in what has previously been called 'property valuation', a more extensive service of property analysis be provided. Generally the approach that should be taken (as discussed in Chapter 1) is that the overall property appraisal should be clearly divided between property valuation for purchase (that is the valuation for market price) and the subsequent analysis of performance. In the first case, this is defined as valuation and in the second case it is defined as analysis; the overall process is generally termed 'property appraisal'. Thus the valuation of a property, that is the calculation of the exchange value of a property, is different from the subsequent analysis of the performance of the investment which is the appraisal of its actual worth. Calculations before and after purchase will not agree because of the lack of perfect knowledge in the market at the time of the transaction and the inability to predict future changes in the cash flow and the risk profile of the investment accurately. Thus the techniques discussed later on in this book can be used to anticipate the market value or else to record and analyse the progress of the investment subsequent to purchase. However, it is still important to understand the difference between these two approaches.

Development valuation techniques

In 1991, a research report was produced by Philip Marshall for the RICS on development valuation techniques (Marshall 1991). The research was intended to investigate the methods and techniques which development companies and their advisers use to value land and projects for development. The research was based on a questionnaire to discover the basic methodology of valuation. The research into the development valuation approach looked at a number of appraisal methods including the residual valuation, residual profit method, cash flow, (DCF), sensitivity analysis, ground rent appraisals, forward funding appraisals and long-term funding appraisals. The research findings reflected how practitioners carried out development valuations. For instance, in the use of rents in the calculation of the gross development value in residual valuations, practitioners were asked whether current rents were used or else the likely rental on completion. In the boom period in property of 1988–89, over 65% of developers admitted they would take a view of the likely rental on completion. In terms of yields used to arrive at the gross development value, the research found that a sensitivity analysis was usually undertaken and the final yield selected on the optimistic side to reflect the keen competition for land. If inflated rental values were taken into account, developers normally inflated building costs over the building period. Interest rates could vary and could be based on LIBOR or the base rate, opportunity costs rates, forward funding rates, internal rates or the gross return yield on gilts (see Chapter 7 for an explanation of financial terms). To calculate the interest, most practitioners used a percentage of total building costs (usually 50%, but some were as low as 40%) and charged interest over the total period. Practitioners tended to base profit estimates on total costs but final estimates depended on the risks involved. The average rate was about 15%. Sensitivity analysis was used in the calculations and cash flows to project the development's viability. DCF methods were not used if the property was going to be traded and probability analysis was also not used. Comparable land prices were used to check residual valuations and the report noted that American and Japanese developers in the UK usually required a breakdown from their advisers of comparable land sales. Finally, nearly all active developers and their advisers used computers with either appraisal programmes purchased ready made, or had developed their own spreadsheets.

Simplified residual valuation

The basis of the calculation for the residual valuation is:

> value of completed development
> *less* cost of carrying out development
> *equals* amount available to pay for the land

Example 4.1: Simplified residual valuation

A proposed office development on city centre site has the following project details:

Gross area		10000 m^2
Rental value		£200 m^2
Building cost		£700 m^2
Profit as a % of cost		20

Appraisal	£	£
Gross Development Value:		
Net lettable area (80% gross)	8 000	
Rental value per m^2	200	
Rental income	1 600 000	
Yield at 10%	10 YP *	
Capital value		16 000 000
Development Costs:		
Building cost		
10 000 m^2 @ £700 per m^2	7 000 000	
Fees (say)	1 000 000	
Interest on costs (say)	3 000 000	
Total Cost	11 000 000	
Profit @ 20% total cost	2 200 000	
Total cost plus profit		13 200 000
Amount left for land purchase		£ 2 800 000

* YP = Year Purchase (see section 4.6).

The costs in a residual valuation which have to be deducted from the gross development value include:

- building costs and fees;
- fees on letting and advertising;
- interest on costs;
- contingencies;
- purchase costs of land (not the land value as this is the residual); costs would include fees on purchase and compensation for tenants to obtain vacant possession.

Examples of costs and other elements of the valuation

1. *Building costs* (from BCIS 1994, pp. 19–24)

Average building cost, 2nd quarter 1994		$£/m^2$
Offices	general	630
	with air conditioning	737
	6 storeys +	844
Retail	shopping centres	398
	hypermarkets, supermarkets up to $1\,000m^2$	299
	$1\,000m^2 – 7\,000m^2$	493
	$7\,000m^2 – 15\,000m^2$	407
	shops, general	388
	retail warehouses	255
Business space	factories, general	282
	purpose built factories	352
	warehouses/stores	286
Residential	housing, mixed development	370
	estate housing, 2 storey	339
	flats, 2 storey	397
	one-off detached houses, (schemes of 3 units or less)	597
	conversions, flats, 1–2 storey	325

Costs per square metre are based on gross internal floor area, and are the national average tender prices for construction works, exclusive of external works, professional fees and VAT. The regional variation for London and the South East is around plus 8 per cent. VAT is payable on new and refurbishment contracts at 17.5 per cent.

The regional and county factors will increase or decrease the cost depending on location for instance:

Regional and county factors (UK mean = 100)
South East excluding Greater London	1.00
Essex	0.98
North west	1.02
South west	0.95
Scotland	1.08
Greater London	1.14
London Postal Districts	1.16
Outer London	1.09

(examples from BCIS, 1994, pp. 13–16)

Gross internal areas are the gross areas measured from the inside of external walls. This measurement contrasts with other measures used in the development process. Planning matters are dealt with on gross external areas whilst rentals are sometimes dealt with on a net internal basis, where common parts and services and accessways are excluded. Rule of thumb guidelines for converting gross internal areas to net internal areas may be: 0% for new industrial/warehouses (class B1 of the Use Classes Order), 10% for industrial generally, 20% for shops, offices and older industrial premises. The gross internal area is defined as the total of all enclosed spaces fulfilling the functional requirement of the building measured to the internal structural face of enclosing walls. It includes areas occupied by partitions, columns, chimney breasts, internal structural or party walls, stairwells, lift wells and the like. Also included are lift, plant and tank rooms and the like above the roof slab (BCIS, 1994, p. 30).

The inflation in building costs may also be an important factor for the project. The BCIS tables give an indication of the regional price index to compare inflation rates in different parts of the country.

The building costs consist of materials, labour, establishment charges and profit. These are the basis for the tender price. The bill of quantities, on which the final cost is based, also includes the preliminaries which in turn includes details of the contract conditions, the contractor's liability, any obligations or restrictions imposed by the employer and the provision of facilities by the contractor. These items are also costed in the price for the contract. Design factors affecting the cost of a building include shape, detail, quality of materials, the use of standard components, maintenance requirement, location, availability of labour, repetition and position on the critical path of the work programme (Hancock 1984, pp. 16–17).

Regional Tender Price Index (example)
1985 mean = 100

Year	Quarter	South and East	Rest of UK
1992	1	105	116
	2	102	111
	3	99	109
	4	100	110
1993	1	98	112
	2	107	109
	3	104	115
	4	103	112
1994	1	102	116
	2	114	122

Source: BCIS (1994), p. 5).

An example of how a building cost can be assessed is given by the BCIS (1994, p. 29); this example estimates the cost for the building of a 400 m^2 public house in Hampshire using the mean building price (this may require additional adjustment) for the second quarter of 1994:

(Table 4 CI/SfB 517) Public House building cost	£610/m^2
(Table 3 location factor) Hampshire	0.95
£/m^2 rate at 2nd quarter 1994	£580/m^2
Gross internal floor area	400 m^2
Mean building price	£232 000

2. Fees

The fees may be assessed at 12.5% of costs to include architects', structural engineers' and quantity surveyors' fees.

3. Contingency

This is between 0 and 3% or more depending on the nature of the project, the contract for construction and possible risk of variation of cost. This is based on total cost of building, including external works and fees and interest charges.

There are three main types of contingency (Hancock,1984, p. 6):

(i)   Design contingency to allow for the working up of initial sketch designs into the detailed final design.

(ii)   Contingency to be inserted into the building contract to cover unforeseen items that occur during the building operation,

(These two types of contingency are normally allowed for in the estimate of the main building costs.)

(iii) Contingency included as a separate item, which we are considering here. This is a general contingency to cover unforeseen costs or time delays in undertaking the project; this does not normally fall within the building cost estimate but is a separate item as part of the overall development costs.

4. *Finance charges*

Finance is charged , as an approximation, as interest on the total building cost for half the building period; this represents the fact that not all the money for the contract will be required at the beginning of the contract but that money will be drawn down as work proceeds. The total cumulative cost is represented by the S curve of construction costs over the building period (see Figure 4.1).

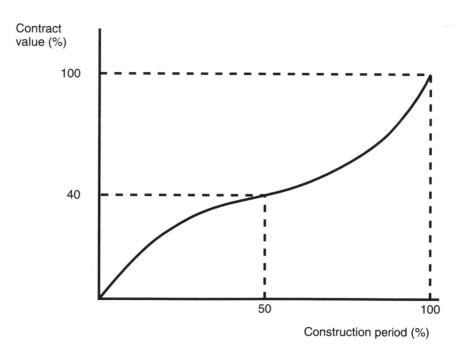

Figure 4.1   *S curve of building costs*

For the fees, as these are front ended in respect of the drawings and cost estimates, the interest is estimated as being on the total fee over two thirds of the building period. The builder is paid monthly but interest on outstanding amounts may be assessed on a monthly or quarterly basis; thus interest should be compounded on the same basis. On a simple analysis, simple interest is used and only compounded if the building period exceeds one year and then on an annual basis. The interest rate can be assessed as a margin over the base rate, currently 6.75% (February 1995). One may use a margin (say) of 3% to reflect the nature of the developer and scheme, giving (say) 10%.

5. *Letting fees*

Generally these are 10% of the initial rents but if there are joint agents, as on a larger scheme, they will operate jointly for a total fee of 15% of the rents. In the present competitive market, agents may be asked to bid for the contract and thus a lower-cost fee structure may be obtained. Advertising, depending on the project, is (say) a spot figure of 0.5–1.0% of the gross development value.

6. *Development period*

The development period includes the planning period, the building contract and the void period. The planning period is the time to get planning permission, drawings prepared and quantities/costs prepared and this time is assumed to be (say) six months as an example. The void period is the time to let the property; this depends on circumstances, in this example three months has been allowed, which is likely to be optimistic. This example assumes nine months for the building contract (see Figure 4.2).

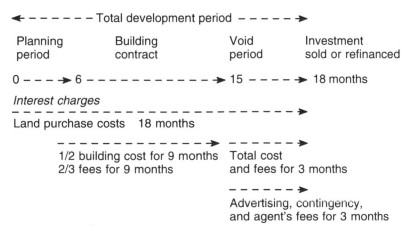

Figure 4.2 *Breakdown of total development period and interest charges*

Thus interest is charged on the whole cost for the void period.

7. Gross development value

This is an investment valuation based on:

> Net income from completed development × Years purchase @ invest-
> ment yield = Gross development value.

8. Developer's profit

This is a percentage based on the gross development value (GDV) or total cost (TC), say 20% total cost or 17% gross development value, i.e.

$$GDV - TC = \text{Profit}$$

if Profit $(P) = 0.2TC$, then $TC = P/0.2$

inserting this value in the original equation: $GDV - (P/0.2) = P$

$$GDV = P + (P/0.2) = \frac{0.2P + P}{0.2} = \frac{1.2P}{0.2}$$

thus $P = GDV/6 = 16.5\% \ GDV$.

9. Residual land value

In practice, the residual value will have to be discounted back over the period of the development and void period to reflect the interest that would need to be paid on the land cost (see section 4.6); this will then give the land cost at the time of purchase, being the beginning of the development.

Notes on valuation

There are so many variables in the residual valuation that inaccuracy can easily occur. Changes in the elements, especially the gross development value, can dramatically alter the residual land value. Valuers can therefore alter the variables to determine the outcome as a form of sensitivity analysis; this is discussed later in this chapter.

1. VAT implications for the developer

The developer should obtain specialist advice on the implications of VAT on any site acquisition. The Finance Bill in 1989 following a judgement of the European Court of Justice in June 1988 (Cadman and Austin-Crowe 1991, p.50) imposed VAT at the standard rate of 17½% on construction costs and interests in rights over and licences to occupy land. The legislation only applies to commercial buildings and not to residential buildings. A vendor, in the case of selling an interest in land or buildings, or landlord in the case of leases and licences, has to opt to charge tax. In the majority of cases, VAT has an impact only on the cash flow of the development project as developers may be able to fully recover all VAT paid on land transactions and construction costs if they charge VAT on a sale of the completed building or on rents from the letting of the completed building. Thus the cash flow implication is that there may be a delay between the payment of VAT and its recovery. An approach to this is to allow a lag of approximately four months between the charge and recovery of the VAT within the residual calculation. The approach for tax planning for a new development project is to identify the methods of disposal and the VAT liability on supplies (see McClenaghan 1990, p.400).

2. *Ground rents*

The residual calculation can be extended to devise a ground rent calculation in situations where there are partnerships between developers and land-owners and the developer takes a lease of the site; these calculations are discussed in more detail in Chapter 5.

4.2   DETAILED RESIDUAL VALUATION

The simplified residual calculation shown in section 4.1 can be developed by addition of more variables and the application of the techniques discussed earlier.

Example 4.2: Detailed development valuation

A site of 9000 square metres is owned by the local authority. A development brief prepared by the local authority has suggested that an appropriate development on the site would be a mixed commercial scheme incorporating:

>   Office space: 5280 m^2 gross
>   Supermarket: 3000 m^2 gross
>   Shop units: 20 at 125 m^2 gross each

The local authority will agree to the demolition of buildings on site. 200 car parking spaces will need to be provided, 50 being accommodated above the supermarket and the rest as surface car parking.
   The *building costs* are as follows:

>   Demolition and site preparation costs — £100 000
>   Offices — £500 per m^2

Standard shop units – £300 per m^2
Supermarket – £250 per m^2
Surface car parking – £400 per space
Roof top car parking – £2 000 per space

The scheme will take 18 months to complete.

Rents:

Office rents are £70 per m^2 on modern leases
Shops/supermarkets are let at £80 per m^2 overall in the locality (based on net retail space)
The yield on the overall scheme is 7%

An appraisal is set out below, including assumptions, to determine whether the scheme is viable and determine the residual value of the land, or overall loss.

Assumptions:

1. The gross area is quoted, so to get a net area deductions are made of 20% for offices, 10% for shops and 10% for supermarket to get the net space.
2. Yield – given at 7%.
3. Sales costs: if the investment is sold on to an institution at the end of development period, then this cost should be deducted from the gross development value. For simplicity, this example assumes that the developer retains the site.
4. Deductions from the gross development value are:

    – total building costs (on gross areas)
    – fees on building costs (12.5%)
    – finance on fees and building costs (building cost for ½ building period and for fees at 2/3 building period as costs are paid out gradually over contract)
    – finance rate is (say) base + 8% = 15% (assumes project is risky)
    – contingency
    – letting fees (15% rental – assumes joint agents)
    – advertising
    – profit as (say) 17% GDV

5. A void or letting period of 3 months is allowed for – interest is calculated on total sum for this period.
6. Amount of residual has to be discounted back to the beginning of the development period (18 months + 3 months void) to give the value of the land now. From this figure purchase costs need to be deducted to get to the net residual value.

Site appraisal:

			£
Gross development value			
Supermarket – 3000 m² gross			
less 10% (say) 2700 m² net			
at £80 per m²			216 000 p.a.
Shops – 20 at 125 m² gross			
less 10% (say) 110 m² net			
at £80 per m² = £8800 x 20			176 000 p.a.
Offices - 5280 m² gross			
less 20% (say) 4224 m² net			
at £70 per m²			295 680 p.a.
Total income			687 680 p.a.
Yield in perp at 7%			14.29 YP
Gross development value (GDV)			9 826 947

	£	£	
Less costs			
Building costs			
5280 m² offices @ £500	2 640 000		
3000 m² supermarket @ £250		750 000	
125 m² shops × 20 × £300		750 000	
Car parking:			
150 at £400		60 000	
50 at £2000		100 000	
Demolition and site cost		100 000	
Total building cost		4 400 000	
Fees at 12.5%		550 000	
Interest on building cost			
for ½ × 18 months at 15%		495 000	
Interest on fees for			
2/3 × 18 months at 15%		82 500	
Total cost		5 527 500	
Interest on total for void			
period (letting period)			
3 months @ 15% p.a.		207 281	
		5 734 781	
add contingency at 3%		172 043	
		5 906 824	
Letting fees at 15% rent (say)		95 000	
Advertising 1% GDV (say)		90 000	
Total development costs		6 091 824	

Gross Development Value (GDV) b.f.		9 826 947
Total development costs b.f.	6 091 824	
plus developer's profit		
at 17% GDV	1 670 581	
Costs plus profit		7 762 405
Value of site in $1\frac{3}{4}$ years		2 064 542
× PV of £1 in $1\frac{3}{4}$ years at 15% (say)		0.783
Value of site now		1 616 536
less acquisition costs at 4%		64 661
Site value		1 551 875
Site value that could be offered		
is (say)	£1 550 000	

Further examples of the residual approach have been provided by Seeley (1995).

4.3   SENSITIVITY AND RISK

Detailed applications of sensitivity and risk are dealt with in Chapter 6, but here an introduction is attempted to the variables involved.

Sensitivity analysis: consideration of the variable factors in the residual valuation

When we look at the residual valuation we can see that there are a number of variables providing inputs to the valuation. A discussion is attempted here of the variables, their nature and the degree of variability.

1. *Land costs*

The land costs may be put in at the asking price, but in practice if the appraisal does not produce a satisfactory developer's yield or profit, the scheme would have to be abandoned or some means found to reduce development costs. Because the land cost is a residual cost, it should therefore be negotiated once the appraisal has been completed.

2. *Ancillary costs of acquisition*

The ancillary costs of acquisition are made up of agents' fees, valuation fees, survey fees, legal fees and stamp duty. Each of these is either the subject of a fixed scale or can be determined accurately prior to purchase. In any event, they comprise a small part of the total development cost, perhaps not more than 0.5 per cent. In Example 4.2, 4% of the land cost was used, which included (say) 1% for valuation fees and 1% for stamp duty. Thus the land cost is 'netted' by the deduction of the acquisition costs and this is done as 4% of the gross land cost. So, from Example 4.2:

	£
Value of site now	1 616 536
less acquisition costs at 4%	64 661
Site value	£1 551 875

Strictly speaking, the acquisition costs are calculated on the net land cost being the actual purchase price, so:

	£
Value of site now	1 616 536
	= 1.04 × site value
Site value =	£1 554 361

Or more precisely, let site value $= S$ £
$(1.04S)$ × Amount of £1 in
$\qquad 1\frac{3}{4}$ years at 15% —   2 064 542
$(1.04S)$ × 1.2771 =   2 064 542

$$S = \frac{£2\,064\,542}{1.3282} = \qquad\qquad £1\,554\,391$$

(See section 4.6 for a discussion of the Amount of £1 formula).

3. *Gross development value*

The gross development value is netted if the completed development is sold off to a financial institution such as a pension fund or insurance company, and a deduction of 3% is generally made. This is taken off the gross development value at the beginning of the calculation to give a net development value (NDV). 3% represents the institution's legal fees and surveyor's expenses including stamp duty on purchase. If there are legal fees and agent's fees to be incurred by the developer on sale of the completed development they can also be deducted from the gross development value, but it is more usual for them to be included in the section of the calculation where letting fees are deducted.

4. *Pre-building contract period*

The period for which the land will be held, and therefore the period for which it has to be financed, is made up of three parts. First the period between the purchase of the land and the start of construction; this may be easy to assess if planning permission is already available. When no planning permission exists, the contract of purchase may be made subject to planning permission being granted and the greater part of the land costs therefore will not be incurred until that time. The second period which has to be financed is the period of construction and the third period is the period for letting and selling. If the property is speculative, you will need to assume that there is no rental income receivable before the completion of construction and that an additional period of perhaps three months needs to be allowed to secure a tenant and arrange for leases to be granted. Where the scheme is pre-let or pre-sold, this period may be eliminated.

5. *Short-term rate of interest*

Having established an estimated period for holding the land, it is necessary to apply an estimated rate of interest on short-term borrowing, to arrive at the cost of holding the land. The developer may have established sources of funds or may have arranged specific short-term funds for the particular scheme. The estimated rate of interest will reflect current rates and possible future trends of rates but in particular the interest rate margin (over base rate or LIBOR) will reflect the risk of the project (see Chapter 7 for an explanation of financial terms).

6. *Area of building*

If there is detailed planning consent, then the area of building is known from this consent; otherwise it will be based on discussion with the local authority and limited by what is physically possible on site. A common plot ratio for industrial buildings is a 1:2 ratio, that is 1 square metre of building to 2 square metres of site, while commercial buildings might be 2:1.

7. *Building costs*

The estimate of the cost of construction is a major element, but this is affected by the level of inflation. The overall rate of increase in the building costs is made up of the increase in the cost of building materials and in the cost of labour. It is usual to allow for foreseeable increases in wages and material costs which can be reasonably estimated for perhaps six months or so ahead. However, despite the foregoing, tender prices may decrease while the cost of labour and materials increases, as occurred during 1990–4, hence it is more usual to use tender price indices and forecast indices for the year ahead as supplied by BCIS.

8. *Professional fees*

In addition to the basic cost of construction, there are professional fees. Given the estimated building costs, they can be calculated fairly accurately, as they are normally related to established scales of charges, for example, those of the RIBA and the RICS; however the scales have now officially been abandoned and charges are often subject to competitive bids and significant discounts on the scale fees. The figure for fees may be made up as follows:

Architect	6.0 per cent
Quantity Surveyor	4.0 per cent
Engineer	2.0 per cent
Building Regulations Approvals, etc.	0.5 per cent
Total	12.5 per cent

9. Building and letting period

The length of the building period is important because it affects the cost of holding the land and the cost of short-term building finance. The normal convention is to assume that the building costs are spread evenly over the building period. The cost of construction has to be financed during the building period and for the period it takes to sell or let the completed project. The void period will also need to take into account rent-free periods offered as an incentive generally or particularly in respect of fitting-out periods. The latter may reach startling proportions, as in the case of the Canary Wharf development in London's Docklands.

10. Agents' fees

The amount of the agents' fees is fairly easy to assess as it is normally charged in relation to some established scale of charges. The normal agents' fees are recommended by the RICS and would normally be 10 per cent of the first year's rent. Stiff competition amongst agents in present markets may reduce this scale fee.

11. Advertising costs

The cost of advertising includes the cost of advertising the property and of preparing and distributing particulars. This item of cost is fairly easy to estimate and is normally a small percentage of total development costs. An advertising consultant would be asked to prepare a budget for costs for the advertising campaign.

12. Rental income

The rental income is an estimate of the rent that will be achieved when the development is completed at the end of the development period. The convention is that appraisals are based on today's costs and rental values, without allowing for inflation or real increases over the period of the development. The conservative convention is to allow for some inflationary effect on building costs but to keep rental values to current levels. The rental income directly determines the developer's yield and indirectly the developer's profit which is related to capital value.

13. *Investor's yield*

Having established the estimate of rental income, the capital value of the completed project is arrived at by capitalising the income at the appropriate investor's yield, making allowance for the cost of disposal. The prime property market is compact and the flow of market intelligence comparatively efficient. Yields do, however, vary over time and, unless the investment is to be pre-sold, that is the terms for the eventual sale are agreed with an investor prior to the start of the development, the developer has to form a view of the yields that will prevail at the end of the project, perhaps some 18 months on. Because of the difficulties of forecasting, it is not unusual to adopt current yields.

14. *Developer's profit*

The developer's profit is dependent on the nature of the project and the type of developer but fundamentally it should also represent the risk involved in the project. Reward will vary directly with the level of risk, additional risk being compensated by additional reward (see the Capital market line in Figure 4.3 which represents this relationship between risk and reward).

The developer's profit is a point figure as a percentage of cost or gross development value but for additional security to funders may be subject to a threshold based on rental cover. This cover means there is a liability to pay the rental, if lettings are difficult, from the profit where guarantees to funders have been made. A pre-let or pre-sale will reduce the risk; if an institution has provided the pre-sale and perhaps the short-term finance for construction of the project, the institution will look to a reduction in the developer's profit by purchasing the property at a higher yield and thus reducing the gross development value at purchase (see Chapter 8).

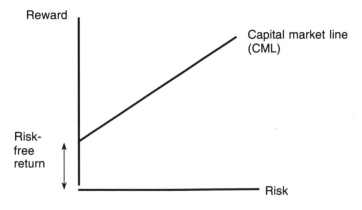

Figure 4.3   *The relationship between risk and reward*

15. *Inflation*

Rents and building costs can be inflated through the development and building period respectively, building costs from the mid-point of the building period but also allowing for inflation in the void period. Such an approach would be less conservative than that shown in Example 4.2 because it is using anticipated rather than existing rental levels. Building costs could be inflated because of the nature of the contract and the problems which may arise on the contract. The problems of increased building costs may be taken into account in the contingency figure (see earlier comments). The inflation of rental figures by developers was apparent in the boom years of the 1980s (see the research carried out by Marshall 1991 mentioned earlier).

A modified residual could be undertaken by allowing for inflation and other adjustments, for instance:

(i) the rental levels used in the calculation of the gross development value can be inflated over the development period from existing rent levels using an Amount of £1 calculation (see section 4.6) to represent the growth in rental values over the period;

(ii) the yield could be adjusted to a quarterly in advance calculation to reflect more accurately the future income flow;

(iii) the cash flow could be extended from the development period into the investment period once the development has been completed and a subsequent analysis carried out. The investment part of the valuation can take into account contemporary techniques such as short-cut DCF approaches, and reflect inducements and voids.

Sensitivity testing

Small changes in individual inputs lead to larger changes in the residual answer; sensitivity testing is a way of examining the effects. A simple example is set out below which shows the effect of changes on two different development appraisals, one with a low land value and the other with a high land value.

Example 4.3: Simple sensitivity testing

	Development on prime site (land cost high in proportion to other costs)	Development on cheap site (land cost low in proportion to other costs)
	£	£
GDV	1 000 000	1 000 000
Total costs		
(inc. finance)	700 000	900 000
Land value	£ 300 000	£ 100 000

Assume three scenarios for the above appraisals:

(i)   value and cost increase by same percentage
(ii)   value increases more than cost
(iii) cost increases more than value.

(i)   *Value and cost increase in the same proportion*
       In this case land value will increase in the same proportion.

(ii)   *Value increases by 30%, cost by 10%.*

	Prime development site	Other site
GDV	1 300 000	1 300 000
Total costs	770 000	990 000
Land value	£ 530 000	£ 310 000
% change	+77%	+210%

Thus, if value increases by more than cost, it affects land value more in the case where the land value is small in proportion to the total value of the development.

(iii) *Value increases 10%, cost by 20%*

	Prime development site	Other site
GDV	1 100 000	1 100 000
Total costs	840 000	1 080 000
Land value	£ 260 000	£ 20 000
% change	−13%	−80%

The effect on the land value in this case where the land value is a small proportion of total value is again more dramatic, illustrating the concept of gearing which is discussed in Chapters 7–10 on finance.

4.4 CALCULATION OF THE DEVELOPMENT PROFIT

The residual valuation gives the answer of how much to pay for the site. If the site value is already known then this can be incorporated into the valuation to work out the developer's profit. Using the figures from Example 4.2, the capital profit on completion can be calculated and the annual profit.

Example 4.4: Capital profit on completion

		£
Expected capital value		9 826 947
Expected total costs:		
	£	
Building cost, fees and finance on		
total	6 091 824	
Land cost	1 550 000	
Finance on land cost @		
15% over $1\frac{3}{4}$ years	429 488 *	
		8 071 312
Residual profit		£ 1 755 635

* This is calculated by compound interest, i.e. (£1 550 000 × (1 + 0.15)$^{1.75}$) −£1 550 000. This is based on the Amount of £1 formula or compound interest (see section 4.6).

Thus instead of the traditional residual calculation to find the site value, which is based on:

Gross development value *less* (Building cost plus profit) *equals* residual site value or land cost
$GDV - (BC + P) = LC.$

This is rearranged to:

Gross development value *less* total cost (which includes land cost) *equals* profit
$GDV - (BC + LC) = P$

From the calculation:

$$\text{Profit as a percentage of total cost} = \frac{\overset{£}{1\,755\,635}}{8\,071\,312} = 21.8\%$$

$$\text{Profit as a percentage of capital value} = \frac{\overset{£}{1\,755\,635}}{9\,826\,947} = 17.9\%$$

Example 4.5: Annual profit if scheme is retained as an investment.

This assumes that the development company has funded the scheme from its own funds or else an investing institution has acted as developer. Assume that the developer requires a 7% long-term yield:

		£
Expected annual income		687 680 p.a.
Expected total costs:		
Building cost, fees and finance on	£	
total	6 091 824	
Land cost	1 550 000	
Finance on land cost @		
15% over $1\frac{3}{4}$ years	429 488	
	£8 071 312	

$$\text{Development yield} = \frac{£687\,680}{£8\,071\,312}\text{ p.a.} = 8.52\% \text{ (Income return on total costs)}$$

Thus any return greater than 7% could be the developer's profit = 1.52%.
So, in the residual valuation approach:

Value − cost = profit on a capital basis and,
Development yield − investment yield = developer's profit on an annual basis.

Rental cover

Taking the expected annual income = £687 680 and the residual profit calculated in Example 4.4 = £1 755 635, then the rental cover is the profit : rental ratio

= £1 755 635 : £687 680 = 2.6 times.

This indicates the cover available from the profit if the rent is guaranteed and has to be paid by the developer if there is no letting of the property. It suggests that the developer could cover 2.6 years of void with the profit from the scheme.

4.5 ALTERNATIVE APPROACHES

The traditional residual technique is not adequate to deal with a more complex development situation where expenditure and income are being made and received at different times over a long time scale. Greater accuracy can be achieved by using cash flow approaches. There are three approaches which could be possible to provide a more realistic approach:

(i)   A cash flow method, using period by period cash flow on which interest can be charged.
(ii) A discounted cash flow (DCF) method, as above except that the flows are discounted back to the present rather than interest added.

(iii) A DCF approach, but building inflation into costs and growth into rents.

Improved techniques do not solve all the difficulties of the calculation. The problem of a residual calculation is that changes in elements of the calculation can seriously affect the final site value. Sensitivity analysis looks at the various elements of the residual calculation in an attempt to distinguish those elements where change will most affect profitability. Attention can then be paid to such factors and steps taken to reduce the uncertainty. The use of cash flow approaches, sensitivity analysis and risk are dealt with in Chapter 6.

The draft consultation paper on the valuation of development land issued by the (RICS 1995, p. 10) summarises the approaches that may be used to assess profit and rate of return in the residual valuation:

When using the residual method, it is usual for the developer to seek a capital profit expressed as a percentage of the total development cost, including interest (the Profit Yield); the other criteria that may be adopted include:

(a) *Initial yield*: the net rental return calculated as the full annual rental on completion of the letting expressed as a percentage of the total development cost. This is useful for assessing whether the developer could service a long-term mortgage loan on the development.

(b) *Cash-on-cash (or equity yield)*: the capital uplift or (more usually) net income (after interest charges on any long-term mortgage loan) expressed as a percentage of the long-term equity finance provided by the developer.

(c) *DCF methods*: the income stream is projected with explicit assumptions about rental growth and discounted back to a net present value (NPV) using an appropriate discount rate; the scheme is deemed viable if NPV exceeds the total development cost. The discount rate allows for a profit margin reflecting the risk and reward elements of the project.

(d) *Equated yield (or internal rate of return, IRR)*: a variant of (c), the IRR is the yield which equates the discounted value of the project with discounted cost (NPV = 0); strictly the equated yield is the same as the IRR but where there is inflation/growth allowed for in the costs and values (see Isaac and Steley 1991, Chapter 5).

(e) *Amount of cover*: the extent to which the rent or sale price can be reduced, or the letting or sale period extended, without suffering an overall loss on the scheme.

4.6   THE INVESTMENT METHOD USED TO CALCULATE VALUE

This section provides an introduction to the investment method to be used in the residual valuation to calculate the gross development value. It looks at the valuation tables used to carry out basic calculations and examines the compound rate of interest formula which is used in the residual valuation. Readers familiar with valuation principles may therefore wish to omit this section.

Introduction

Most investors seek to obtain a return on their invested money either as an annual income or a capital gain; the investment method of valuation is traditionally concerned with the former.

Where the investor has a known sum of money to invest on which a particular return is required, the income can be readily calculated from:

$$\text{Income} = \text{Capital} \times \frac{i}{100}$$

where i = rate of return required as a percentage.

For example, if £1 000 is to be invested with a required rate of return of 8%, the income will be:

$$\text{Income} = £10\,000 \times \frac{8}{100} = £800$$

In this type of problem the capital is known and the income is to be calculated. In the case of real property the income (rent) is known, either from the capital rent passing under the lease or estimated from the letting of similar comparable properties and the capital value is usually calculated. The formula above has to be changed so that the capital becomes the subject:

$$\text{Capital} = \text{Income} \times \frac{100}{i}$$

For instance, what capital sum should be paid for an investment producing £8000 per annum when a return of 8% is required?

$$\text{Capital} = £800 \times \frac{100}{8} = £10\,000$$

This process is known as 'capitalising' the income, in other words converting an annual income into a capital sum. It is essential that the income capitalised is 'net', that is clear of any expenses incurred by the investor under the lease. The formula can be modified to:

$$C = NI \times \frac{100}{i}$$

where C = Capital
       NI = Net income
       i = Rate of return.

For given rates of return $100/i$ will be constant, for example:

Rate of return (%)	100/i
10	10
8	12.5
12	8.33

This constant is known as the Present Value (PV) of £1 per annum, or more commonly in real property valuation, Years Purchase (abbreviated to YP). The formula can thus be finally modified to:

$$C = NI \times YP$$

The YP calculated by using $100/i$ will only apply to incomes received in perpetuity, which are those received from freehold interests let at a full market rent or rack rent. Incomes to be received for shorter periods use a YP which must be calculated using a more complex formula but tables of constants are available and *Parry's Valuation and Conversion Tables* are most commonly used (Davidson 1990). The historic approach of *Parry's Tables* was to assume that the rental income was received annually in arrear whereas in practice it was received quarterly in advance. Although the tables have now been modified, much traditional valuation uses the original assumption for simplicity. However, whatever income basis is used, the two essential inputs required for the calculation are: (i) the period of time the investment is to last in terms of years, and (ii) the rate of return required, usually known as the yield.

To summarise, to estimate the capital value of an interest in real property using the traditional investment method, three inputs are required:

(i)   the net income to be received,
(ii) the period for which the net income will be received,
(iii) the required yield.

(i) and (ii) will be obtained from the lease of the subject property or, if the property is unlet, an estimate of the rental value will be obtained from lettings of comparable properties. (iii) will be obtained from analysis of sales of comparable investments. A valuer must therefore have knowledge of two separate markets; the letting and investment markets.

Example 4.6: Simple investment valuation

Assume prime shops in a certain location have a yield of 4%. The income from the shop you are interested in is £200 000 net p.a. How much would you pay for the freehold?

Net income	£ 200 000 p.a. x
Years purchase @ 4% in perpetuity	25YP*
Capital value	£5 000 000

$$* \text{ YP} = \frac{100}{\text{Yield}} = \frac{100\%}{4\%} = 25$$

The tables used in the investment method

In order to understand the basis of the traditional method and the calculation using compounding and discounting factors in investment calculations, we need to consider the tables which underpin the appraisals. In dealing with investment situations, we are considering the purchase of an asset to generate an income stream over a period of time; thus we are converting the value of an income stream in the future into a present capital sum. The basis of the traditional approaches, the tables used in *Parry's Tables* (Davidson 1990), is about the conversion of present and future sums and the conversions of capital and income streams. The tables deal with the process of compounding and discounting; for instance, the Amount of £1 table will add compound interest to an initial sum to give a future capital sum. The six main options of conversion are:

- Capital to income, and vice versa
- Present sums to future sums, and vice versa
- The compounding of sums into the future, and discounting back to the present.

Summary of the valuation tables (see Box 4.1)

1. *Amount of £1*

This table provides the amount £1 will accumulate to over n years at an interest rate of $i\%$ p.a. It thus compounds up from a present capital sum to a future capital sum. The approach is commonly known as compound interest, and the formula is

$$A(\text{Amount of £1}) = (1 + i)^n$$

SUMMARY OF VALUATION TABLES			
Option	Cashflow		Formula
	Now	Future	
1. Amount of £1 (A)	Capital sum	Capital sum	$A = (1+i)^n$
	compounding ⟶		
2. PV of £1 (PV)	Capital sum	Capital sum	$PV = \dfrac{1}{A}$
	⟵ *discounting*		
3. Amount of £1 p.a.	Income	Capital sum	$\dfrac{A-1}{i}$
	compounding ⟶		
4. ASF to produce £1 (ASF)	Income	Capital sum	$ASF = \dfrac{i}{A-1}$
	⟵ *discounting*		
5. Annuity £1 will purchase	Capital sum	Income	$\dfrac{i}{1-PV}$
	compounding ⟶		
6. PV of £1 p.a. (YP)	Capital sum	Income	$YP = \dfrac{(1-PV)}{i}$
	⟵ *discounting*		(single rate)

Source: Isaac and Steley (1991), p. 5.

Box 4.1 *Summary of valuation tables*

2. PV of £1

The present value of £1 gives the sum which needs to be invested at the interest rate *i* to accumulate to £1 in *n* years. *i* discounts a future capital sum to a present capital sum; it is the process of the Amount of £1 in reverse and the formula is

$$1/A$$

3. Amount of £1 p.a.

This is the amount to which £1 invested annually will accumulate in *n* years. It is thus compounding a present income stream to a future capital sum and the formula is

$$(A-1)/i$$

4. Annual sinking fund (ASF) to produce £1

This is the amount which needs to be invested annually to accumulate to £1 in n years at an interest rate $i\%$. It thus discounts back the future capital sum to a present income stream.

5. Annuity £1 will purchase

This is the income stream that will be generated over n years by an original investment of £1. The income produced will be consumed as part capital and part interest on capital. Assuming the rates of consumption are the same, a single rate approach gives an equation

$$i/(1 - PV)$$

If the rates differ, then the formula

$$(i + s)$$

needs to be used, where s is the annual sinking fund formula (see above) at a different interest rate from i. Note that this is the way a mortgage is calculated: the Building Society provides the initial capital sum and expects repayments of equal amounts throughout the loan period (assuming fixed-rate money), but the repayments consist of interest and capital (that is, the sinking fund).

6. PV of £1 p.a.

The present value of £1 p.a. is the present value of the right to receive £1 pa over n years. The future income stream is discounted back to the present value and is the opposite of the annuity calculation. Thus the formulation for a single rate is

$$(1 - PV)/i$$

or for the dual rate,

$$1/(i + s)$$

where s is the annual sinking fund at the sinking fund rate. This approach is commonly known as the Year's Purchase and gives the present value of a future stream of rental income.

The compound interest formula

As can be seen from the valuation table, the formula for compound interest is the same as the amount of £1 formula (A) where:

$$A = (1 + i)^n$$

where i is the interest rate for a period, and
        n is the number of periods.

These must coincide, that is if the formula is calculated on an annual basis, then n is the number of years and i the annual interest rate, so interest is compounded annually. If n is the number of months and i the monthly interest rate then the calculation is compounded monthly.
    Thus
On an *annual* basis:
The future value of £1 in 2 years at an interest rate of 10% p.a. =

$$£1 \times (1 + 0.10)^2 = £1.21$$

On a *quarterly* basis:
The future value of £1 in 8 quarters at a quarterly rate of 2½%, interest being compounded quarterly =

$$£1 \times (1 + 0.025)^8 = £1.22$$

Note that 2½% compounded quarterly gives an annual rate greater than 10%:

$$£1 \times (1 + 0.025)^4 = £1.1038, \text{ interest is } £0.1038 = 10.38\%$$

REFERENCES

Baum, A. and Crosby, N. (1988) *Property Investment Appraisal*, Routledge, London.
Baum, A. and Crosby, N. (1995) *Property Investment Appraisal*, Routledge, London.
Building Cost Information Service (BCIS) (1994) *Quarterly Review of Building Prices*, BCIS, issue no. 55, September.
Britton, W., Davies, K. and Johnson, T. (1990) *Modern Methods of Valuation*, Estates Gazette, London.
Butler, D. and Richmond, D. (1990) *Advanced Valuation*, Macmillan, London.
Cadman, D. and Austin-Crowe, L. (1991) *Property Development*, E. & F.N. Spon, London.
Davidson, A.W.(1990) *'Parry's Valuation and Investment Tables'*, Estates Gazette, London.
Hancock, P. (1984) *Building Costs and Contracts*, Centre of Advanced Land Use Studies, College of Estate Management, Reading.
Isaac, D. and Steley, T. (1991) *Property Valuation Techniques*, Macmillan Press, London.
Marshall, P. (1991) 'Development Valuation Techniques', Research Technical Paper, RICS, London.

Marshall, P. and Kennedy, C. (1992) 'Development Valuation Techniques', *Journal of Property Valuation and Investment*, vol. 11, no. 1, pp. 57–66.

McClenaghan, T. (1990) 'The Expert Series: VAT and Property: A Practical Guide', *Journal of Valuation*, vol. 8, no. 4, pp. 394–402.

Morley, S. (1988) 'The Residual Method of Valuation', in C. Darlow (ed.), *Valuation and Development Appraisal*, Estates Gazette, London.

Newall, M. (1989) 'Development Appraisals', *Journal of Valuation*, vol. 7, no. 2, pp. 123–33.

Ratcliffe, J. (1983) 'The Valuation of Development Properties', *Journal of Valuation*, vol. 1, no. 1, pp. 24–31; no. 2, pp. 142–52; no. 3, pp. 268–74.

Ratcliffe, J. and Rapley, N. (1984) 'Development Properties', in W. H. Rees (ed.), *Principles into Practice*, Estates Gazette, London.

Royal Institution of Chartered Surveyors (RICS) (1995) *Valuation of Development Land*, Draft Consultation Paper, RICS, London, January.

Seeley I. H. (1995) *Building Economics*, Macmillan Press, London.

Whipple, R. T. M. (1988) 'Evaluating Development Projects', *Journal of Valuation*, vol. 6, no. 3, pp. 253–86.

5 Ground Rents and Partnership Schemes

5.1 CALCULATION OF GROUND RENTS

The capital value of a development site as calculated in Chapter 4 can be used in situations where the freeholder of the land retains the land interest. These arrangements are called 'partnership arrangements', and often the landowner is a local authority with a land bank or a statutory authority with surplus property or a major landowner wishing to efficiently manage its estate. In these cases the landowners may feel that there is not the development expertise within their organisations to carry out the development alone. The developer together with a funder thus forms one side of a partnership, with the landowner on the other. In the 1980s this was a common form of development arrangement with local authorities. In these arrangements the landowner will retain the freehold and thus retains an interest in the development together with an opportunity to share in the growth of the development. The landowner then grants a lease, usually a long lease of (say) 125 years to the developer to carry out the project. The landowner then receives an annual ground rent for the land rather than taking a capital sum on the sale. This arrangement has enabled major landowners historically to develop their lands and yet still maintain some interest, ongoing return and control. In particular this approach has advantages in town centre situations where land assembly is difficult and risky, or in new development situations where the nature of the market has not yet been established and where risks may frighten off developers, funders and investors. In these situations by partnership arrangements the balance between risk and reward can be traded-off. Partnership arrangements in this trade-off also offer the opportunity for more innovative funding arrangements as in sale and leaseback and finance leaseback situations; these aspects are investigated in Chapters 7–10 on finance, in particular project finance.

In order to remove the element of risk from the equation completely, local authorities may take a lease and leaseback arrangement or an overriding lease of the property to give guarantees to the rents and thus enable the developer to obtain funding. In these situations the local authority grants a 125 year lease to the developer, who then leases back the property at a guaranteed rent for (say) 25 years to the local authority. The local authority then lets the premises on occupational leases; this arrangement is shown in Figure 5.1. By guaranteeing the rent in this way the developer can obtain

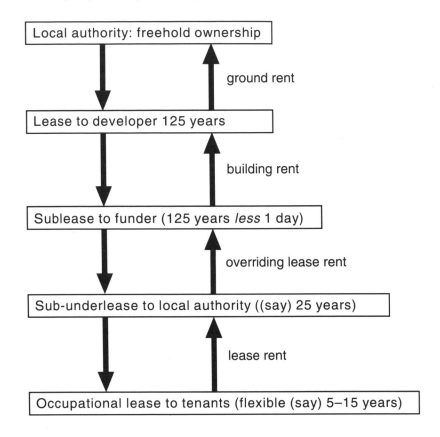

Figure 5.1   *Example of a lease structure in a partnership arrangement*

finance. The local authority has control over the leases and can use the space to further policies of local economic regeneration or employment. If successful, there will be an excess of rent received over the guaranteed rent to be paid to the developer. Variations on this form of guaranteed payment are also discussed in Chapter 7 on project finance. The calculation of the ground rent is shown in Example 5.1.

Example 5.1: Ground rent calculation

> Valuation of a 125-year lease with 5-year rent reviews.
> Estimated income   £500 000 p.a.
> Yield   7% freehold: long lease (say) 7.5%
> Finance costs   15%

	£	£
Estimated costs	£5 000 000 (all costs except land)	
Profit	20% costs	

Calculation:

	£	£
Income		500 000 p.a.
Actual cost	5 000 000	
Yield @ 7.5%, decapitalise by	0.075	
Return for risk and profit (20% of 7.5%) (say)	0.015	
Sinking fund: long lease therefore	Nil	
Total development yield		0.09
Developer's costs and profit		450 000 p.a.
Ground rent available		50 000 p.a.

Future rent growth apportionment:

The future rent is divided up on the original proportions agreed, it is thus a proportional arrangement:

$$\text{Future growth apportioned} \quad \frac{50\,000\text{ p.a.}}{500\,000\text{ p.a.}} \text{ to local authority/landowner} = \frac{ground\ rent}{total\ income}$$

$$= 10\%$$

$$\text{Developer's return} \quad \frac{450\,000\text{ p.a.}}{500\,000\text{ p.a.}}$$

$$= 90\%$$

At review, income is divided accordingly in the same proportion.
Return to local authority/landowner:

Assume historic site purchase costs to be £750 000 including fees and disturbance costs.

	£
Site purchase cost	750 000
Interest during development period 3 years @ 13%	332 000
Total cost on completion	£1 082 000
Return =	$\dfrac{50\,000}{1\,082\,000} = 4.6\%$
Total cost £1 082 000 @ 13%* =	140 700 p.a.
less ground rent	50 000 p.a.
deficit	£90 700 p.a.
* cost of borrowing.	

5.2   EQUITY-SHARING AND PARTNERSHIPS

Participation

Participation arrangements involve the sharing of the additional return which arises over a period from the time of the estimated outcome to the actual outcome on completion. In this case, let us assume there has been a growth in income over the development period and an inflation in building costs. Let us assume a 50:50 share in the growth in the net income over the development period.

Example 5.2: Participation arrangement

	£
Estimated income:	500 000 p.a.
Actual income (estimated *plus* (say) 20%)	600 000 p.a.
Estimated costs:	5 000 000
Actual costs (estimated *plus* (say) 10%)	5 500 000

The original ground rent was £50 000 p.a. but now there is agreement that any excess of return over the position set out in the estimated position is shared 50:50.

Calculation:

	£	£
Actual income		600 000 p.a.
Actual cost	5 500 000	
Decapitalise by the development yield	0.09	
		495 000 p.a.
Residue		105 000 p.a.
less ground rent		50 000 p.a.
Excess		55 000 p.a.
		£
thus: 50% excess to local authority		27 500 p.a.
plus original ground rent		50 000 p.a.
Revised ground rent		77 500 p.a.

Future growth apportioned $\dfrac{77\,500 \text{ p.a.}}{600\,000 \text{ p.a.}}$ to local authority

$= 12.9\%$

So developer gets 87.1%.

Equity-sharing arrangements

Equity-sharing arrangements are summarised in Figure 5.2; the main elements of the different arrangements are discussed below.

4 slice

The approach is the same as in the participation arrangement shown in Example 5.2. The charges to the property are as follows:

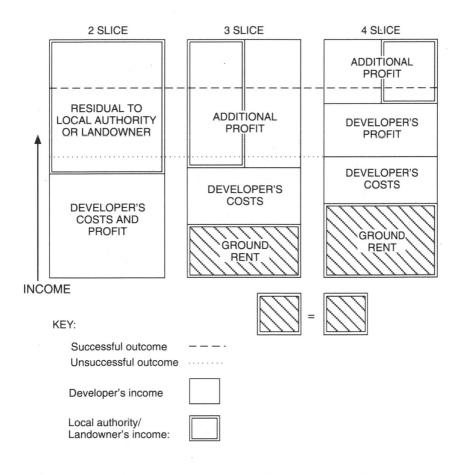

Note: Horizontal division of income is called 'slicing'; hence 'top slice'.
        Vertical division is called 'side by side' or 'back to back'.

Figure 5.2 *Equity sharing: a summary*

1st charge: the ground rent to the local authority or landowner
2nd charge: the developer's costs also known as the 'building rent' (0.075 on cost)
3rd charge: the developer's profit (0.015 on cost)
4th charge: the residue or 'top slice', in this case split 50:50.

This arrangement is also shown in Figure 5.3, which shows the priority of charge.

3 slice

The approach is the same as in the participation approach, but with no developer's profit. Here the developer is taking a substantial risk and may ask for a lower ground rent to be payable.

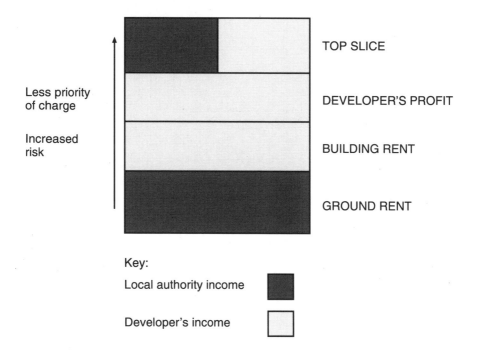

Figure 5.3   *4 slice equity-sharing*

Example 5.3: 3 slice approach

Calculation:

	£	£
Actual income		600 000 p.a.
Actual cost	5 500 000	
Decapitalise by the developer's costs	0.075	
		412 500 p.a.
Residue		187 500 p.a.
less ground rent		20 000 p.a.
Excess		167 500 p.a.
		£
thus: 50% excess to local authority		83 750 p.a.
plus original ground rent		20 000 p.a.
Equity rent payable		£103 750 p.a.

Future growth apportioned $\dfrac{103750 \text{ p.a.}}{600000 \text{ p.a.}}$ to local authority or landowner

$$= 17.3\%.$$

So developer gets 82.7%.

1st charge:	The ground rent to the local authority or landowner
2nd charge:	The developer's costs, also known as the 'building rent' (0.075 on cost)
3rd charge:	The residue.

2 slice

Here the local authority or the landowner is taking all the risk if something goes wrong; they may ask the developer to take less profit on this basis, perhaps by reducing the development yield to 8.5%.

Example 5.4: 2 slice approach

Calculation:

	£	£
Actual income		600 000 p.a.
Actual cost	5 500 000	
Decapitalise by the development yield	0.085	
		467 500 p.a.
Residue to local authority/landowner		132 500 p.a.

Future growth apportioned $\dfrac{132500 \text{ p.a.}}{600000 \text{ p.a.}}$ to local authority or landowner

$$= 22.1\%$$

So developer gets 77.9%.

1st charge: The developer's costs and profit.
2nd charge: The residue to the local authority or landowner.

Notes on equity-sharing arrangements

The risk element will always hit the top slice of the income stream if anything goes wrong, as can be seen in Figure 5.3. On rent growth the returns have been worked out on apportioned returns, as at the date of completion of the scheme. So, in the participation arrangement the proportionate share was 12.9% to the local authority/landowner and 87.1% to the developer. This arrangement then serves to divide the proceeds at each subsequent review.

If the 4 slice method was used and the proportions were recalculated at each rent review, then there would be a gearing effect on the review as the residue increases in proportion to the total income. Thus the local authority's/landowner's 50% of the top slice would increase and the developer's share decrease (see Figure 5.4). Box 5.1 summarises these equity-sharing schemes.

5.3   ADVANTAGES OF PARTNERSHIPS

There are a number of advantages for the main parties in the partnership approach, and these are summarised in this section.

Advantages of partnerships for the developer

(i)   Land assembly: compulsory purchase may be the only means to complete the site and a local authority may be able to provide these powers. It would certainly help to reduce the development period.

(ii)   The local authority can assist on planning, Building Regulations and highway matters. In partnership it could also provide good publicity. Other major landowners in partnership may be able to influence the local authority in these areas.

(iii) If the local authority or landowner provides the site, there are no site acquisition costs nor finance charges on site costs to be carried until development.

(iv)   The local authority or landowner may be able to apply for grants to subsidise development costs, for instance:

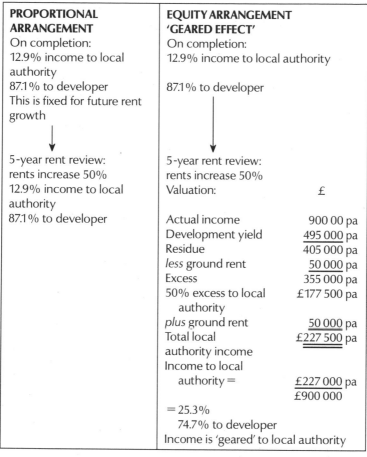

PROPORTIONAL ARRANGEMENT	EQUITY ARRANGEMENT 'GEARED EFFECT'	
On completion:	On completion:	
12.9% income to local authority	12.9% income to local authority	
87.1% to developer	87.1% to developer	
This is fixed for future rent growth		
↓	↓	
5-year rent review:	5-year rent review:	
rents increase 50%	rents increase 50%	
12.9% income to local authority	Valuation:	£
87.1% to developer		
	Actual income	900 00 pa
	Development yield	495 000 pa
	Residue	405 000 pa
	less ground rent	50 000 pa
	Excess	355 000 pa
	50% excess to local authority	£177 500 pa
	plus ground rent	50 000 pa
	Total local authority income	£227 500 pa
	Income to local authority =	£227 000 pa
		£900 000
	= 25.3%	
	74.7% to developer	
	Income is 'geared' to local authority	

Figure 5.4   *Proportional and equity-sharing (sliced) arrangements for future growth: example from participation calculation (Example 5.2)*

      — land grants to improve soil/ground conditions;
      — development grants to help subsidise schemes that don't quite add up financially.

Advantages of partnerships for the local authority

(i)   The local authority can use partnership arrangements to encourage development and initiate schemes. It can provide 'pump priming' finance, infrastructure, subsidies or land.

(ii)   The local authority has more control over what is being developed if it is actually involved in the development. 'Positive planning' as

---

SUMMARY OF EQUITY-SHARING SCHEMES

---

4 slice

    (i)   As for 3 slice but the ground rent is the full amount
    (ii)   The developer's costs are the second slice
    (iii) The allowance for the developer's profit is the third slice
    (iv) The additional profit is split between the parties.

3 slice

    (i)   The ground rent is the first charge, then the developer's costs
    (ii)   The additional profit is split between the partners
    (iii) The ground rent is smaller as there is no developer's profit
    (iv) The risk borne by the landowner is more as compared to the four slice method, as the ground rent is less.

2 slice

    (i)   Developer has first charge, with the residual going to the landowner as the top slice
    (ii)   If scheme is unsuccessful, then the landowner has little return
    (iii) If the scheme is successful, then the return to the landowner is very high
    (iv) There is little risk for the developer
    (v)   The position is safe for the developer, so there is no incentive to ensure maximum success.

Box 5.1   *Summary of equity-sharing schemes (see Figure 5.2)*

        envisaged in the Community Land Act legislation in the 1970s for instance. This control is greater than can be achieved by planning legislation.

(iii)   Partnerships complement the skills of the two parties. The local authority can provide backup on engineering matters, sewers, roads, transport, and planning, whereas the private partner can provide project management and financial expertise and development knowledge. Developers can also take some of the risk out of the development, because of their experience.

(iv)   Partnerships may allow developments to be funded in the market. Private funds may be attracted to a partnership scheme whereas they may not be to a local authority scheme. The partner is often chosen for expertise in raising funds.

(v)   By proportionate rent-sharing arrangements, the local authority can share in future growth in rents in the scheme.

Similar advantages may be available for other types of landowner besides the local authority. An example of a partnership arrangement is set out in Example 5.5.

Example 5.5: The application of a partnership arrangements using a hypothetical example

A local authority own a town centre site of 1 hectare. The buildings on site have no value and the local authority want the site developed. The development brief suggests the following mixed scheme:

Office space (m^2)   6000
Supermarket (m^2)   3000
Shop units each 120 m^2 x 20 units
Car parking spaces   200, including roofspace

The appraisal is set out in Figure 5.5, together with the calculation of the residual value for the land.

The local authority has subsequently indicated that they may wish to participate in the scheme. They require an initial ground rent of £100 000 p.a. with a premium. The rents are likely to increase over the period by 10% Details of a suitable equity-sharing arrangement are set out below. The suggested approach is outlined using a spreadsheet structure, note the layout and note that there may be rounding differences as the spreadsheet is working to more precise numbers not visible in the figures displayed in the example.

Assumptions:						
	rents per m^2 p.a.			£140	offices	
				£250	shop units	
				£200	supermarket	
	investment yield %		7.00	long leasehold %		7.50
	building cost per m^2			£850	offices	
				£460	shop units	
				£420	supermarket	
	short-term finance % p.a.			17		
	car parking spaces		150	@	£500	surface
			50	@	£2000	rooftop
	planning period (months)			0		
	building period (months)			18		
	void period (months)			3		
Site appraisal						
Gross development value						
Supermarket: gross area			3000	m^2		
net area @	90	%	2700	m^2		
rental per m^2			£200			
total rent					£540 000	p.a.

total rent b.f.						£540 000	p.a.
Shops: gross area		each		120	m²		
net area @	90	%		108	m²		
rental per m²				£250			
number of units				20			
total rent						£540 000	pa
Offices: gross area				6000	m²		
net area @	80	%		4800	m²		
rental per m²				£140			
total rent						£672 000	p.a.
Total income from scheme						£1 752 000	p.a.
YP perp @	7	% yield				14.29	YP
Gross development value						£25 028 571	
Less **costs:**							
Building costs				£	£		
	3000	m² supermarket @		420	1 260 000		
	2400	m² shops @		460	1 104 000		
	6 000	m² offices @		850	5 100 000		
Car park		150	spaces @	500	75 000		
		50	spaces @	2 000	100 000		
Demolition and site cost					100 000		
Total building cost					7 739 000		
Fees @	12.50	%			967 375		
Interest on 1/2 building cost for 18 months @ 17%					986 723		(simple interest)
Interest on 2/3 fees for 18 months @ 17%					164 437		
Total cost					9 857 535		
Interest on total for void (letting) for 3 months 17%					418 945		
Contingency on total cost 3%					308 294		
					10 584 774		
Letting fees @		15	% rent		262 800		
Advertising @		1	% G.D.V.		250 286		
Total development costs					11 097 860		
Plus developer's profit 17%GDV					4 254 857		
Costs *plus* profit						15 352 717	
Value of site in		1.75	years			9 675 854	
P V £1 in	1.75	years @		17	%	0.7598	
Value of site now						7 351 298	
less acquisition costs				4	%	294 052	
Site value						7 057 247	
				say	£7 060 000		

Equity participation:						
Assuming no increase in costs, allow for 50:50 participation on increased income.						
Original position:						
Expected income p.a.						£1752 000
Costs:						
Development costs *less* profit					£11 097 860	
Developer's yield:						
Investment yield				7.50	% p.a.	
Profit @	20	%		1.50	% p.a.	
Total yield required on costs					9.00	% p.a.
Rent to developer						£998 807
Balance of income to landowner (ground rent)						£753 193
Ground rent to local authority =			£100 000			
Balance of ground rent =			£653 193			
Premium = balance/development yield = balance/0.09			£7 257 695			
Actual position:						
Actual income p.a. +10%						£1 927 200
Costs:						
Development costs *less* profit					£11 097 860	
Premium					£7 257 695	
Total costs					£18 355 556	
Developer's yield:						
Investment yield				7.50	% pa	
Profit @	20	%		1.50	% p.a.	
Total yield required on costs					9.00	% p.a.
Rent to developer						£1 652 000
Ground rent						£100 000
Residue						£175 200
split 50 : 50		£87 600	each			
Income to local authority $= \dfrac{\text{ground rent } + 50\% \text{ residue}}{\text{income}} =$						9.7%
Income on review on a proportional basis =				9.7%		

Figure 5.5   *Appraisal of partnership arrangements in Example 5.5, and calculation of residual value for the land.*

REFERENCES

Darlow, C. (ed.) (1988) *Valuation and Development Appraisal,* Estates Gazette, London.
Morley, S. (1988) 'Partnership Schemes and Ground Rent Calculations', in C. Darlow (ed.), *Valuation and Development Appraisal,* Estates Gazette, London.

6　Cash Flow Approaches

6.1　USE OF CASH FLOW METHODS

Introduction

This chapter looks at cash flow methods in property development appraisals. Cash flows into the future are forecasts, but valuations and forecasts are fundamentally different. This aspect has been discussed to a degree in Chapter 4, but essentially the valuation is about market price as a snapshot in time. It may be based on assumptions as to what will happen in the future but it is not a forecast A forecast will be concerned entirely with the future. In development appraisals assumptions need to be made about project costs and future rents, and potential changes can be incorporated. Formal forecasting is used in property development, but its overall lack of use is based on the problems of risk and uncertainty in the development process (Schiller 1994, p. 4). Cash flow approaches are aided by computers and the use of spreadsheets for calculations involving cash flow statements is vital. Some texts suggest the use of bespoke computer programs (Darlow 1988). These bespoke programs can examine the answers relating to changes of inputs into the calculations, but it is difficult to examine the changes in detail as they occur; for this, a spreadsheet is more useful. The Lotus 1–2–3 spreadsheet is a useful tool for development appraisals and the examples in this book have been calculated using this software.

The traditional method of residual valuation is the most commonly used approach in the financial analysis of development proposals. However, the increasing complexity of investment markets and the size and complexity of development projects have required more sophisticated techniques for analysis. As with investment markets, much of the push for greater detail and analysis in appraisal lies with the demands and examples set by the major funders of schemes, the financial institutions, the insurance companies and the pension funds. They make demands for better analysis when they are providing funds and provide an example in the quality of analysis used in-house when they are project managing or dealing with their own portfolio. In addition, other lenders – banks, individuals and organisations in joint ventures – have established their own standards to ensure that their money does not get into trouble. The financial sector and the investment market deal internationally and with a number of asset classes, so techniques have been adopted from experiences in the US and the use of analysis in investment appraisal has been utilised from examples used in the management of portfolios of shares and gilts. Economic analysis, providing a wider setting to the micro-economic financial analysis used in property development, has been applied both in the valuation to ensure that the outcome is appropriate to the market and in the subsequent analysis of the investment. These developments are reflected in the move in property appraisal in the UK from the traditional definition of open market value to the concept of estimated realisation price and the need for more explicit forecasting.

At a basic level, the traditional valuation can be developed by using a cash flow approach which divides up the timescale of development into periods to which the interest periods can be more precisely applied. The simple analysis of the application of interest charges to building costs and fees for half or two thirds of the building period respectively is therefore flawed because if the 'S curve' of cumulative building costs is applied, costs will tend to accumulate more in the later stages of development, for instance in relation to the high cost of services and finishes in buildings. In this case, the 'rough' residual calculation can be seen to be overestimating the costs. In a competitive situation, the 'refined' cash flow approach will throw up lower costs and, assuming other elements equal, a 'higher' site value than the 'rough' calculation. Thus the 'refined' approach would tend to ensure that the developer won the purchase or tender.

Cash flows can also enable more explicit assumptions to be put into the appraisal: changes over time, for instance changes in interest rates, can be accommodated; these changes cannot be accommodated in the 'snapshot' traditional residual valuation. In a period of inflation, allowance can be made for inflation on costs and, by including revenue and costs in the calculation, growth and inflation can be applied to various revenues and rents. The cash flow can make allowance for the timing of possible one-off payments or allow for deductions or allowances based on the size of the various elements, tax deductions and capital allowances for instance.

The argument about using cash flow approaches (including discounted cash flow) against the traditional Years Purchase approach of valuation is extensive. Problems arise because the price paid in the market may not reflect the present worth of the future cash flow and these problems have been discussed earlier when it was suggested that appraisal needs to distinguish between the valuation of a purchase price and the analysis of the worth of an investment. A discounted cash flow (DCF) approach appears to be the only realistic approach to dealing with over-rented property (where the rent passing under the lease is higher than the existing market rental). In the present recessionary market, the use of traditional techniques may no longer be defended, thus traditional methods may not be able to cope with issues such as rent-free periods, reverse premiums, tenant incentives, bad debts, negative growth and over-rented properties (French 1994).

Development appraisal: the use of cash flows to improve the traditional residual

Cash flows can assist in the calculation of costs over the development period. The basic residual method is unaltered but the cash flow approach gives a more detailed calculation of the scheme's total costs and thus the finance costs. In the cash flow approach, all development costs are divided into monthly (or quarterly or annual) amounts. The net cash flows are calculated and short-term finance allowed for each period. Cash flows deal more accurately with the build-up of total construction costs over the period. In Figure 6.1 the build-up of costs can be seen and, depending on the shape of the S curve, the simplified example shows that over the period to the half-way stage only 40 per cent of the contract value may have been spent.

There are thus two errors in the traditional residual:

(i)　It is assumed that the total money borrowed will bear interest over half the building period. This is inaccurate because:

(a)　it bears no relation to actual incidence of costs which may differ from month to month over the period;

(b)　interest compounds monthly or quarterly over the period depending on the arrangements with the lender; the simple

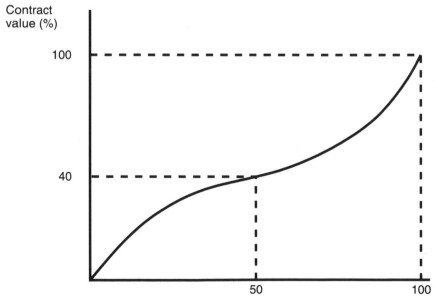

Figure 6.1　*S curve of building costs*

interest formula of the traditional residual, or even compounding interest annually is an over-simplification.

(ii)   The build-up of building costs as shown in the S curve suggests that costs are loaded to the end of the building period. In the example only 40 per cent of the costs are incurred halfway through the period. This may be because ground and initial works may be cheaper. This will depend on circumstances but in many cases this is a fair assumption. Any building with complex service provision in the form of lifts or air conditioning or with expensive finishes will exaggerate this tendency. The traditional method will thus allow for too much interest.

To summarise, cash flow statements are useful in certain situations:

(i)   in showing the effect of inflation in rents and building costs over time;
(ii)   in sensitivity analysis, to examine the effect of changes on the elements of cost;
(iii)   when including tax in the calculation;
(iv)   when taking into account a phased development and partial disposal;
(v)   in showing the debt outstanding at any point; and,
(vi)   in showing the time of peak cash outlay.

Cash flows are a necessity for certain developments, for instance:

(i)   residential estates with phased disposal, say where a new phase of houses are being built and an existing phase is being sold off to fund the cost of the new phase;
(ii)   complex central area shopping schemes with complex phasing and funding;
(iii)   industrial estates or business parks with a programme of disposal of sites and completed buildings to minimise cash outlay;
(iv)   New Town developments with a phased implementation of schemes to develop infrastructure and social provision.

When considering the finance of a project, DCF techniques can be useful if the scheme is to be retained and financed by mortgage and leaseback as the net return can be seen. Morley (1988a, pp. 73–7) suggests three general approaches to the use of cash flow statements: the period by period cash flow, net terminal value approach, and a DCF approach. The advantages and disadvantages of the three approaches are summarised in Box 6.1. Example 6.1 sets out a calculation in a spreadsheet format using these three approaches.

CASH FLOW APPRAISAL		
PERIOD BY PERIOD	**NET TERMINAL VALUE**	**DISCOUNTED CASH FLOW**
Interest accrues quarterly according to how the bank charges or monthly for payments to the building contractor Interest on the previous quarter is added to the next	Like the residual valuation, it adds interest on the outstanding amount to the end of the construction period	It converts the period payments to present day value
Advantages The debt is shown for each period, it copes with interest rate changes	Quicker, logical extension to the traditional residual	Quickest approach, the internal rate of return (IRR) is calculated
Disadvantages Laborious	Not flexible	Not related to how cost is evolved. Does not show the total debt

Box 6.1   *Cash flow appraisal: alternative approaches*

Example 6.1: Cash flow methods

USE OF CASH FLOW METHODS						
EXAMPLE:						
Value a site for development. Outgoings, buildings costs and fees breakdown as follows, excluding finance:						
Year 1		£		Year 2	£	
1st quarter		90 000		5	120 000	
2		50 000		6	160 000	
3		120 000		7	170 000	
4		140 000		8	150 000	

The builder is usually paid monthly, so a monthly cash flow is needed for this; the developer uses a quarterly cash flow as interest is usually charged on a quarterly basis.

Income from the scheme is £200 000 and it could be sold at a 8 per cent yield for £2 500 000 on completion of the works. Finance is 4 per cent per quarter (17 per cent p.a.). The return for risk and profit is 20 per cent capital value.

1. TRADITIONAL RESIDUAL						
				£	£	£
Income				200 000		
YP perp @	8	%		12.5		
Gross development value					2 500 000	
less costs:			£			
Building cost + fees			1 000 000			
Finance @	17	% for 1/2				
costs for	2	years	170 000			
Total costs				1 170 000		
Return for risk and profit						
20	% capital value			500 000		
Costs *plus* profit					1 670 000	
Site value on completion					830 000	
PV £1	2	years @	17	%	0.730514	
Site value today					606 326	
(including purchase costs)						

2. PERIOD BY PERIOD CASH FLOW						
Period: 3 months	Total costs £	Income £	Net flow £	Capital outstanding from previous period	Interest @ 4.00% (on d)	Capital outstanding
	a	*b*	*c = b + a*	*d*	*e*	*f = c + d + e*
1	−90 000	0	−90 000	0	0	−90 000
2	−50 000	0	−50 000	−90 000	−3 600	−143 600
3	−120 000	0	−120 000	−143 600	−5 744	−269 344
4	−140 000	0	−140 000	−269 344	−10 774	−420 118
5	−120 000	0	−120 000	−420 118	−16 805	−556 922
6	−160 000	0	−160 000	−556 922	−22 277	−739 199
7	−170 000	0	−170 000	−739 199	−29 568	−938 767
8	−150 000	0	−150 000	−938 767	−37 551	−1 126 318
					£	
Capital value					2 500 000	
less: Outstanding debt				1 126 318		
and return for risk and profit						
20	% capital value			500 000		
Costs *plus* profit					1 626 318	
Site value on completion					873 682	
PV £1	2	years @	17	%	0.730514	
Site value today					638 237	
(including purchase costs)						

3	NET TERMINAL VALUE						
Period	Net flow		Interest until		Net outlay		
	as above		completion @		on completion		
	£		4.00%		£		
			% (see below)				
1	−90 000		1.315932		−118 434		
2	−50 000		1.265319		−63 266		
3	−120 000		1.216653		−145 998		
4	−140 000		1.169859		−163 780		
5	−120 000		1.124864		−134 984		
6	−160 000		1.0816		−173 056		
7	−170 000		1.04		−176 800		
8	−150 000		1		−150 000		
					−1 126 318		

This gives the same answer as above.

Interest on completion is the Amount of £1 for the remainder of the project, in period 1 it is the Amount of £1 in 7 quarters @ 4%.

4.	DISCOUNTED CASH FLOW						
Period	Net flow		PV £1 @		PV of		
	as above		4.00%		cash flow		
	£		%		£		
1	−90 000		0.961538		−86 538		
2	−50 000		0.924556		−46 228		
3	−120 000		0.888996		−106 680		
4	−140 000		0.854804		−119 673		
5	−120 000		0.821927		−98 631		
6	−160 000		0.790315		−126 450		
7	−170 000		0.759918		−129 186		
8	−150 000		0.73069		−109 604		
Total cost					−822 990		
− Profit	−500 000		0.73069		−365 345		
+ Value	2 500 000		0.73069		1 826 726		
			Site value today		638 391		

Present value of £1 is based on the PV £1 @ 4% for the period shown in the first column, i.e. for period 1 it is $1/((1 + 0.04)^1)$, in this case value and profit are discounted back to the present time, this means that the site value calculated is already at present value.

The main differences between the approaches can thus be summarised:

Period by period

1. The interest is assessed quarterly on the outstanding amount from the previous quarter.
2. This is a more accurate statement of cost *plus* interest, the total cost is deducted from the gross development value to get to the site value.
3. The site value needs to be discounted back to the present in this calculation.

Net terminal value

1. The interest per quarter is assessed to the end of the project.
2. As 2 and 3 above in the period by period cash flow approach.

Discounted cash flow

1. The cost and interest is present valued for the period involved.
2. The value and profit is present valued and the site value worked out.
3. The site value is already at present value.

Development valuations and the cash flow approach

The valuation of properties having development potential uses the residual method. The basis of this method as seen in earlier chapters is an estimate of the development value *less* costs to give the residual value of the site. The development costs include all the costs to complete the development such as the building costs and ancillary costs related to landscaping and servicing. In addition, costs relating to fees, funding costs and the developers' profit will also need to be included. The sum available for land acquisition is at the completion of the development as calculated by the residual valuation and includes the costs of borrowing the amount for acquisition throughout the development period.

This sum for land acquisition thus needs to be discounted back to the present day to find the acquisition price now. In acquiring the site, there will be legal, valuation and stamp duty fees which will need to be paid and these are usually allowed for at 3 per cent of the amount of the site value. With development, there will be problems of retaining the development while there is no income available. This will happen where there is speculative development which has not been presold or pre-let. This increases the risk to the developer and to the financier. An obvious way of reducing the funding problem and the risk of voids is to phase the developments so that cash inflows can be generated. For example, in residential schemes, this may be fairly straightforward. The residential development can proceed in various phases where the first phase, for instance, is sold to finance the construction costs of later phases. In the past commercial development schemes did not readily allow for phasing. This is because tenants do not welcome occupying premises with construction continuing around them. This can affect their business and profitability. However, business and retail parks and industrial estates do lend themselves to phasing of development, therefore considerably reducing the funding requirements as well as the risk to the developer, which increases the longer a scheme takes to complete (Isaac and Steley 1991).

Example 6.2: A development appraisal using a cash flow (from Isaac and Steley 1991, Example 13.2)

An office development has been proposed. The office block will have a gross floor area of 1100 m^2 and the net lettable floor area will be 80 per cent of the gross area. An investment yield of 8 per cent is expected to be obtained on a net rental value of £320 per m^2. Construction is planned to commence six months after the site is acquired and building will take 15 months to complete. The premises will be let and sold as an investment six months after completion. Funding can be obtained at an interest rate of 17 per cent per annum.

The conventional residual valuation is shown in Table 6.1. The net development value is based on the capitalised net rent, less the fees incurred on disposal. The building costs will be estimated on the gross internal area and the total design fees are taken at 13 per cent of costs as well as a contingency allowance of 5 per cent for the costs and the fees. Finance is taken for half the construction period as indicated in earlier chapters, followed by six months during which the finance will be paid on the total cost including the building finance. This is for the void period. The site purchase amount will have to be financed from the date of purchase and therefore the final sum is discounted for the total period of 27 months being the development period for the project. The resultant net present value of £1 109 634 is available for the purchase of the site at the beginning of the project. The cash flow approach is then set out in Table 6.2. In the cash flow approach, interest is paid at the end of each quarter, local authority fees and part of the design fees being paid in the first quarter with construction commencing in the third quarter. It is usual for the retention to be held by the developer, part being released on completion and the remainder at the end of the defects liability period, generally six months. This retention allows for any minor defects to be remedied. Had the offices been let before being sold as an investment, the rent received would have been entered as an income with a corresponding reduction in borrowing. On this cash flow basis, an offer of £1 180 348 could be made for the site.

The two treatments of this simple example illustrate that the basis of the traditional residual valuation for development purposes remains unchanged, it is the deduction of development costs from the developed value. The cash flow approach gives a much more accurate valuation by requiring the valuer to give detailed consideration as to all the costs elements likely to arise during the project. Computer models do not provide an easy solution, they

Table 6.1   *Conventional residual valuation for an office development*

Gross floor area	1100 m^2		
Net floor area	880 m^2		
Net income	880 m^2 @ £320/m^2	£281 600	
YP in perp. @ 8%		12.5	
Gross development value		£3 520 000	
Less sale costs @		140 000	
Net developed value			£3 379 200
Development costs			
Building costs	1100 m^2 @ £625/m^2	687 500	
Fees:			
Architect, etc.	13.00%	89 375	
Local authority	2.5%	17 188	
Contingencies	5.0%	39 703	
Total		833 766	
Finance costs			
Construction costs	833 766		
7.5 months @ 17%	0.1021	85 961	
Letting time			
Accrued amount	919 727		
6 months @ 17%	0.0817	75 142	
Letting cost			
Agent 10% of rent	28 160		
Legal 2%	5 632	33 792	
Developer's profit			
20% Gross development value		704 000	
Total development costs			1 732 661
Amount for site on completion			1 646 539
PV £1 for 2.25 years @ 17%			0.702
Amount for site acquisition			1 155 870
Less acquisition fees @ 40%			46 236
Amount for site			1 109 634
Estimated capital value of site			£1 110 000

Note: Quarterly rate used.

only enable otherwise tedious and repetitive calculations to be avoided. Frequently, the purchase price of the site is known, in which case a developer will need to know the profit to be made from a project. In using the cash flow, the acquisition costs can be included as a development expense in the residual valuation and thus the resulting residue is the amount of profit generated. Viability statements showing profit expressed as a return on gross development value or total cost can also be prepared and are invaluable for monitoring the development project; changes in interest rates, delays in

Table 6.2 Cash flow valuation for an office development

Period number		1	2	3	4	5	6	7	8	9
Expenditure										
Site: Cost										
Fees										
Contractor: cost				68 750	120 312	144 375	171 875	182 187		
contingency				3 438	6 016	7 219	8 594	9 109		
less: retention				−3 609	−6 316	−7 580	−9 023	−9 565		
release: retention									18 047	18 047
Fees: Architect		30 000								4 375
Local Authority		17 188								
Developer's required profit										704 000
Letting fees				11 000	11 000	11 000	11 000	11 000		33 792
Balance b.f.	0.12		49 077	51 042	135 849	277 543	449 873	657 631	884 404	938 577
Total monthly expenditure		47 188	49 077	130 620	266 860	432 557	632 318	850 363	902 451	1 698 791
Income										
Sale										3 520 000
less Agent's fees @	0.04									140 800
Total net income		0	0	0	0	0	0	0	0	3 379 200
Outstanding balance		−47 188	−49 077	−130 620	−266 860	−432 577	−632 318	−850 363	−902 451	1 680 409
Interest on balance		−1 889	−1 965	−5 229	−10 683	−17 316	−25 313	−34 041	−36 126	67 269
Cumulative balance c.f.		−49 077	−51 042	−135 849	−277 543	−499 873	−657 631	−884 404	−938 577	1 747 678
Balance at end of project				£1 747 678						
PV £1 @ 0.04003/quarter		9 quarters		0.702						
Present amount for site				£1 227 562						
Acquisition fees		4%		£47 214						
Site value					£1 180 348					

Note: Quarterly rate used.

construction programme and variation in cost and sales forecasts can be readily inserted to project the resulting profit level. There is no doubt that the traditional residual valuation still has its use, especially where a quick appraisal is required, but in the present competitive market where the dividing line between success and failure is so fine, then detailed consideration of the cash flow is of prime importance.

The use of predicted values and costs

Current estimates can easily be overtaken by time; the research by Marshall (1991) suggested that in the late 1980s the bullish market used growth figures to increase rental values in the calculation of the gross development value. The use of predicted values in the calculation by the application of inflation to the cost figures and forecasted growth rates for the rental levels is subject to the risk of errors in estimation. This risk may be less than the equivalent risk of using current figures in an environment of change where approaches to the prediction of that change can be made.

Estimates of the future and consideration of risk and the probability of outcomes are discussed later in the chapter. Property developments, as with other major investment projects, have a long time scale; the environment is changing with ever-increasing rapidity, the danger will be that the estimates will be inaccurate. But consider the danger of taking no action; many business and personal decisions involve the need to take decisions, the decisions may turn out to be more or less a success or a disaster but not to make a decision in a rapidly changing environment is surely to court the certainty of disaster. The explicit approach of looking to the future and making adjustments accordingly may be flawed but is likely to be the only option. The problems of forecasting changes can be alleviated by the application of better techniques, the use of data arising from extensive research and the use of computing hardware/software to handle the demands of the techniques and the weight of data.

Strictly speaking, if a market rate of interest is used to discount and compound the elements within the residual valuation, then these elements should be at market rates. A market discount rate will include an inflation element and therefore should be applied to a current cost, not an historic one envisaged at the original time of appraisal. The current cost will have the inflation allowance built in.

Morley (1988a, pp. 84–7) looks at the prospects for forecasting costs using an historic analysis of changes in building cost inflation using data provided by the Building Cost Information Service (BCIS) and also the prospects for rental forecasting using an example from the retail sector (the Hillier Parker forecast of shop rents). An approach to building-in predicted costs and values into the cash flow would involve the cash flow being broken down into its elements of cost and appropriate inflation rates applied. These total costs can then be increased by the interest charges to completion. Finally, the building and finances costs can be incorporated into a residual valuation with a rental figure in which a growth rate has been applied. This approach is shown in a simplified manner in Example 6.3. There will need to be a refinement in the cash flow to allow for the delay in payment of the contractor (say 4 weeks) and a retention allowance of 3–5 per cent deducted from each monthly payment, with half repaid on completion and the other half six months after completion.

Example 6.3: Cash flow with inflated costs and expected rents

Assume a project with the following criteria:
Gross development value:

Full rental value	£ 100 000
YP @ 5%	20YP
Capital value	£2 000 000

Period of development: 1 year, cash flow divided into 4 quarters.

Costs	Building cost £	Fees £
Period 1	200 000	
2	200 000	
3	200 000	50 000
4	200 000	50 000

	% per quarter
Growth rate for rent	1
Inflation rate for building costs	3
Inflation rate for fees	2
Interest rate	4

Step 1: Apply inflation to costs (£)

Period	Current estimate: bldg costs	Inflation @ 0.03 per quarter	Inflated cost: bldg. costs	Current estimate: fees	Inflation @ 0.02 per quarter	Inflated cost: fees	Total cost
1	200 000	1	200 000				200 000
2	200 000	1.03	206 000				206 000
3	200 000	1.0609	212 180	50 000	1.0404	52 020	264 200
4	200 000	1.092727	218 545.4	50 000	1.061208	53 060.4	271 605.8

Assumes costs incurred at the beginning of the period thus inflation applied to remaining periods; e.g. for period 1 inflation $= (1 + i)^n$ where i is the growth rate per quarter, n is existing period *less* 1.

Step 2:	Include interest						
Period	Total cost	Interest @ 0.04 per quarter	Cost to completion				
1	200 000	1.124864	224 973				
2	206 000	1.0816	222 810				
3	264 200	1.04	274 768				
4	271 605.8	1	271 606				
		Total	994 156				

Step 3: Valuation with growth rate applied to rent:

				£			
Present estimated rental				100 000			
Rental growth 4 quarters @			0.01	1.040604			
Future estimated income				104 060			
YP in perpetuity @		5	%	20			
Capital value				2 081 208			
Less cost and finance			994 156				
Risk and profit @	0.2						
	capital value			416 242			
Total				1 410 398			
Site value				670 810			
PV of £1 in 4 quarters @			0.04	0.854804			
Site value today (including acquisition costs)				573 411			

This calculation is taken from a spreadsheet; note the layout and note that there may be rounding differences as the spreadsheet is working to more precise figures not visible on the display.

6.2 COMPUTER SPREADSHEETS

Computer software is critical for property development appraisal; in addition to databases to provide the evidence and analysis for valuation and property transactions, the spreadsheet is also an important tool to be used by valuation surveyors in calculations.

The spreadsheet was introduced generally into business at the beginning of the 1980s. The spreadsheet consists of a computer program which displays on the computer screen a number of cells. Each cell is given location co-ordinates rather like a map reference and these co-ordinates provide an address in which to put input data and a means by which the relationship between each of the cells can be described. By knowing the addresses of the various cells, by installing data within the cells and by instructing the computer as to the relationship between the cells, it is possible to build up a complex calculation across a number of cells and obtain an answer to the calculation. The power of the spreadsheet is its ability to recalculate instantly when one or a number of the inputs into the cells is changed. The investment calculation can thus be changed to allow access of a number of 'what if' scenarios. It may also be used with the input of very simple data to ensure that the calculation process that has been put into the spreadsheet is correct before elaborate calculation. The use of the spreadsheet comes into its own when dealing with complex valuation methods, particularly when dealing with discounted cash flow calculations and attempting to apply growth rates or risk probabilities to variables as discussed earlier.

The development of the spreadsheet came mainly in the area of accounting where it can be seen that the tool was very powerful in managing the complex financial calculations as contained in the accounts of companies and being able to give solutions for the final accounts.

Spreadsheets used to facilitate development appraisal

A spreadsheet is the equivalent of a piece of paper divided into a grid of rows and columns. In a computer, it can be considered as an electronic grid. The rows and columns are either number or lettered and each box formed by the grid is known as a cell and will have a unique reference. The size of the grid will depend on the spreadsheet program and that can be considerable, enabling quite extensive and complex calculations to be undertaken. Where calculations such as a residual valuation or viability statement will follow a structured format, templates can be set up in the programme; all that needs to be done is for the relevant data to be inserted in the appropriate cells and the required result is immediately obtained. Although data can be overwritten in any cell, it is possible to lock cells containing essential formulae in the program thereby preventing any accidental alteration to the structure of the program. There are differences in the figures produced from the spreadsheet and those in other worked examples in this book because the spreadsheet is capable of greater accuracy in the calculation.

The spreadsheet has the ability to calculate 'what if' calculations. This is because, as is appreciated in residual valuations, relatively minor changes in any one of the input variables can produce considerably greater change in the resulting land value as a residual. Appraisers therefore need to pose questions such as what if the interest changes? What if the building costs increase? Formerly, it would have been necessary to undertake a series of repetitive manual calculations, changing the data each time to produce answers to these questions. It can readily be seen that the spreadsheets allow such data changes to be made, instantly producing answers to 'what if' problems (Isaac and Steley 1991, p. 141).

An example of a spreadsheet which was used to develop a cash flow analysis is shown in Example 6.4; here a sensitivity analysis was used for instance in repetitive calculations where the outcomes were tested with a range of yields

Example 6.4: Example of the use of spreadsheet analysis

BUSINESS PARK EQUITY SCHEMES: INVESTMENT SCENARIO 1				
Initial yield	9.00%		Reversion yield	7.50%
Loan: value ratio	70.00%		Rental per m^2	£75.00
Property:		PHASE 1		
Gross area:		4 000	m^2	
Rent p.m^2.:		£75.00		
Rental value:		£300 000		
Yield:		9.00%	Reversion yield	7.50%
Capital value: £		3 333 333	Loan: value ratio	70%
Sale year		3		
Rent review year:		5		
Total costs:		£3 082 893		

YEAR			1992/93	1993/94	1994/95	1995/96
CAPITAL GROWTH						
Growth rate of rent				−3.00%		6.00%
Amount of £1				0.97	0.97	1.0282
Rent with growth				291 000	291 000	308 460
Yield:						7.50%
Capital value of term and reversion:						4 105 128
INTEREST						
Investment loan interest rate				14.50%	14.50%	14.50%
Investment loan b.f.			(2 333 333)	(2 333 333)	(2 371 667)	(2 415 558)
Loan interest			0	(338 333)	(343 892)	(350 256)
Rental income			0	300 000	300 000	300 000
Investment loan balance			(2 333 333)	(2 371 667)	(2 415 558)	(2 465 814)
Interest on cost shortfall				16.00%	15.00%	14.00%

CASH FLOW Year end March			1992/93	1993/94	1994/95	1995/96
Total b.f.			0	(749 560)	(876 879)	(1 015 996)
Interest on shortfall			0	(127 319)	(139 117)	(149 883)
Construction costs			(3 082 893)	0	0	0
Sale of investment						4 105 128
Loan capital (repayment)			2 333 333			(2 465 814)
Total c.f.			(749 560)	(876 879)	(1 015 996)	473 435
Cash flow for NPV			0	0	0	473 435

NPV @ 17% = <u>£295 599</u>
This compares with a net value at the present time of £3 333 333 *less* total costs
£3 082 893 = £250 440
Notes:
1. The present capital value is based on the rental of £7.50 per m² capitalised at 9% yield.
2. The sale price at the end of year 3 is based on the capital value of the term and reversion, assuming a 5-year rent review. The reversionary yield is 7.5 % and the income has been inflated at the anticipated growth rates to year 3.
3. Debt interest is compounded quarterly, it is assumed that 70% of value is charged the lower rate and the balance of interest *less* rental income is rolled up to year 3.
4. The remainder of the debt is charged at the higher rate and also rolled up to year 3.
5. The NPV of the net income in year 3 is discounted back at 17%, an opportunity cost rate.

between 7 and 10 per cent. It is not intended to describe the elements of this spreadsheet in detail but it is intended to give an example of its use; for instance, in the spreadsheet it can be seen that variables can be altered over the life of the cash flow; for instance the growth rate of the rents has been changed over the periods. Also the spreadsheet can incorporate quite complex calculations in a single cell, the figure for the capital value of the term and reversion involves the term and reversion calculation in a single cell.

Expert systems

Expert systems are models and simulations which are at the leading edge of sophistication. These models and simulations attempt to copy decision-making processes in certain contexts by asking questions of the data provided, in the same way that an enquiring professional might. This process simulates the thought and decision-making processes of the brain so that appropriate responses are made in the same way. Expert systems, if appropriately modelled, can avoid the subjectivity of some decision-making and appraisal. On the other hand, there is no allowance for subjectivity and wider consideration which may improve the quality of the decision made.

6.3   SENSITIVITY ANALYSIS AND RISK

Risk is related to return but it is important to distinguish between risk and uncertainty. Whereas risk can be assessed in terms of its probability and therefore insured against or allowed for, this is not possible with uncertainty. Risk also needs to be distinguished in its application to an individual asset or to a portfolio of assets. Risk relating to a portfolio is more concerned with investment strategy and portfolio analysis, and this is discussed later.

Allowance for risk can be applied in a number of ways; first it can be applied to the discount rate used in the calculation or secondly it can be applied to the cash flow which arises from the investment. In the first case, for instance, if a risk-free rate is 5 per cent and the risk premium is 2 per cent then this premium could be added to the risk-free rate to give a discount rate of 7 per cent which is therefore appropriate for the risk taken. If the risk is applied to the cash flow, then this flow has to be varied within a range of acceptable values and thus the output of the calculation can be assessed accordingly. The result can be found by using a statistical analysis assigning probability to the incidence of the cash flows and thus the result can be even more accurately defined.

Sensitivity analysis

The aim of sensitivity testing is to examine the effects of changes in variables on the residual value and the basic method involves changing one variable at a time, recalculating the value and analysing the result. The percentage change in the variable is compared with the percentage change in the residual amount. If a small percentage change in the variables produces a large percentage change in the residual amount then this variable is very sensitive (Butler and Richmond 1990, p. 111). Sensitivity analysis has been developed as a means of identifying the independent variable which causes the greatest change in the dependent variable (Baum and Crosby 1995, p. 246).

Examples of approaches to sensitivity analysis are now considered. These approaches require repetitive calculations and therefore will need computer assistance, for instance a spreadsheet. The medium of a book such as this to indicate approaches makes it difficult to show these approaches properly, since the presentation of a number of different calculations would make reading the text particularly difficult. So it is pointless setting out the figures to a particular example in the cases provided; the reader will learn about the approach by carrying out the calculations alone and will learn about the construction of the appraisal by constructing the appraisal method on a spreadsheet.

Simple sensitivity testing

Here the individual variables are changed one at a time and the effect of these changes on the result is seen. Percentage changes in the result or output can be seen relative to the changes in the input variables. A simple sensitivity test was carried out in Chapter 4. An approach to this would be to draw up a matrix of site values for different variables, i.e.:

Variable 1:	Investment capitalisation rate	5%	6%	7%
Variable 2:	£100/m^2	site value 1	site value 2	site value 3
Estimated	£110/m^2	site value 4	site value 5	site value 6,
rental value	£120/m^2			etc. . .

Or alternatively, the following approach shows which variables to focus on:

Change in variable (say) +10%	Change in residual value	Change in profit
Rental growth	+x%	+y%, etc. . . . .
Investment yield		
Building cost		
Finance cost		
Building period		
Development period		

A spider diagram will show changes in the variables plotted against the residual value or level of developer's profit; see Figure 6.2 for an example.

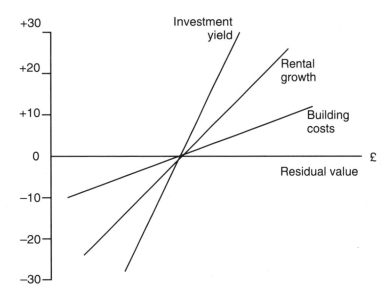

Figure 6.2   *Spider diagram*

Scenario testing

This involves changing a combination of a number of inputs and the output then is calculated with this combination of changes. This can be done in a number of ways, for example a combination of factors which are the expected variables can be used, for example the expected rental and yield of a future deal. In addition to this expected or realistic outcome, an optimistic scenario and a pessimistic scenario taking more optimistic or less optimistic outcomes can also be assessed, as follows:

Variable	Optimistic	Expected	Pessimistic
Rental growth	e.g. 7%	5%	3% etc. . . .
Investment yield			
Building cost			
Finance cost			
Building period			
Development period			
RESULTS			
Profit			
Residual Value			

Probability

Where a model for appraisal contains several or many uncertain inputs, predicted output is problematic and sensitivity analysis is of limited use. The output will be a range rather than a single value, and the problem is how to define the range and distribution; this is done by probabilistic modelling (Mollart 1994). In a more sophisticated form of sensitivity analysis, probability can be taken into account. This assesses the probability of the inputs being at a certain level and therefore can provide an even more sophisticated result. The probabilities are assigned to the input variables according to how likely these variables will be at certain levels. For instance, if there is a 50 per cent chance of the rent being say £120 per m^2, then the probability is assigned at 0.5 and included in the calculation accordingly. By running a computer program with the assigned probabilities which picks up the inputs on the basis of the probability, for instance, a 50 per cent chance of picking a rent of £120 and then by running the program a number of times, an average output can be assessed. This approach is called a Monte Carlo simulation (for more information on sensitivity analysis, see Morley 1988a and Byrne and Cadman 1984).

A basic approach to probability would look like that in Example 6.5.

Example 6.5: Probability

Probability of rental growth:

Rental growth	(a)	7%	5%	3%
Probability	(b%)	10%	60%	30%
Chance	(b)	0.1	0.6	0.3
Expected outcome	(a × b)	0.7	3.0	0.9

The weighted probability of rental growth = 0.7%+3.0%+0.9%= 4.6% This figure can then be used in the scenario test in the previous section instead of the single estimate figures (Isaac and Steley 1991, p. 111).

Analysing risk requires that the distribution of returns be defined in some way and this requires that the range and distribution of the inputs be defined and incorporated. The analysis used is probabilistic modelling; where the value of a variable cannot be predicted with certainty it is usually possible to set a range within which it will almost certainly fall, furthermore it will be possible to say that some values for the variable are more likely than others. This identifying of the range and associated probabilities for the values of variables typifies probability analysis (Mollart 1994, p. 90).

Probabilistic modelling generally falls into two categories; algebraic and simulation. The algebraic approach normally used is the Hillier method but this has severe limitations and simulations are more useful in this analysis. Monte Carlo simulation (MCS) is the simulation model most referred to and these routines can be run on a spreadsheet. Previously these were crude but with the advent of a spreadsheet add-in, @RISK this enables the simulation to be more easily carried out (Mollart 1994). The key feature of the Monte Carlo simulation is that input variables which cannot be stated with certainty are treated as distributions of some sort. When the simulation is run, a value for each variable is selected at random from the range of possible values which are then fed into the appraisal model being used to give a possible value from the output. Through a process of iteration this is repeated many times, thus simulating the range of possible outcomes. So long as sufficient iterations have been undertaken, a distribution of the possible outcomes can be produced to provide a measure of risk for the project.

Simulation

To summarise the use of simulation, the computer valuation is run like a Monte Carlo simulation which picks up the variables at random but within a range according to the probability ascribed to the variable; the simulation may then be run 1000 times. This then gives a range of results, say, for the residual value or profit. The mean is then calculated for the value or profit and the standard deviation is calculated. Assuming that the range of results is a normal distribution in statistical terms, there is a 95 per cent likelihood that the result will fall in the range of the mean ±2 standard deviations. The standard deviation is an indication of the variability of the results and there-fore represents risk. The developer may choose to avoid the risk by choice of variables – if risk averse – to limit the downside possibilities, that is the result falling below an acceptable range of values.

Aspects of risk are discussed in the next section. The use of computers to handle the analysis can save a lot of time. @RISK is a spreadsheet add-in which is available for the major spreadsheets. @RISK adds-in a number of facilities to enable the simulation to be carried out easily:

- it enables input variables to be specified as distributions instead of single point estimates;
- using a simple execute command, it performs as many iterations as specified i.e. 1000;
- it carries out a detailed statistical analysis of the resulting distribution;
- it generates a graphical output in a range of formats. (Mollart 1994)

Risk

The decision-maker's attitude to risk can be seen in terms of the utility function of the individual/corporate entity (see Figure 6.3).

The risk adverse developer will require more reward for more risk than the risk neutral developer and much more than the risk seeking developer. These curves all represent risk avoidance in the sense that all require more reward for more risk, but the classification is determined by the extent of the additional return required. Generally most investors are considered to be risk averse, that is preferring less risk to more risk, and there is evidence to suggest that all investors are risk averse when making important investment decisions (Brown 1991, p. 11). The risk profiles of developer–investors will change over time and will change relative to the project being considered. The risk indifference curves shown in Figure 6.3 can be adapted to show the return expected in the market and the actual trade-off of risk and reward, as shown in Figure 6.4.

Baum and Crosby (1988) have adopted DCF approaches to analyse prop-erty investments; however, many international investment markets are still reliant on basic initial yield analysis. Baum and Crosby recognise three levels of analysis, the individual investment or project return using NPV or IRR techniques (NPV is better; see Baum and Crosby 1988 or Hargitay and Yu 1993); a second level is calculation of the individual risk and the third is portfolio risk. The analysis of return without consideration of risk is pointless, the return will vary with risk and expected return will be higher in a risky situation. Individual risk will need to be considered and also the influence of

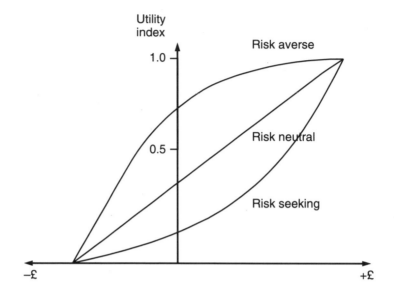

Source: Lumby (1991), p. 183.
Figure 6.3   *Utility functions illustrating attitudes to risk*

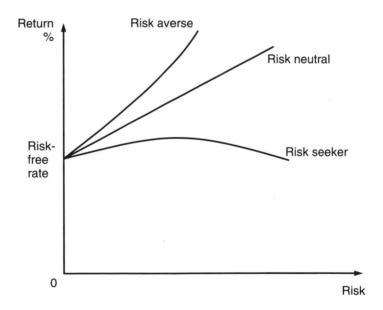

Figure 6.4   *Risk/return trade-off*

choosing a particular investment or project relative to the rest of the portfolio of investments/projects held (portfolio risk).

To summarise, the levels of analysis suggested by Baum and Crosby are thus:

(i)   calculation of NPV or IRR;
(ii) calculation of individual risk;
(iii) portfolio risk.

Definition of risk

Investment and development are considered risky because the investor–developer is unsure about the actual return which will be realised from the investment, so that risk is related to the uncertainty of future returns from an investment. There is a spectrum of uncertainty, see Figure 6.5.

Certainty is where there is precise knowledge of the outcome; risk is a situation where alternative outcomes are identified, together with a definite statement of the probabilities of such outcomes. Partial uncertainty is where alternative outcomes can be identified, but without the knowledge of the probabilities of such outcomes. Total uncertainty is where even the alternative outcomes cannot be identified. Thus if risk is regarded as the extent to which the actual outcome of an action or decision may diverge from the expected outcome, an action or decision is risk-free when the consequences are known with certainty. To a rational investor–developer who is averse to risk, the possibility of a lower than expected return has more importance than the possibility of a higher than expected return, the former case is therefore termed the 'downside risk'.

Definitions of risk may be descriptive or analytical:

* *Descriptive definitions* are related to sources and elements of risk and are used:
   – for classification of projects on the basis of the risk associated with them (see Chapter 4, where a descriptive analysis was undertaken on the components of the calculation for the residual valuation);

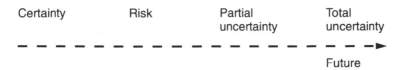

Source: Hargitay and Yu (1993), p. 35.
Figure 6.5 *Definition of risk*

– to determine the risk premium for use in a discount rate (see later in this chapter).
- *Analytical definitions* provide definitions of risk in terms of probability or variability, i.e.:
  – the probability of loss;
  – the probability that the developer–investor will not receive the expected or required rate of return;
  – the deviation of realised return from the expected return;
  – the variance or volatility of returns. (Hargitay and Yu 1993, p. 35)

Portfolio theory also tells us that total risk will have two components, systematic and unsystematic risk; see Table 6.3.

Systematic risk may have a number of elements: these relate to variations in the market, business cycles, inflation and financial interest rates for example. Unsystematic risk will cover elements such as business risk (associated with the product, markets, strategy), financial risk (associated with financial structure – see Chapters 7–10 on finance), liquidity risks and other specific risks related to the industrial sector in which the project takes place, the nature of the property and its location, etc.

Investment risks in development projects are concerned with future events which by their nature are uncertain. A rational approach to risk associated with the development process must include a strategy for dealing with risk such as:

(i)   recognition and definition of risk and its various components;
(ii)   quantification and measurement of risk;
(iii) the analysis of risk;
(iv)   a response to risk.

In a risk–return trade-off. the risks associated with a development project must be adequately compensated for by the expected returns generated. A

Table 6.3 *Components of risk from portfolio theory*

Systematic risk	Unsystematic risk (or specific risk)
• Caused by factors which affect *all* projects/ investments • e.g. Changes in general economic/ political/social environment. • Investor–developer has no control	• Affects only a particular investment • e.g. way a project has been financed, so more debt, more risk • Investor–developer has limited control by taking the appropriate investment–development decisions

suitable combination of discounting and probability criteria is the best solution (Hargitay and Yu 1993, p. 155). In investment decision-making, risk is defined as the extent to which the actual outcome of a decision may diverge from the expected outcome. Statistical measures such as measures of standard deviation and variance can be used as the absolute measure of variability of the actual outcome and the expected outcome.

The methods of risk analysis indicated can thus be classified in detail, as in Table 6.4.

Detailed analysis of these approaches is beyond the scope of this book and you are referred to the following texts for an introduction to this rapidly developing area: Byrne and Cadman (1984), Baum and Crosby (1995), Dubben and Sayce (1991) and Hargitay and Yu (1993). The descriptive methods of risk analysis have been outlined elsewhere in this chapter in relation to sensitivity testing, scenarios and simulations. The mean variance rule is used in projects and suggests that project A is preferred to project B where at least one of the following situations arises:

(i)   the expected return of A is greater than B and A's variance is less than or equal to B (expected return $A > B$, variance $A \leq B$);

(ii)   the expected return of A is equal to or greater than B and A's variance is less than B's (expected return of $A \geq B$, variance $A < B$).

The variance is a statistical measure of dispersion around the mean expected value and is a measure of risk as discussed earlier. For a background to these statistical measures see Hargitay and Yu (1993) or Brown (1991). Finally, amongst these descriptive measures is beta analysis; this concerns Portfolio theory and the earlier discussion of systematic and unsystematic risk; for further reading on this you are again referred to Hargitay and Yu (1993) and Brown (1991).

Table 6.4   *Risk analysis*

Methods which attempt a description of the riskiness of a project	Methods which attempt the incorporation of perceived risk in appraisal models
• Expected value/variance methods (mean variance method) • Sensitivity analysis • Scenario testing • Simulations • Beta analysis	• Risk adjusted discount rate method (RADR) • Certainty equivalent method • Sliced income approach

The methods which attempt to incorporate risk into appraisal models are discussed in Baum and Crosby (1995, Chapter 8) and I will outline a brief summary of these methods here.

Risk adjusted discount rate (RADR)

The market interest rate or discount rate,

$$I = (1 + i)(1 + d)(1 + r) - 1$$

where i is the time preference allowance
d is the inflation premium
r is the risk premium (see Isaac and Steley 1991, p. 105).

The risk-free rate (RFR) is a function of i and d only so that:

$$I = (1 + RFR)(1 + r) - 1$$

In practice the equation used is $I = RFR + r$ (Risk-free rate + Risk premium).
    The effective difference is small (see Isaac and Steley 1991, p. 105). The use of the risk adjusted rate implies that more return is required to compensate for more risk, but the problem is the estimation of how much.

Certainty equivalent techniques

This approach uses the statistical techniques of the mean and standard deviation to indicate the position where a risk averse investor–developer would be happy. Taking a normal statistical distribution as shown in Figure 6.6, ±1 standard deviation of the distribution from the mean will incorporate 68 per cent of the range of outcomes and the downside risk in this situation is defined as the area below the curve, more than 1 standard deviation less than the mean. This area will incorporate only 16 per cent (half the balance) of the distribution. Using this position the distribution tells us that the developer–investor has an 84 per cent chance of bettering the position. Thus in this approach the mean and standard deviation are calculated and at this point noted above and this is used in the analysis (the mean expected value - 1 standard deviation). In practice this expected value will be calculated from the probability calculation shown earlier.

The certainty equivalent approach is in five stages:

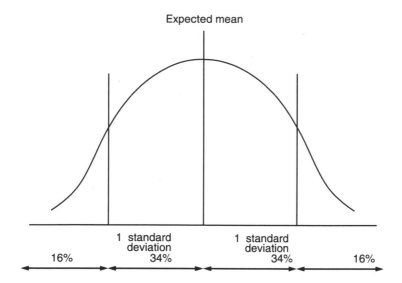

Figure 6.6 *Distribution under a normal curve: the downside risk is the 16 per cent of outcomes on the left side of the diagram below the curve*

1. Calculate the expected value:

    Expected value $(\bar{r}) = \Sigma(p \times \hat{r})$
    where $p = $ the probability of the sample
    and $\hat{r} = $ each sample outcome

2. Calculate the variance

    Variance $(\sigma^2) = \Sigma(p)(\hat{r} - \bar{r})^2$

3. Calculate the standard deviation

    Standard deviation (population) $= \sqrt{\text{variance}} = \sigma$

4. Calculate certainty equivalents

5. Redo calculation with certainty equivalent variables.

The calculation which follows is done with the aid of a spreadsheet structure; note the layout and note that there may be rounding differences as the spreadsheet is working to more precise numbers not visible in the figures displayed in the example.

Example 6.6: Application of certainty equivalent approach

RESIDUAL VALUATION					
Income				£200 000	
YP perp @		8	%	12.5	
Gross development value					2 500 000
less costs:			£		
Building cost + fees			1 000 000		
Finance @		17	% for 1/2		
costs for		2	years	170 000	
Total costs				1 170 000	
Return for risk and profit					
	20	% capital value		500 000	
Costs plus profit					1 670 000
Site value on completion					830 000
PV £1		2	years	17 %	0.7305136
Site value today (including purchase costs)					606 326
(1) Calculate the expected value					
Assume two variables: income and yield					
Income:	outcome	probability =		sample outcome	
	$\hat{r}$	p		$(p \times \hat{r})$	
	180 000	0.3		54 000	
	200 000	0.6		120 000	
	220 000	0.1		22 000	
Expected value $(\bar{r}) = \Sigma(p \times \hat{r})$			total	196 000	
Yield:	outcome	probability =		sample outcome	
	$\hat{r}$	p		$(p \times \hat{r})$	
	0.07	0.1		0.007	
	0.08	0.5		0.04	
	0.09	0.4		0.036	
Expected value $(\bar{r}) = \Sigma(p \times \hat{r})$			total	0.083	

(2) Calculate the variance					
Income:					
outcome	expected			probability	
$(\hat{r})$	value $(\bar{r})$	$(\hat{r}-\bar{r})$	$(\hat{r}-\bar{r})^2$	p	$p(\hat{r}-\bar{r})^2$
180 000	196 000	−16 000	256 000 000	0.3	76 800 000
200 000	196 000	4 000	16 000 000	0.6	9 600 000
220 000	196 000	24 000	576 000 000	0.1	57 600 000
Variance $(\sigma^2) = \Sigma(p)(\hat{r}-\bar{r})^2$					144 000 000
Yield:					
outcome	expected			probability	
$(\hat{r})$	value $(\bar{r})$	$(\hat{r}-\bar{r})$	$(\hat{r}-\bar{r})^2$	p	$p(\hat{r}-\bar{r})^2$
0.07	0.083	−0.013	0.000169	0.1	0.0000169
0.08	0.083	−0.003	0.000009	0.5	0.0000045
0.09	0.083	0.007	0.000049	0.4	0.0000196
Variance $(\sigma^2) = \Sigma(p)(\hat{r}-\bar{r})^2$					0.000041

(3) Calculate the standard deviation		
Income: s.d. = variance = σ		12 000
Yield: s.d. = $\sqrt{\text{variance}}$ = σ		0.006403

(4) Calculate certainty equivalents		
= expected value − standard deviation		
Income:	196 000 −12 000 =	184 000
Yield:	0.083 +0.006403 =	0.089403

(for the yield the risk is of a higher yield/lower YP/less value so it is the upper end of the range we do not want = expected value + standard deviation)

(5) **Reinsert values in calculation**					
RESIDUAL VALUATION (CERTAINTY EQUIVALENT)					
Income				£184 000	
YP perp @	8.940312	%		11.2	
Gross development value					2 058 094
less costs:			£		
Building cost + fees			1 000 000		
Finance @	17	% for 1/2			
costs for	2	years	170 000		
Total costs				1 170 000	
Return for risk and profit					
	20	% capital value		411 619	
Costs plus profit					1 581 619
Site value on completion					476 475
PV £1	2	years @		17	%	0.7305136
Site value today (including purchase costs)					348 071

Sliced income approach

This approach develops risk adjustment and certainty equivalent techniques to provide an overall method which may be suitable in property appraisal. Like the hardcore method or layer approach (see Isaac and Steley 1991, Chapter 6), it distinguishes layers of income which are less risky (core income) and more risky (top slice). The guaranteed income could thus be valued at a risk-free rate whilst the overage or top slice income (calculated with the hardcore/layer method) is then discounted at a highly risk-adjusted rate. The top slice income is calculated by comparing the expected value of the total income stream with the level of the risk-free core income. Baum and Crosby (1995) suggest that this method can be used in situations where a core rental is guaranteed, or with turnover rents where there is a core element with an addition which is profit or turnover related. In development valuations the concept could be applied in partnership arrangements; as discussed in Chapter 5, the various slices as shown in the approaches would have differing risk levels.

A summary of the possible advantages and disadvantages of the various steps of risk analysis drawn from Baum and Crosby's work is made in Table 6.5.

Baum's approach to risk analysis is summarised in Box 6.2.

Development appraisals using cash flow approaches

Using some of the approaches indicated in this chapter, Whipple (1988) has outlined a more involved process for evaluating development projects. Whipple suggests an analytical process for evaluating a development project:

- initial screening of the project using a traditional residual approach;
- modelling the cash inflows and outflows for the project without allowance for finance costs;
- carrying out a sensitivity analysis of the projected outcome with changes in the variables, supplemented by a risk analysis;
- quantifying the effect the project will have on the corporate accounts of the developer, with appropriate adjustments for tax and tax allowances.

Table 6.5   *Risk analysis steps: advantages and disadvantages*

Level of analysis	Examples	Advantages	Disadvantages
1. Sensitivity analysis	Scenario testing, expected returns, probability, simulation	Investor retains decision responsibility	No simple decision rule, range of results
2. Risk adjusted discount rate	RADR, certainty equivalent techniques, sliced income approach	Provides objective decision rule	Decision made by subjective risk adjustment, adviser may replace risk/return indifference of investor with own
3. Mean–variance analysis	Coefficient of IRR/NPV variation	Has separate measures of risk and return, investor can be more subjective about risk/return trade-off	Deals with *individual* project risk
4. Portfolio analysis	Beta analysis	Deals with the effect on portfolio of carrying out the project	Difficult to estimate betas (measures of systematic risk)

AN APPROACH TO RISK ANALYSIS: A SUMMARY

Baum suggests that there are four levels of risk analysis that can be used:

(i)   **Sensitivity analysis**
(ii) **Risk adjustment techniques**
(iii) **Mean variance criterion**
(iv) **Portfolio risk analysis**

Sensitivity analysis involves the changing of the variables from the best estimates, for instance, the effect of a 10 per cent change in a variable can be contrasted with the effect of a 10 per cent change in another variable; thus the results are checked against the product of individual changes to determine how the changes in the inputs will affect changes in the final result. This form of sensitivity analysis will indicate those variables which are most sensitive to change in the sense that they will affect the final result more.

Risk adjustment techniques can include the adjustment of the discount rates to account for risk, for instance, an increase of 2 per cent could be used in the investment decision to indicate risk. In **certainty equivalent techniques**, the aproach uses assigned probabilities to alternative capital values and costs. Standard deviations are calculated. Using statistical techniques in a normal distribution of results, it is expected that 68 per cent of the results will fall within 1 standard deviation from the mean of the results. Thus the equation is calculated using the variables at the position 1 standard deviation below the mean. This conservative approach is intended to convert the variable risky estimates into relatively certain ones. A third type of risk adjustment technique is the sliced income approach which can adopt different interest rates for the layers of income. A guaranteed income could be discounted at a risk-free rate, whereas the average or additional bonus would be discounted at a higher rate then the overall risk adjusted discount rate.

The **mean variance criterion** can be used to choose between two investment arrangements by adopting the rule that project *A* is chosen if the NPV of *A* is greater than the NPV of *B* and the risk of *A* is less than the risk of *B*. The risk is a separate measure using the standard deviation of the data. The approach to this analysis is to list the possible NPVs of the cash flow using a matrix of the key variables; for instance in an investment valuation this could be growth in income against the yield on the resale valuation. If there are three possible outcomes for each of the two variables, then the matrix will be 3×3 having 9 different cases. The assigned probability is 1 in 3 $\times$ 1 in 3 or $0.333 \times 0.333 = 0.1111$. Using this probability, the expected value of the NPV can be calculated and the standard deviation can also be calculated from the data. The decision rule for choosing between two similar projects is thus dependent on the mean variance criterion where the expected NPV is the measure of return and the standard deviation is a measure of risk. Where there are a number of possible present values, then a Monte Carlo simulation can be used.

In **portfolio analysis** investments are chosen which are advantageous in their effect on risk and return on the *total* investor's portfolio.

Source: Baum 1987.

Box 6.2   *An approach to risk analysis: a summary*

The valuations approach taken by Whipple and termed by him a 'contemporary valuation' consists of five stages:

   (i)   *Establish client's requirement*
       Define value, rights to be valued and the nature of the data required. Also indicate the time and nature of disposal.

   (ii) *Define uses*
       Define the uses for which a market demand exists but for which the use is also economically and politically feasible.

   (iii) *Select probable use*
       Select the most profitable use subject to caveats that it will be developed without political/social consequences.

   (iv) *Identify buyer type*
       The buyer type may have different requirements to the rest of the market.

   (v)   *Estimation of probable price*
       This uses three methods as appropriate:
       (a) Inference from past transactions of comparable properties developed on the same basis;
       (b) Simulation of the most probable buyers' price-fixing process
       (c) Otherwise use a normative model, adopting the criteria you believe to have influence in determining the price.

   (vi) The resulting estimate is then adjusted for special circumstances and the result is tested for sensitivity.

REFERENCES

Arnison, C. and Barrett, A. (1984) 'Valuations of Development Sites using the Stochastic Decision Tree Method,' *Journal of Valuation*, vol. 3 no. 2, pp. 126–33.

Baum, A. (1987) 'An Approach to Risk Analysis', Henry Stewart Conference, *Property Investment Appraisal and Analysis*, Cafe Royal, London, 1 December.

Baum, A. and Crosby, N. (1988) *Property Investment Appraisal*, Routledge, London.

Baum, A. and Crosby, N. (1995) *Property Investment Appraisal*, Routledge, London.

Brown, G. (1986) 'A Certainty Equivalent Expectations Model for Estimating the Systematic Risk of Property Investments' *Journal of Valuation*, vol. 6, no. 1, pp. 17–41.

Brown, G R (1991) *Property Investment and the Capital Markets*, E. & F. N. Spon, London.

Butler, D. and Richmond, D. (1990) *Advanced Valuation*, Macmillan, London.

Byrne, P. and Cadman, D. (1984) *Risk, Uncertainty and Decision Making in Property Development*, E. & F. N. Spon, London.

Chapman, C. B. (1991) 'Risk', in P. Venmore-Rowland, P. Brandon and T. Mole (eds), *Investment, Procurement and Performance in Construction*, RICS, London.

Darlow, C. (ed.) (1988) *Valuation and Development Appraisal*, Estates Gazette, London.

Dixon, T. J., Hargitay, S. E. and Bevan, O. A. (1991) *Microcomputers in Property*, E. & F. N. Spon, London.

Dubben, N. and Sayce, S. (1991) *Property Portfolio Management: An Introduction,* Routledge, London.

Duckworth, W. E., Gear, A. E. and Lockett, A. G. (1977) *A Guide to Operational Research,* Chapman & Hall, London.

Estates Gazette (1995), 'Mainly for Students: Spreadsheets and Valuations', Estates Gazette, 21 January, pp. 116–19.

Flanagan, R. and Norman, G. (1993) *Risk Management and Construction,* Blackwell, Oxford.

French, N. (1994) Editorial: 'Market Values and DCF', *Journal of Property Valuation and Investment,* vol. 12, no. 1, pp. 4–6.

Hargitay, S. E. and Yu, S.-M. (1993) *Property Investment Decisions,* E. & F. N. Spon, London.

Isaac, D. and Steley, T. (1991) *Property Valuation Techniques,* Macmillan Press, London.

Lumby, S. (1991) *Investment Appraisal and Financing Decisions,* Chapman & Hall, London.

Marshall, P. (1991) 'Development Valuation Techniques', *Research Technical Paper,* RICS, London.

Mollart, R. (1988) 'Computer briefing: Monte Carlo simulation using Lotus 1–2–3' *Journal of Valuation,* vol. 6, no. 4, pp. 419–33.

Mollart, R. (1994) 'Software Review: Using @Risk for Risk Analysis', *Journal of Property Valuation and Investment,* vol. 12 no.3 pp. 89–94.

Morley, S. (1988a) 'Financial Appraisal – Cashflow Approach', in C. Darlow (ed.) *Valuation and Development Appraisal,* Estates Gazette, London.

Morley, S. (1988b) 'Financial Appraisal – Sensitivity and Probability', in C. Darlow (ed.) *Valuation and Development Appraisal,* Estates Gazette, London.

Newall, M. (1989) 'Development Appraisals', *Journal of Valuation,* vol. 7, no. 2, pp. 123–33.

Pearce, B. (1989) 'Forecasting: An Overview', paper in seminar: *Application of Forecasting Techniques to the Property Market,* RICS/SPR Seminars, Spring 1989.

Schiller, R. (1994) 'Comment: The Interface between Valuation and Forecasting', *Journal of Property Valuation and Investment,* vol. 12, no. 4, pp. 3–6.

Whipple, R. T. M. (1988) 'Evaluating Development Projects', *Journal of Valuation,* vol. 6, no. 3, pp. 253–86.

7 Financing Property Development

7.1 INTRODUCTION

A property or building can be owner-occupied or rented, the latter being an investment property. In the present market (1995) it may of course be vacant, resulting from being surplus to the owner's requirements or a poor investment! A large proportion of property is owner-occupied but most of the conventional property texts and theories are applied to an investment market. Property finance is money raised on the back of existing properties or raised for the purpose of expenditure on properties. Whether the property is owner-occupied or an investment property may alter the criteria for the raising and application of the funds, but the fundamental concepts of finance may well be the same. For instance, funds could be raised internally or externally by an organisation but the criteria for the internal loan or transfer of funds may well need to match those in the market. In this book, the presentation is mainly about the application of funds to property in the investment market and funds are considered to be private rather than public sector monies. This is to make the analysis simpler but, as has already been said, the principles and concepts of finance could well be similar.

The investment market for property cannot be seen in isolation from other investment markets. The application of funds to property has to reflect competition from other forms of investment. The decision to invest in a particular area will be a comparison of return and security, for instance, and thus knowledge of alternative investments and knowledge of the application of finance to other investments could be very important. This can clearly be seen in the securitisation and unitisation of property which are discussed in Chapter 9. Another important point to be made concerns the nature of the lender and the property to which finance is applied. At its simplest the financial arrangement may deal with an individual purchasing a single property with a single loan, but it is rarely this basic. Finance is generally raised by corporate entities such as property companies, using existing property and other assets as collateral for the purchase of a portfolio of assets which may include property assets, but perhaps not exclusively.

Finally it is important to realise the significance of property and its finance to the economy. The importance can be shown in three different ways: as a factor of production, as a corporate asset and as an investment. As a factor of production, property provides the space in which economic activity and production takes place and the efficiency and costs of such space will affect the cost of goods and services produced. As a corporate asset, it forms the major part of asset value in the company's balance sheet and the majority of corporate debt is secured against it. As an investment, it is one of the major types of investment held by individual investors and the financial institutions on which pensions and assurance benefits depend (Fraser 1993, p. 3).

The structure of the investment market

There are three major areas of traditional investment opportunity (ignoring gold, commodities and works of art); these are fixed interest securities, company stocks and shares, and real property. The Stock Exchange provides a market for listed shares and certain fixed interest securities such as those issued by the government, local authorities and public bodies. The market in real property contrasts with that of company shares and other securities. The property market is fragmented and dispersed whilst that of shares and other securities is highly centralised. The London Stock Market is an example of this centralisation. The centralisation of markets assists the transferability of investments, as does the fact that stock and shares can be traded in small units thereby assisting transferability. Compared with other traditional investment opportunities, real property investment has the distinguishing features of being heterogeneous, generally indivisible and having inherent problems of management. The problems of managing property assets may include collecting rents, dealing with repairs and renewals and lease negotiation; these problems mean that real property is likely to be an unattractive proposition for the small investor. A decentralised market, such as exists for property, will tend to have high costs of transfer of investments and also there will be an imperfect knowledge of transactions in the market.

These factors affecting the real property market makes property difficult to value. There is no centralised market price to rely on and the value may be too difficult to assess unless a comparable transaction has recently taken place. The problems of valuation relate to difficulties of trying to relate comparable transactions to properties being valued, or even trying to assess what transactions could be considered comparable. Because of the nature of the real property market, individual investors have tended to withdraw from the market. This is also due to the channelling of savings into collective organisations, such as pension funds and insurance companies rather than individuals using their savings for direct investment.

Property company shares

Property company shares provide a medium for indirect investment in property which deals with some of the disadvantages of direct investment previously outlined. Equities are available in smaller units and can be easily traded. Property shares have been viewed as an effective protection against inflation because of the durability of property. Shares of a property investment company where most of the revenue to the company is derived from rental income also provides the investor with a high degree of income security. Thus property shares traditionally were seen to provide both an element of protection against the effects of inflation and greater security to the investor.

Two types of property company are discernible. The investment company holds property for long periods normally and takes its revenue from rental income. The trading company will develop and sell property, earning revenues on disposal of the property rather than through income. Because of different tax positions the functions of investment and trading should be kept separate, but the most extensive developers will also often be investment companies which may or may not retain a completed development within the portfolio of the investment company.

7.2   METHODS OF FINANCE, HISTORY AND DEVELOPMENT

History of property finance

In the post-war era in the 1950s and 1960s, the modern property developer emerged and property companies established themselves. The stimulation to development was based on the shortage of property in a period of low inflation. This meant that rental levels of developments increased dramatically during the period whilst building costs were static. The other major stimulants to the developers were fixed interest rates and the ability to finance deals with 100 per cent debt finance without any equity input. The growth of property companies was on the back of a strategy of refinancing the development on a fixed interest mortgage for 20–30 years. The financial institutions provided finance for the developments during this period and there was some link-up between developers and institutions. Over this period, the institutions, generally insurance companies, started to insist on having a greater share in the equity returns available; they thus purchased shares in the property companies and also made their mortgage debenture loans convertible to shares so that an increased equity stake could be obtained if the development schemes were a success.

However, the taxation structure in the late 1960s affected these arrangements. The financial institutions were termed gross funds (not paying tax), they suffered from the taxation of income and dividends under these arrangements and thus new financial structures emerged. In the late 1960s and early 1970s developers began using sale and leaseback arrangements; the development was financed in the development stage using short-term bank finance and was sold on completion. As time wore on, a shortage of schemes became apparent and the institutions (originally the insurance companies but subsequently also the pensions funds) purchased development sites directly from property developers and then tied them to a building agreement and agreement for lease on completion of the development.

The crash of 1974–5 showed how the economic indications had changed since the 1950s and 1960s. High interest rates, lessened demand and inflation of costs meant that profit levels were not achieved because of increased capital costs and income voids during which interest arrears accumulated. In the 1980s and 1990s the usual approach to funding was that the funder was invited to purchase the site and provide funds for the building contract. Interest would be rolled up during the development period and added to the development costs. On completion and letting of the building, the profit on development was paid over. On this basis developers built up a large turnover matching their site funding and project management skills with the institutional investors. Such approaches greatly reduced the risk exposure of the developer to the project. Forward funding meant that the project was financed for the development period at a lower interest rate than market levels, but subsequently the capital sum received by the developer at the end of the project was reduced by valuing at a higher yield to recoup the interest lost.

Methods of finance used in the market are outlined below. This overview looks at debt finance, joint venture arrangements and mezzanine finance.

Debt finance

Clearing banks and, to a lesser extent, merchant banks have been prepared to provide loans for property development. Generally the loans have been secured on collateral beyond the property to be developed. Interest is charged on a fixed or variable basis. Non-recourse finance is now more popular. It can be defined as loans on property unsupported by outside collateral. Finance is available from banks for up to 70 per cent loan: value ratio without outside security being provided. Banks take first charge over the site and advance monies during the development phase. Interest rates are a margin over the London Inter Bank Offered Rate (LIBOR), say between 1 per cent and 2 per cent, but this is reduced with pre-let or pre-sale.

Loans generally have limited recourse with developer undertakings to:

- pay cost overruns
- inject equity stakes, either up-front or side-by-side
- pay interest post-completion
- complete within certain time limits
- complete within certain cost limits.

Banks will normally allow interest to be capitalised during the construction period and developers generally include this as a construction cost thus not affecting profits in their accounts during the development process.

Some of the main types of debt finance available are:

Commercial mortgages

These are straightforward loans where the interest rate is either paid currently or capitalised. The principal is either amortised over the term of the loan or repaid by a single payment at the end. The interest rate can be fixed or variable and other capital market instruments can be used including caps (compensating for interest rate rises over a certain rate) and floors (preventing interest rate falls below a certain level). These instruments are used to minimise interest rate fluctuations thereby reducing risk and obtaining finer pricing of the loans. The length of loans will vary but the maximum for many banks is five years, although insurance companies and building societies may lend up to 25 years or more.

Equity participation or convertible mortgages

This structure allows the lender to share in the uplift of the value of the property for a reduction in the interest rate payable. The mortgage loan outstanding can be converted into the ordinary shares of the company who is lending the money.

Mortgage debenture issue

This is a traditional method of raising corporate finance. It involves a loan raised on a debenture issue which is secured against the property or other assets, and yields either a fixed or index-linked return.

Multi-option facility

In this structure, a group of banks agree to provide cash advances at a predetermined margin for a certain period.

Deep discounted bonds

Deep discounted bonds are a method of raising long-term finance with a low initial interest rate. Interest payments can be stepped to accord with rent review and there are also tax advantages. Bonds can be placed with institutional investors and can be very finely priced. It is anticipated that bond issues will become increasingly used to finance major projects to overcome the need to refinance on completion of the development.

Joint ventures

There are a number of different types of joint venture; the concept involves the coming together of two or more parties to undertake a transaction. Joint ventures are a useful means of bringing parties together with different interests in order to complete deals.

The reasons for increased use of joint ventures in property development include:

(i)   Bank of England pressure to reduce the level of bank debt in the property sector;
(ii)   increased risk in property development;
(iii) lack of equity in the property market, with property companies less able to raise new funds in the Stock Market;
(iv)   demand from overseas investors, who have a preference for joint venture arrangements.

Forms of joint venture structures are:

(i)   limited liability companies;
(ii)   partnership, where one party must have unlimited liability;
(iii) profit participation.

The decision on creating a joint venture will depend on the purposes of the joint venture:

(i)   whether this is for one property or for one of a number of schemes;
(ii)   the tax situation;
(iii) the stamp duty considerations.

On negotiation of a joint venture agreement important points to consider are:

(i)   the level of funding to be provided;
(ii)   the development period/time;
(iii) who will control the decision-making process;
(iv)   how the profit is going to be distributed;
(v)   what the provisions are for dissolution in the event of failure;
(vi)   how disputes are to be settled.

Mezzanine finance

There is often a gap between the costs of development and limited recourse loans and this is filled by a mezzanine loan. The amount of mezzanine finance varies but can take debt up to 95 per cent of cost. Mezzanine funders require rates of return between 30 and 40 per cent, secured on a subordinated loan with a share of profit, normally side-by-side with a cap at an agreed level. Should the project run into problems, the priority return that the mezzanine funder seeks can quickly diminish any profit. Interest payable on the mezzanine finance can be capitalised, producing cash flow benefits.

Comparison of loan terms

There are four main areas to be considered prior to entering into a loan facility to ensure that a suitable structure related to the lender's requirements can be arranged. These are cost, flexibility, risk and accounting presentation:

- *Cost*
  The best rates are available for the best quality covenants. Where the lending institution takes more risk, a higher return is required. For a non-recourse transaction the interest rate margin over LIBOR required by the lender is increased.
- *Flexibility*
  The greater the level of security and recourse, the less likely there is to be any restriction on management control. Flexibility depends on interest rate structure.
- *Risk*
  The greater the lender's risk, the greater the cost to the borrower.
- *Accounting*
  A number of creative packages are available which can remove debt from the balance sheet.

Market overview

Bank of England property lending figures are showing that there is too much debt and too little equity in the market. Banks have continued to lend on the basis that the institutions or foreign investors would be around to refinance the projects. Big Bang and the deregulation of the financial services market sparked an increase in property lending by the foreign banks; £31 billion of debt is outstanding. If restrictions on loans are introduced, the property sector could collapse.

Despite the slowdown in the economy, property transactions are still being financed and some international banks regard the current situation as an opportunity to increase their market share. American Banks have reduced their exposure. Clearing banks are now taking a cautious approach and with property values falling they will have to be very careful not to cause a collapse through unwarranted liquidations. The problems arising from the collapse of Rush & Tompkins, a major building contractor, in 1990, and the domino effect triggered by the collapse demonstrates this. Building Societies have become increasingly active but the demise of one or two of their major investments has caused them to reappraise the situation.

Few banks are now lending on speculative schemes and even pre-let schemes can only be financed where an exit route for the financier can be clearly demonstrated. The borrower must be prepared to provide guarantees for any cost overruns and interest during the cost period. Equity injections may be required by the developer and the bank will demand a substantial level of recourse. The amount of equity initially required has increased. Most banks are not prepared to lend above 70 per cent of cost and often insist on a developer putting in equity up front.

By comparison, banks are still keen to lend on good quality investment property although they are not comfortable about capitalising interest over long periods. This creates difficulties with reversionary properties. Loans of up to 80 per cent of investment value are available and can be exceeded if mortgage indemnity policies are used or the bank receives a share of profits.

In terms of future prospects, there is clearly a need for further liquidity in the property sector through increased equity. More funds may enter the market through Authorised Property Unit Trusts, but despite the tax transparency they are unlikely to be successful in the short term because of falling property values and high interest rates. The London Futures and Options Exchange which collapsed soon after its commencement in 1991 introduced a property futures contract which provided liquidity in the market; whilst it existed investors were able to increase their exposure to the property market by purchasing contracts which could be used to hedge the risks of a trading or investment portfolio. The use of financial derivatives such as swaps, options and futures can be a very risky business for the unwary, inexperienced or those who become over-committed. The experience of Barings, the merchant bank, which collapsed due to enormous losses in futures trading on the Japanese market is evidence of this.

In today's market any loan structure which capitalises interest will carry great weight because of the need to provide funds to refinance development facilities. In the last few years deep discounted bond issues have increased in popularity. Convertible mortgages offer another alternative, whereby the borrower provides the lender or investor with equity in the scheme in return for a higher loan advance and reduced obligation. Both discounted bonds and convertible mortgages have suffered recently because of higher interest rates in international markets. To conclude, until new investments or investment products bolster the amount of equity in the market property, loans on new transactions will be difficult to secure.

Finance for small companies

Finance for small companies is extremely important and this is a specialist area. Four stages in the financing needs of small companies can be distinguished. These are:

(i)   *Venture capital*
       These are the funds necessary to meet the start up costs of a new company.
(ii)   *Development capital*
       This capital is needed to finance expansion once the initial phase of establishing the company has been completed.
(iii) *Increasing the number of shareholders*
       This finance is needed when it becomes necessary to widen the equity base of the company. In situations like this the loan capital may have reached an undesirable level for the future financial stability of the company, thus the gearing is too high.
(iv)   *Acquiring a Stock Exchange listing*

The smaller firm would generally suffer a number of disadvantages in the market. Small borrowers generally would have to pay higher rates of interest. In addition, many small firms lack knowledge about potential sources of finance. Thus, because of problems related to credit and interest rates, the general condition of the economy will affect smaller firms more acutely than larger ones. The other problems that small firms face in raising finance is that they are very wary of entering into debt arrangements. There are a number of reasons for this, including fear of losing control over the company as well as fear of not being able to meet the conditions related to the loans. Possible sources of funding for small firms include: merchant banks, who provide medium- and long-term loans and equity interests; specialist funders such as Investors in Industry who provide loans and equity interest for venture and development capital and finance houses and leasing companies who provide finance for equipment and vehicle financing. There are also monies available from factoring houses who provide cash for debts and the clearing banks who provide overdraft facilities. Insurance companies provide some financing for property and, finally, there is government funding through a number of intermediary bodies for financing technological innovation.

7.3   SOURCES OF FINANCE

The main lenders in the market are:

(i)   High Street/Clearing Banks
(ii)   Foreign Banks

(iii)   Building Societies
(iv)   Merchant Banks
(v)   Insurance Companies
(vi)   Finance Houses.

Data on the sources of money flowing into property is shown in Table 7.1.

High Street/Clearing Banks

The big four clearing banks are Lloyds, Barclays, National Westminster and Midland. These are probably the first port of call for people looking for loans, especially if they have established relationships as account holders. However, these banks are conservative and may view new transactions related to property in a less than enthusiastic way. Smaller High Street Banks such as the Royal Bank of Scotland, The Bank of Scotland, Yorkshire Bank and the Clydesdale Bank may be more useful potential funders. The smaller banks are likely to have less of a bad debt problem and may want to increase market share. The larger banks are burdened at the moment by over-exposure to the

Table 7.1   *New money into property*

£ million

Year	Pension funds	Insurance companies	Banks	Property companies	Overseas	Total
1980	908	855	72	147	100	2082
1981	843	1073	469	97	70	2552
1982	797	1059	822	263	120	3061
1983	680	845	934	83	85	2627
1984	997	744	963	237	65	3006
1985	590	815	1691	344	90	3530
1986	434	821	2224	737	150	4306
1987	240	755	3998	2300	290	7583
1988	312	1102	7954	761	1897	12026
1989	92	1510	10622	1647	3267	17138
1990	−491	1080	7066	164	3269	11088
1991	467	1483	678	1270	1551	5449
1992	349	600	−1708	334	1232	807
1993[a]	299	232	−3248	1957	1514	754
1994[b]	−282	1868	−1546	1280	−	1320

Notes: [a] Overseas figures to September
[b] Not including overseas; 1994 figures first 2 quarters only; to September for property companies
Source: Evans (1993), p. 76; CSO (1994).

property sector, the emphasis at the present time is on debt repayment rather than new lending. British clearing banks' exposure to the property sector at the critical period to the end of the 1980s is shown in Figure 7.1.

Foreign banks

The foreign banks tend to be more aggressive sources of property finance, or were in the early 1990s, but by 1993 they were showing less interest. They are useful sources of funding particularly for quality and corporate transactions. The collapse of BCCI made borrowers wary of dealing with foreign banks: the collapse of a bank halfway through a development may mean that it could take years to unwind the legal problems and thus would put the borrower's own financial position at risk.

Building societies

The building societies fared badly in the 1990–5 slump in the property market. In the late 1980s, their inexperience and desire for market share in commercial property lending led to substantial bad debt. They are now putting their respective houses in order with rationalisation and more qualified staff and are likely to be an important source of commercial finance in the future.

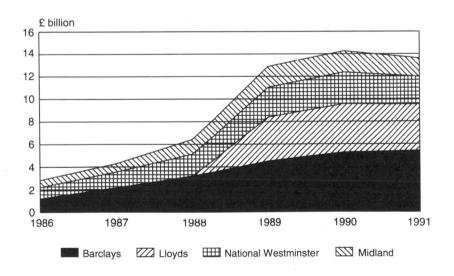

Notes: No figures for Lloyds 1986–8.
Source: IBCA; Scott (1992), p. 348.
Figure 7.1   *British clearing banks, UK property lending; 1986–91*

Merchant banks

Merchant banks rarely lend their own money but act as advisers and especially concentrate on large corporate transactions. They are unlikely to be interested in ordinary debt transactions because there would be little opportunity to use their expertise and add value to such a transaction.

Insurance companies

The insurance companies are limited providers of funds. They do, however, offer the attraction of long-term, fixed rate funds priced over gilts which can be useful in certain transactions.

Finance houses

In essence, the finance houses have been the principal providers of funding to the secondary leisure and retailing markets, providing finance for the purchase of freehold shops, pubs, restaurants and hotels. Their small trader exposure has made them particularly vulnerable to this latest recession which has resulted in most of them leaving the market.

The growth of institutional investment

Institutions investing in the capital market in the UK are suppliers of finance to companies. These institutional investors include insurance companies, pension funds, investment trusts and unit trusts. Since 1945 institutional investors have increased their share of finance to firms at the expense of private individual investors. At the turn of the century, individual investors were very important on the Stock Markets but since that time progressive taxation and increased egalitarianism have reduced the differences in income between the very rich and poor and thus enabled the poorer sections of society to accumulate some form of insurance within the insurance companies' funds. Thus, with the decline of the large private investors, there has been an increase in the amount of investment from the less affluent sections of society. These people have tended to invest their money in building societies, in unit trusts, insurance companies and saving banks and these institutions have in turn provided their funds to the Stock Markets.

Government finance

Government finance is available to developers to assist in developing sites in certain locations under certain criteria. The loans available include money for

City Grants and allowances in Enterprise Zones and urban development corporation (UDC) areas. Assistance is also provided through the Simplified Planning Zones.

The City Grant came into operation on 3 May 1988. This replaced the Urban Development Grant, and the Urban Regeneration Grant. To qualify for a City Grant, it is necessary for the developer to prove that the development project would not proceed without such a grant and that the project would benefit a run down city area. Development projects must be worth over £200 000 when completed to qualify for grant aid. City Grant can be applied in the Urban Development Corporation areas and also in the 57 inner city regions which have been designated as target areas. In addition, to obtain a funding, there should be some private sector funding for the development. The amount of grant obtainable depends upon the difference between costs and value. Cost must exceed value in order to qualify. In March 1993 it was announced that the Urban Programme of government funding would be phased out; this formed a major part of the government's urban renewal expenditure along with City Grants, Derelict Land Grants, Urban Development Corporations , City Action Teams and City Challenge (see Balchin *et al.*, 1995 p. 272). Under the Leasehold Reform, Housing and Urban Development Act 1993 the government established English Partnerships (EPs) to take over policy decision-making, to complement regional policy, administer the English Industrial Estates Corporation, buy and develop inner city sites, assume the responsibility of the Urban Programme to award City Grants and Derelict Land Grants and administer City Challenge. A Single Regeneration Budget was created in 1994 to include expenditure on UDCs, EP activities, Housing Action Trusts (HATs) and other programmes.

Money for property development is also available from the EU especially funds for run down or economically depressed locations. This source of funds has been discussed in Chapter 3.

7.4 LENDING CRITERIA

The cost and availability of lending is a function of the value of any particular project and the amount of cost to be financed. The nature of the development is important, and also the design, mix, location and likely demand. The letting conditions are important as are whether or not the investment is pre-let or speculative. The quality of the tenant who will be providing the cash flow to the investment will also be important. Other criteria are the track record of the developer and the strength of security. Finally, the duration of the loan will be important as well as the details of repayment, for instance, the anticipated regularity of repayments and the size/amount of repayments prior to redemption.

Most lenders look for the same aspects of a lending proposal which in simplified terms are the four 'Cs':

- Character
- Cashstake
- Capability
- Collateral.

Character

This relates to the trading history or development experience of a borrower. In respect of a property developer or an investment company, the lender will want to know whether the borrower has the experience to complete the development, manage the investment or run the business, if applicable. The lender will also be interested in whether the client is respectable and trustworthy. The lender may also cynically wonder why the borrower's own High Street bank will not lend the money.

Cashstake

This relates to how much equity (the borrower's own money) is going into the transaction. In addition, the bank will want to know where the equity has come from:

(i)   is it lent from someone else?
(ii)   is it from other profitable activities?
(iii) is it simply a surplus which has arisen on the revaluation of property?
(iv)   is it already pledged as security?
(v)   is it legally acquired money – not laundered money?

Capability

Does the borrower have the capability to service the loan, that is to pay the interest when it arises and the capital as and when repayment is required? Does the borrower have accounts or a business plan to show his/her present financial position and any estimate of future cash flow?

Collateral

The lender will want to know what security will be offered for the loan, its value and its saleability. The lender will want to know who valued the security and on what basis. The lender will need to assess the extent of the loan which would be exposed to the value of that security. Finally, will personal guarantees be given by the borrower?

7.5   GLOSSARY OF FINANCIAL AND PROPERTY TERMS

Basis point   One hundredth of 1 per cent, used in interest rate calculations, for instance 5 basis points is 0.05 per cent.

Cap   A means of providing an interest rate ceiling for a variable rate loan by the use of an insurance policy.

Collar   Provides a ceiling and floor for interest rate movements for a variable interest loan.

Covenant   The financial status of a party involved in a property transaction.

Deficit financing   The financing of a project in such a way that the cash flows in the early years of the project are insufficient to cover the interest on debt payable.

Discount   Bonds with below market coupons (interest rate payable) trade at a discount below par (the nominal value).

Finance lease   This involves the sale and leaseback with a financial institution; there may be tax advantages in such an arrangement without loss of control over the asset.

Gearing   The ratio of interest-bearing debt to the shareholder's funds, basically the ratio of debt to equity ('debt: equity ratio') which gives an indication of the financial standing of the company. A highly geared company has a high proportion of debt. (The American term is leverage.) Strictly, in academic texts it is defined as the ratio of debt to *total* capital.

Ground rent   An annual payment for the inclusion of the land element in a development proposal.

Interest capitalisation   The process of rolling up interest on a project and adding the interest to the costs of the project, the total being shown in accounts as the asset value.

Joint venture   Two or more parties, working together, sharing the rewards and risks of the project.

Loan: value ratio   The level of the loan expressed as a percentage of value.

Margin   The interest rate payable over a base rate to reflect the risk of the project or the parties involved. Commonly used as a margin above LIBOR (London Interbank Offered Rate).

Mezzanine finance   Above a conventional loan to a value limit of (say) 70 per cent certain lenders will lend additional monies known as mezzanine finance. This is priced at a higher rate than the senior debt (the initial advance)

	and may include profit-sharing to reflect the increased risk.
Overage	The growth in capital value over the development period which is available to be shared between vendor and developer.
Pre-let	The letting of a development before the completion of the project. This reduces the risk of voids and improves the funding position.
Ratchet basis	Used on profit participation transactions; whereas the overall profit increases, the proportion of profit received can increase or fall.
Recourse	The ability of the lender in a loan situation to have recourse to the assets of the company receiving the loan in the event of default. These assets are in addition to the assets immediately involved in the project for which the loan was made. In a non-recourse situation the lender can only have recourse to the project and its underlying assets.
Rental void	The period of time a completed development is unlet and thus not income producing. During this period it is also not usually possible to sell the completed project.
Senior and junior debt	These are different levels of debt with different priorities for repayment, security and with different arrangements for repayment. Senior debt usually has first charge on the security.
Swap	An interest rate swap is an agreement between two parties to swap their interest rate obligations, normally from a variable interest rate to a fixed one. A swap option is an option to change to a fixed rate in the future at preset terms.

7.6   CASE STUDY: FINANCE FOR THE SMALLER DEVELOPMENT/BUILDING COMPANY AND CONTRACTOR
(from Jones and Isaac 1994)

Introduction

The days of taking your local bank manager out for a pleasant lunch and expecting to see your overdraft limit increased on your return to work are long gone. The big clearing banks are still licking the wounds of their 1980s lending policies. The local manager may only be a puppet with the regional or head office pulling the strings.

For those who have only relied on their local branch of one of the big four, this can create a real dilemma. Where do I turn to fund my next project? How can I avoid being charged excessively?

To answer these questions we must first look at what is available in terms of finance, remove some of the mystique of the financial world and finally outline the ways of properly approaching a new lender.

What is available

There are a myriad of ways to raise finance for a particular project, including:

- Corporate methods
  - Debt capital
  - Debenture stock
  - Unsecured loan stock
  - Share capital
  - Preference shares
  - Ordinary shares
  - Convertibles
  - Warrants
- Finance leases
- Commercial mortgages.

We shall concentrate here on commercial mortgages as the other types of structure are usually only available for larger more complex transactions and are therefore beyond the scope of this section.

Commercial mortgages

Commercial mortgages themselves offer a wide variety of options and are available from building societies, clearing banks, international banks and insurance companies. There are many types of structure from short-term bridging finance to 30-year terms. A mortgage can be repaid in a variety of ways, and through the use of capital market instruments the interest rate risk can be reduced.

Repayment structures

There are a variety of different structures available. A combination of each can also be used.

- *Bullet repayment*
  This is commonly used in short-to medium-term loans where the

borrower repays interest only for the duration of the loan. The capital sum is then repaid at the end.

- *Capital and interest*
  This is the most common type of repayment structure where capital and interest are repaid over a longer period of up to 25 years.
- *Interest only*
  Only interest on the loan is payable, with the capital being repaid by, for example, an endowment or pension policy.
- *Pension schemes*
  These can offer a tax efficient investment strategy for commercial property purchases. The facility is appropriate for individuals, or people in partnership. Rents on the property are paid into a linked pension fund. Funds from existing pension facilities go towards a deposit on the property with the lending source providing the remainder. The main advantages are that contributions to the scheme attract tax relief at up to 40 per cent and any growth in value of property held in the fund is free of capital gains tax.
- *Capital holiday*
  Interest is payable for an initial agreed period usually up to five years. Thereafter, capital and interest are repayable for the remainder of the loan. This has obvious attractions in minimising outgoings during the first few years of the loan, which in turn will help cash flow.

Interest rate structures

The rate of interest payable by a borrower will be made up of a 'base' rate plus a fixed margin. The base rate charged can take a number of forms:

- *Variable rates*
  The interest rate is normally set periodically at three-, six-, nine or 12 month intervals. The rate may either be set by the lender (for example, finance house or building society case rates) or a variable rate such as LIBOR (London Interbank Offered Rate) may be offered.
- *Fixed rates*
  A fixed rate mortgage will eliminate any exposure to a rise in interest rates and conversely any benefits from falling interest rates. Only a few lenders offer long-term fixed rate mortgages and they are mainly clearing banks and insurance companies.

Interest rate hedging instruments

There are a number of capital market instruments available that can reduce a borrower's exposure to interest rate movements.

- *Interest rate caps*
  An interest rate cap is effectively an insurance policy. In return for a premium, a borrower is compensated by a bank or insurance company should interest rates rise above the level at which the cap is agreed.

- *Interest rate collars*
  An interest rate collar limits the volatility of future interest rate payments. It provides both a ceiling, by way of an interest rate cap, and a floor within which the interest rate can move. In addition to the cap, a floor will be taken out with a bank. Should interest rates fall below the floor the borrower will pay to the bank the difference between the interest payment due at the level of the floor and that due at the prevailing interest rate.

  Therefore where interest rates rise above the agreed cap rate, the bank would compensate the borrower and conversely where interest rates fall below the agreed floor, the borrower would compensate the bank. By arranging such a collar the cost of finance should be significantly cheaper than for a cap alone.

- *Interest rate swap*
  An interest rate swap is an agreement between two parties to swap their interest payment obligations with each other. Typically, banks act as intermediaries to arrange the swap and this enables a borrower to exchange floating money for a fixed interest obligation.

The main disadvantage of fixing interest rates is that there will be breakage costs if the loan is repaid. These costs can be substantial.

Loan : value ratio

Although loans of up to 85 per cent of open market value are available, most lenders will look at providing a loan of between 70 per cent to 75 per cent, with the difference between the purchase price and loan being provided from the borrower's own resources. However, the additional equity may be provided by allowing the lender to take an additional charge over an additional unencumbered property, such as a director's own home.

Interest rate margin

A margin on top of the interest rate set by the lender will also be payable. This margin is dependent upon the individual lender's assessment of the borrower's financial strength and reflects the risk to the lender of entering into the transaction. The margin is usually between 0.50 per cent and 4.00 per cent.

Servicing

It must be possible for the business to create cash surpluses from its trading activities not only for the repayment of the loan but for tax, living expenses and future expenditure.

As a rule of thumb the net profit figure shown in the accounts should be twice the amount of all interest charges to include bank borrowing, factoring, overdraft charges, etc. However where, for example, a rented property will be replaced by a freehold property, the rental saving should be added back to the net profit figure. Box 7.1 illustrates an example of double interest cover:

Other costs relating to a mortgage

It is likely that the lender will charge an arrangement fee of between 0.5 per cent to 1.0 per cent of the amount of the advance. An independent valuation will need to be undertaken at a cost of between 0.125 per cent and 0.2 per cent of the value and the borrower will also be liable for the lender's legal fees.

Information required to approach a lender

When you approach a lender to obtain funds you should ensure that you are clear on what finance you require and also ensure that you provide sufficient background information as follows:

DOUBLE INTEREST COVER		
	£	£
Loan Amount:	450 000	
Company's latest audited accounts indicate:		
Net profit before tax	217 000	
Add back rent saving	19 000	
Net profit		236 000
This year's finance charges from cash flow		
Bank overdraft interest	55 000	
Hire purchase interest	20 000	
£450 000 loan @ 9%	40 500	
Total interest payable		116 000
Ratio of net profit: interest payable = £236 000 : £116 000		
= 2.03, therefore OK		

Box 7.1   *Example of double interest cover*

- *Amount and purpose*
  Specify the amount you wish to borrow and its purpose, e.g. acquisition of property, goodwill, fixtures and fittings, etc.
- *Borrower's details*
  The borrowing company's name, trading and registered address, accountant, banker and solicitor, together with the company's authorised and paid up share capital and a breakdown of shareholders and their respective holdings.
- *Directors'/shareholders' details*
  CVs of the directors/shareholders and the background or history of any parent company. Where the borrower is a sole trader or partnership, the lenders will require CVs together with personal asset and liability statements and copies of partnership agreements where relevant.
- *Accounts*
  3 years' audited accounts for the borrower.
- *Bank borrowing*
  A breakdown of all current borrowings, i.e. mortgages, overdrafts, hire purchase agreements and leasing, identifying each lender and how each facility is secured.
- *Development activity*
  Where the borrower is building or extending premises, the lenders need full details of the development to include a description, breakdown of costs, details of warranties, copies of planning permission, details of contractor and building contract and a full set of drawings.
- *Financial status*
  The amount and availability of borrower's equity together with cash flow forecasts to support borrowing requests.
- *Background*
  Other relevant information.

Recent research has shown that the presentation of funding proposals is very important in obtaining finance (Isaac and O'Grady 1993).

Conclusions

There are a number of possible ways of obtaining finance for a builder or contractor concerned with smaller developments. The size of the borrower restricts the opportunities available and this section has therefore concentrated on the use of commercial mortgages. The advantages and disadvantages of commercial mortgages are summarised in Box 7.2.

COMMERCIAL MORTGAGES: ADVANTAGES AND DISADVANTAGES

Advantages

- Ease of arranging
- Low set up costs
- Present low interest rates offer cash flow advantages
- No tax risk.

Disadvantages

- On balance sheet
- Increased gearing, thereby reducing flexibility in the future
- Additional equity may be required if values fall
- Large equity input required through cash or additional security; this makes it relatively expensive in terms of opportunity cost.

Box 7.2   *Advantages and disadvantages of commercial mortgages*

REFERENCES

Balchin, P. N., Bull, G. H. and Kieve, J. L. (1995) *Urban Land Economics and Public Policy*, 5th edn, Macmillan Press, London.

Bank of England (1994a) *Quarterly Bulletin*, vol. 34, no. 3, August.

Bank of England (1994b) *Quarterly Bulletin*, vol. 34, no. 4, November.

Berkley, R. (1991) 'Raising Commercial Property Finance in a Difficult Market', *Journal of Property Finance*, vol. 1, no. 4, pp. 523–9.

Brett, M. (1983) 'Indirect Investment in Property', in C. Darlow (ed.), *Valuation and Investment Appraisal*, Estates Gazette, London.

Brett, M. (1990) *Property and Money*, Estates Gazette, London.

Cadman, D. and Austin-Crowe, L. (1991) *Property Development*, E. & F. N. Spon, London.

Cadman, D. and Catalano, A. (1983) *Property Development in the UK - Evolution and Change*, College of Estate Management, Reading.

Central Statistical Office (CSO) (1994) *Financial Statistics*, CSO, London, November.

Chesterton Financial (1994) *Property Lending Survey*, Chesterton Financial, London, February.

Chesterton Financial/CSW (1993) *Property Confidence Barometer*, Chesterton Financial, London, July.

D. J. Freeman (1994), *The Language of Property Finance*, D. J. Freeman, London.

Darlow, C. (1988c) 'The Supply and Sources of Finance', in C. Darlow (ed.) *Valuation and Development Appraisal*, Estates Gazette, London.

Darlow, C. (1988a) 'Corporate and Share Capital Funding' in C. Darlow (ed.) *Valuation and Development Appraisal*, Estates Gazette, London.

Darlow, C. (1988b) 'Direct Project Funding' in C. Darlow (ed.) *Valuation and Development Appraisal*, Estates Gazette, London.

Debenham, Tewson and Chinnocks (1984) *Property Investment in Britain*, Debenham, Tewson and Chinnocks, London.

DTZ Debenham Thorpe (1993) *Money into Property*, DTZ Debenham Thorpe, London, August.

Dubben, N. and Sayce, S. (1991) *Property Portfolio Management*, Routledge, London.

Evans, P. H. (1993) 'Statistical Review', *Journal of Property Finance*, vol. 4, no. 2, pp. 75–82.

Fraser, W. D. (1993) *Principles of Property Investment and Pricing*, 2nd edition, Macmillan Press, London.

Isaac, D. and O'Grady, M. (1993) 'Thorough Approach the Key to Development Funding', *Property Valuer*, Dublin, Winter.

Jones, T. and Isaac, D. (1994) 'Finance for the Smaller Building Company and Contractor', *Chartered Institute of Building Directory*, CIOB/Macmillan, London.

Pike, R. and Neale, B. (1993) *Corporate Finance and Investment*, Prentice-Hall, London.

Riley, M. and Isaac, D. (1993) 'Commercial Property Lending: Confidence Survey' *Journal of Property Finance*, vol. 4, no. 3.

Riley, M. and Isaac, D. (1994) 'Property Lending Survey 1994' *Journal of Property Finance*, vol. 5, no. 1, pp. 45–51.

Ross, S. A., Westerfield, R. W. and Jaffe, J. F. (1993) *Corporate Finance*, Irwin, Boston.

Savills (1989) *Financing Property 1989*, Savills, London.

Savills (1993a) *Financing Property 1993*, Savills, London.

Savills (1993b) *Investment and Economic Outlook*, Savills, London, issue 3, October.

Scott, I. P. (1992) 'Debt, Liquidity and Secondary Trading in Property Debt', *Journal of Property Finance*, vol. 3, no. 3, pp. 347–55.

Venmore-Rowland, P. (1991) 'Vehicles for Property Investment' in P. Venmore-Rowland, P. Brandon and T. Mole (eds), *Investment, Procurement and Performance in Construction*, RICS, London.

8 Classification of Development Finance

8.1 INTRODUCTION

The cash flow approach to the firm and the balance sheet model will be discussed in Chapter 10. These approaches, besides looking at the application of company funds for the purchase of assets, also differentiate between the sources of the funds, in particular the difference between long-term debt and shareholders' equity in the firm. An understanding of the difference between equity and debt is fundamental to an understanding of how finance works. The structure of finance can analysed in two different ways:

- *Debt v. equity.*
- *Project v. corporate funding.*

In the past most interest in property finance concentrated on project finance, but with the size of schemes increasing and innovatory techniques of funding derived from the USA and other economic sectors, there is now more interest in corporate finance. Generally, firms offer two basic types of securities to investors: debt securities are contractual obligations to repay corporate borrowing whilst equity securities are shares of common stock and preferred stock that represent non-contractual claims on the residual cash flow of the firm. Issues of debt and equity that are publicly sold by the firm are then traded on the financial markets. These distinctions between equity and debt and between project and corporate finance are clarified in the following paragraphs.

Debt v. equity

Equity is money and resources provided by the developer, partners, investors and funds who participate in the risk and profit of the scheme. Debt finance basically consists of loans raised from banks and other sources against the project (project specific) and non-project specific loans raised in the market. This is not always a useful distinction as corporate funding, the raising of finance against the assets of a company, can be based on equity as well as debt.

Project v. corporate finance

Project finance is finance provided where the principal or only security for the finance is the property itself, although supporting guarantees and additional collateral may also be requested. Corporate finance is finance raised on the back of the corporate entity rather than the project. Traditionally, property and other companies provided funds for new projects from retained earnings, the issue of new shares and borrowings. In the post-war era, fixed interest mortgages and debentures were also used. Nowadays there may be a complex corporate package of different types of funds.

Using the parameters above the funding matrix can distinguish amongst the financing methods available, and this is shown in Box 8.1.

Capital structure

Financing arrangements determine how the value of a company is sliced up. The persons or institutions that buy debt from the firm are creditors. The holders of the equity shares are shareholders. The size of the company's balance sheet will determine how well the company has made its investment decisions. The size of the firm is its value in the financial markets:

$$V = D + E$$

Value of company = Value of debt + Value of equity

(Ross *et al.*1993, p. 6)

Corporate securities issued are a contingent claim on the value of the company. The shareholder's claim on the value of the company is a residual after payment to the debtholder; they get nothing if the value of the company is equal to or less than the amount promised to the debt holders.

In Figure 8.1, F is the promised payoff to debtholders. $X-F$ is the payoff to equity shareholders if $X-F > 0$; if not then payoff $= 0$.

FUNDING MATRIX		
	CORPORATE FUNDING	PROJECT FINANCE
EQUITY FINANCE	Share issues	Partnership funds Single asset unitisation
DEBT FINANCE	Loan stock Fixed interest debentures	Bank overdrafts Short-term funds for development

Box 8.1   *Funding matrix*

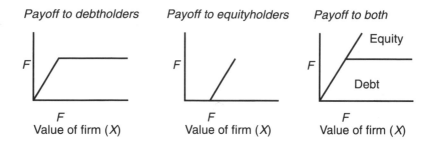

Source: Ross *et al.* (1993), p. 12.
Figure 8.1   *Payoffs to debt and equity*

Financial markets

The financial markets are composed of the money markets and the capital markets. Money markets are the markets for debt securities that pay off in the short term (usually less than one year). Capital markets are the markets for long-term debt and equity shares. Primary markets are used when governments or companies initially sell securities. Companies offer their shares through public placings or public offerings, and this is discussed in greater detail later in this chapter. Secondary markets come into operation for the resale of securities. Debt and equity are traded in the security markets; there is a distinction between auction markets and dealer markets: equity securities tend to be sold in auction markets (like the Stock Exchange); debt securities are sold in dealer markets. Auction markets differ from dealer markets in two ways:

(i)   Trading in an auction exchange takes place at a single site on the floor of the exchange or with a centralised screen system. In October 1986, the Stock Exchange changed its system of trading, post-'Big Bang' (the deregulation of the Stock Exchange), from trading on the floor of the exchange to an electronic market place. The Stock Exchange Automated Quotation System (SEAQ) moved the system of trading into dealing rooms equipped with computer screens.

(ii)   The transaction prices of shares traded on the auction exchange are communicated almost immediately to the public by means of computers and other devices; this is not so in dealer markets (Ross *et al.* 1993, p. 23).

Direct investment versus property vehicles

The concept of project versus corporate finance can be looked at from a different perspective, that of direct investment in property as against investment through a property vehicle. Venmore-Rowland (1991) has considered the advantages and disadvantages of investment by these two approaches and these are shown in Box 8.2.

DIRECT INVESTMENT AND PROPERTY VEHICLES

DIRECT INVESTMENT

Advantages
- Low risk relative to equities
- Diversification benefits
- Hedge against inflation
- Good for matching inflation-prone long-term liabilities

Disadvantages
- Illiquid
- Management intensive
- Minimum portfolio size required

PROPERTY VEHICLES

Advantages
- Liquidity
- Divisibility
- Management expertise
- Specialisation of vehicle
- Gearing
- Can shift weight/exposure
- Income benefits from the discount to net asset value

Disadvantages
- Loss of control
- Tax slippage
- Short-term, relatively poor performance
- High correlation to Stock Market

Box 8.2   *Direct investment and property vehicles*

There are two factors which are working in opposite directions in the investment strategy: correlation to other investments and liquidity. Correlation is an important criterion to obtain a diversified portfolio of investments and therefore to spread risks. Direct property investment has a relatively low correlation to equities but is more illiquid. Property vehicles are liquid but are more highly correlated to equities (Venmore-Rowland 1991, p. 7).

8.2   CATEGORIES OF FINANCE

This section is based on a suggested classification by Brett (1990, pp. 147–51), and is summarised in Box 8.3.

CATEGORIES OF FINANCE

Debt or equity
Project finance or corporate finance
Loan or traded security
Secured of unsecured
Fixed rate or variable rate
Long-term or short-term
Recourse, non–recourse, limited recourse

Main criteria

DEBT or EQUITY
PROJECT or CORPORATE FINANCE

Finance matrix

	Debt	Equity
Project Finance		
Corporate Finance		

Box 8.3   *Summary of categories of finance*

Debt or equity

The distinction between debt and equity depends on whether the money is borrowed (debt) and here the lender has no direct involvement in the project, or whether the money has been invested on the basis of sharing both the risk and the returns of the project (equity). Borrowed money needs to be repaid and interest will be paid on the outstanding amount until the debt is repaid. The equity return for the person who puts up the money is determined by the success of the enterprise. The person shares the profits and if there are none then there is no return.

The most obvious form of equity is ordinary share capital. Equity shares can also exist in development situations where a financier is entitled to a share in profits of the scheme. There are also deferred forms of equity like convertible loans, which start as debt instruments paying a fixed rate of interest but later the loans may be converted into equity shares.

Project finance or corporate finance

Project finance is the money borrowed for a project, usually a development project. The loan is based on the project itself and this becomes the main security. A larger company may be able to borrow on the strength of the assets of the company itself rather than its individual projects; this is asset based or corporate finance. Interest will generally be lower for corporate loans than for project loans because there will be more collateral available for security rather than relying on the risk of a single project. Many companies are undertaking developments of such a size that they dwarf the company's own resources, and the developer may then be concerned that, if anything goes wrong with the project, the lenders may have recourse to other assets of the company, which may undermine the company's financial position. In this case each development may need to be financed separately on a project basis, and may try to make the project 'off balance sheet' if possible.

Loan or traded security

Borrowed money may simply be a simple loan or a bond in the form of an instrument (a negotiable piece of paper) which is transferable. This is a form of IOU note and is called a security rather than a straight-forward loan and this can be sold on to other investors. The purchasers receive interest each year and also have the right for the original cost to be repaid at the end of the agreed duration of the security. If the purchasers do not wish to wait for this repayment date they can sell the rights to other investors, who then become entitled to receive the interest and the eventual repayment monies. Securities of this kind are bought and sold on the Stock Market.

Secured and unsecured

Lenders will normally require security for the money they provide; they want collateral (security) for the loans and thus will charge assets to cover the loan, either the specific assets of a business related to the project or the assets of a business as a whole. If the borrower fails to pay the interest or capital repayments as required then the lender can then put a receiver into the company and the receiver will repay the loans from the proceeds of the sale of the company's assets or other available revenues. A secured loan is safer than an unsecured loan but well established companies may be able to raise unsecured loans because the safeguard for the lender is the company's established profit record out of which the interest can be paid. Most borrowings in the euromarkets are unsecured, as are borrowings in the commercial paper market. The company's name and standing are the main guarantees.

Fixed rate or variable rate (floating rate) interest

Sometimes the rate of interest is agreed at the outset of the loan and remains unchanged over the life of the loan. With other loans, the interest rate will change according to movements in money market rates or other rates agreed. For large scale floating rate borrowings, the most common yardstick of interest rates is the London Interbank Offered Rate or LIBOR. This is the rate of interest at which the banks themselves are prepared to lend to each other. It is agreed at the outset, say, that the company will pay a margin over the LIBOR rate, say 2.5 percentage points (or 250 basis points, which is the same thing, as a basis point is .01%) over LIBOR. You can choose a LIBOR floating rate and then fix it. Short term borrowings are most likely to be at the floating rate of interest. Long term borrowings such as mortgage debentures are more likely to be at a fixed rate. The borrower can buy a cap for floating rate borrowing. This is a form of insurance policy which means that whatever happens to interest rates in general, a maximum limit is set to the interest rate that a borrower will have to pay.

Long-term or short-term

Loans are usually over a period between one and 30 years. This range contains short and long-term loans but the boundaries of the two and the intermediate area between are not clearly defined. Many people consider one–two years to be short-term, equivalent to the development period for most projects, two-seven years as medium-term and more than seven years as long-term. Overdrafts are technically payable on demand and thus are short- term borrowing but many companies have an overdraft outstanding almost indefinitely. With a multi-option facility (MOF), a company might technically be borrowing for three months at a time. At the end of three months it repays the original loans and takes out new ones for another three months. If the facility runs for five years, effectively it has the use of five year money by 'rolling over' (Brett 1990, p. 150).

Recourse, non-recourse or limited recourse loans

If the loan for a particular project or for a particular subsidiary company is guaranteed by the parent, the lender has recourse to the parent, so can claim on the assets of the parent. If the only security for the lender is the project itself, as in a pure form of project based finance and the parent company has given no guarantees, the loan is non-recourse. A non-recourse loan is very unlikely to be granted in practice, banks would generally requires the loans to be limited recourse. The parent may have guaranteed interest payments but is under no obligation to repay the loan itself in these circumstances. A limited recourse loan would still depend on the reputation of the borrower and the track record of the company as well as the quality of the project itself.

Domestic or euromarket loans

Loans can be raised in the UK or in the euromarkets. Euromarket loans can be in sterling abroad (eurosterling) or other currencies (eurodollar). A company may well raise monies in the euromarkets in different currencies and then swap to sterling if sterling is not popular at the time of raising the funds. The terms and conditions of operation in the European market can be different; for instance euro-loans are often unsecured.

8.3   PROJECT BASED FUNDING

Financial arrangements can be made to suit the requirements of the borrower or of the scheme. The merchant banks are the most sophisticated part of the development lending market. Note that in many projects the initial rents may not cover repayments until the first rent review; this is called deficit financing.

Types of finance available

- Bridging finance
- Forward sale
- Mortgage
- Drop lock loan
- Sale and leaseback
- Project management fee
- General funding.

Bridging finance

This is a loan generally up to three years. Interest is rolled up until the development is sold and thus the developer must be able to pay the interest and principal on completion of the development. This is done by selling the scheme or refinancing the bridging finance with long-term loans. Commercial banks would require, in order to provide finance:

(a)   security over and above the project, i.e. other assets which are not charged;
(b)   an interest rate of 2–4 per cent above base rate (or LIBOR).

Commercial Banks are not interested in an equity stake. Merchant banks may only require the project as security, but may charge a higher margin, say 4–6 per cent above base and will want an equity share (profits share).

A forward sale

A contract for a future sale can encourage short-term funds because the bank will know that it will get its money back within a period of time.

Alternatively, the party providing the future sale contract may also provide bridging finance. If the investment yield for the scheme was 6 per cent, then the forward sale might take place at 6 ½ per cent. A forward sale with bridging finance might be 7 per cent.

Mortgage

In the 1960s, fixed interest mortgages were used to finance the expansion of many of the large property companies. Interest rates were low and repayments could be serviced from rents. Because of the difference between cost and value projects could be 100 per cent financed.

	£
e.g. New development:	
– Rents	1 000 000 p.a.
– Yield @ 6 ½%	15.38
– Capital value	1 538 000
– Maximum mortgage @ 60% capital value	£922 800
	£
Cost of development	900 000
Mortgage repayments @ 8 ½% over 25 years	88 000 p.a.
Less rental income	100 000 p.a.
Surplus income to developer	£12 000 p.a.

Note: 1. Developer has 100 per cent funding.
2. Developer has income surplus from day 1.
3. Developer takes *all* increase on review.

Nowadays, inflation has undermined the use of the mortgage funding. Mortgages are generally 10–25 years with an advance up to two thirds of the valuation. The interest rate is gilts plus (say) 1 ½ per cent and income must cover repayments. The equivalent gilt rate is the yield on government stocks of equivalent duration.

Drop lock loan

This is really a mechanism for managing the interest rate rather than a separate type of funding arrangement. This general funding arrangement allows for an agreed sum to be released which is secured on the developer's assets. It allows the developer to have access to predetermined amounts of money over a given period of time. Loans are 10–15 years and the option to exercise must be taken up in three–seven years. The base rate is agreed and, if market rate falls to that level, the loan is locked in at that rate, otherwise it varies.

Sale and leaseback

Here a base rent is agreed beforehand, arrangements are as for equity partnership situations – e.g. top slice, side by side, etc. So the freeholder takes a ground rent/base rent and participates in increases in income. Variations on this are:

- *Lease guarantee*: if the development is not let in (say) six months, the developer receives a profit from the funder but takes a lease back guarantee at the base rent. The guarantee is extinguished on letting.
- *Profit erosion*: the developer stakes his profit against voids; the guarantee is for two–four years and is useful if the developer is weak and unwilling to provide a lease back.
- *Priority yield*: the fund sets the return at (say) 6 ½ per cent, the target is 7 ½ per cent (1 per cent for developer) and, if the return is over the target, it is split (say) 50:50.

Project management fee

This is not a very popular arrangement. Here the funder acquires the site and employs the development team. The developer acts as a project manager for a fee plus a bonus if the scheme is successful.

General funding

This is based on the status and assets of the borrower not on the specific project and thus is, strictly, corporate funding. The bank will look at the borrower's accounts and will want to see:

- a good quality property assets on modern leases;
- a good portfolio mix;
- a realistic development programme;
- not all assets pledged;
- a healthy proportion of equity.

The financial agreement

In structuring the financial arrangement, the funder will aim to control certain aspects of the scheme, including:

- the criteria by which tenants are selected and leasehold terms agreed;
- negotiations conducted and agreements concluded with third parties;
- entry by the developer into any legal agreements such as planning agreements (s. 106 agreements) with the local authority and consequent liability if the developer defaults;
- the nature and level of indemnity policies and collateral warranties held or offered by the developer, the professional team, the contractor and subcontractors, so that in the event of failure, the developer can be dismissed and the funder can assume full authority for the completion of the scheme;
- tax implications of the project;
- the method by which the final purchase price of the completed project is agreed.

Practical problems may arise from the wording of financial agreements, and some are listed below:

- design documentation attached to the agreement should clearly and precisely set out the objectives of the scheme;
- a developer is well advised to try to restrict the number of outside consultants whom the funder appoints to act – usually as advisers – on his behalf for the project; a single firm of surveyors should be enough;
- the need to obtain written approval for the appointment of subcontractors should be avoided by agreeing a list of nominated subcontractors;
- a clear understanding of the definition of the date of practical completion should be established; where possible, the site visits of the developer's architect and the funder's surveyor should be synchronised;
- the date when the funder finally values the scheme and the payment is made should be explicit, and should not depend on the actions of third parties;
- access to the site by the funder's surveyors, and facilities to inspect and test materials and workmanship, should be kept within reasonable bounds; the surveyors should also inform the developer of any apparent defects when they discover them;
- a procedure for arbitration should be agreed;
- it may be necessary for the developer to consider the inclusion of a 'walkabout' clause so that he can approach other sources of finance if a top-up of funds is required;
- some mitigation should be allowed for delays that push the completion date beyond that agreed, especially where such delays are beyond the developer's control. (Ratcliffe 1984).

8.4   CASE STUDY: PROPERTY LENDING SURVEY, 1994

Introduction

The Property Lending Survey is a survey of major property lenders which commenced in 1990 and has been carried out on an annual basis since. The survey is a joint project between Chesterton Financial, the financial services section of Chesterton International and the University of Greenwich. A section of the survey has looked repeatedly at the issues of interest rates and the security required. The 1994 survey gave the following results.

Summary of results

The survey was carried out in December 1993 and January 1994 and 85 banks and financial institutions responded to the questionnaire; this was an increase in the total sample from 76 in 1993 but in some cases, because of lack of commitment to lending in the market, the information provided was limited. This survey is the fifth in a series following on from those carried out in 1990, 1991, 1992 and 1993. In the sample replying, the UK banks made up 50 per cent and the rest were foreign banks made up of European (26 per cent), Japanese (11 per cent), North American (6 per cent), Middle Eastern (5 per cent), Far Eastern (excluding Japan) (1 per cent) and others (1 per cent). The nationality of the respondents was broadly in line with the make up of those replying in 1993 but there was a larger response from European banks. Respondents to the survey will tend to have a greater interest in property lending and thus the results set out in this survey may tend to be more positive than the market generally, although it is noticeable that the results in 1994 do reflect a more positive interest in property in terms of numbers committed to lending, especially in development. Terms remain comparable with 1993 in respect of investment lending but margins have increased for development lending, the range of advances has widened generally and the average maximum advances have increased. This reflects the new interest in property but also a realistic approach to its pricing. The attractiveness of different locations for lending on property has remained basically the same; previous surveys had seen a decline in the appeal of Central London for lending but this decline has now been arrested. No particular location appeared to be encouraging fresh interest.

The Property Lending Survey 1994 found that the average size of a property loan book was £485 million, which was an increase on 1993 and the range of the loan books had also increased from a minimum of £3 million to several billion quoted, thus some sizeable lenders had affected the historic results, as this range was wider than 1993 and compared to a range between £12 million and £1500 million in 1992. Many of these larger lenders were European banks.

What was more significant, in 1993 only 25 per cent of the respondents expected to increase their loan books; this was a dip in confidence following increased interest in 1991–2 whereas in 1994 73 per cent of respondents said they would increase their loan books at an average of £85m. Of course, those likely to be more aggressive are also those likely to want to indicate their requirements and thus it could be assumed that those who were silent on the extent of the increase may have smaller additional requirements. The level of response, though, was encouraging in the 1994 survey given the paucity of information from some lenders in 1993 in this area.

The average split of property portfolios in the loan books in the survey was 13 per cent development and 87 per cent investment compared to 21 per cent development and 79 per cent investment in 1993; this continues a trend of reduction of development properties in portfolios (25 per cent in 1992, 32 per cent in 1991 and 43 per cent in 1990). The reasons for this reduction have been indicated before in the surveys and are due to the ongoing completion of existing developments and the shelving of new developments, together with lack of finance for speculative schemes. These comments were reflected in the decreasing proportions prepared to undertake development lending in general in previous surveys, although this recovered slightly in 1994. 54 per cent of respondents said they would undertake development finance compared to 48 per cent in 1993, but this is still markedly lower than the 63 per cent in 1992. Lending on speculative development has also lifted slightly from 12 per cent to 19 per cent in 1994; however if this analysis is done on a sample of respondents lending on development property this represents 31 per cent. When asked their views on speculative development lending, 15 per cent of respondents would lend under given conditions (double the figure of 7 per cent in 1993), the remainder would lend only in exceptional circumstances or not at all. The real interest of the property lender was in investment lending (up to 86 per cent of respondents willing to lend compared to 70 per cent last year) and lending for owner-occupiers.

Lenders in 1993 were less cautious and, in respect of their general view on property lending, 52 per cent were more 'bullish' compared to 7 per cent in 1994; there is thus a distinct change in confidence which has been reflected in other surveys and it now remains for this to pass into lending and more competitive pricing. Only 5 per cent were more cautious about lending this year, about the same as last year reflecting those institutions wary of reentering the market.

Each year additional questions of current interest are asked and in 1994 respondents were asked to comment on how satisfied they were with the Government's handling of the economy. 48 per cent said they were dissatisfied or very dissatisfied, but when this question had been asked last year a massive 92 per cent said they were dissatisfied or very dissatisfied. For both years no one was very satisfied. Respondents were also asked whether they felt the Bank of England should be allowed to adopt a more independent role and 83 per cent felt it should. On the question of property valuation 82 per cent of respondents were generally happy with the quality of the property valuations they received, but most felt that the quality could be improved by the use of more yield and rental comparables.

Additional questions were asked of lenders in the areas of lending on shorter leases; how attitudes to public sector lending may have been changed following the government's private finance initiative; what strategies would have impact on reducing the overall level of property debt. Finally, the issue of a secondary debt market was raised. On the question of shorter leases a clear majority of lenders were prepared to consider lending on a property (limited or non-recourse) with a lease of 11 years or more. The government's private finance initiative was found to have little impact on lending attitudes to the public sector. The clear favourites for reducing the £35 billion of property debt were increased institutional investment and rights issues, with write-offs and debt to equity swaps less popular. On the issue of a secondary debt market, most thought one would develop over the next two years but there was little response to the likely scale of the market with suggestions of a size up to £5 billion, although a large number thought it would be small, say less than £500 million.

Investment

Most lending institutions still appear keen to lend on good quality investment property and this increased from 1993. The proportion lending on investment property was 86 per cent in 1994 compared to 70 per cent in 1993 and to around 95 per cent for the years 1990–2. The proportion lending to owner-occupiers has gone up to 74 per cent compared to 64 per cent for 1993, 48 per cent for 1992, 74 per cent for 1991 and 66 per cent for 1990. This may be due to the influence of building societies in the survey; their commercial lending departments were expanded over this period.

The lending term for investment loans ranged from one to 30 years, although the average was 13 years as for the previous two years. Bridging loans are provided by 30 per cent of the lenders, an increase from 1993. The amount that lenders are prepared to lend as a proportion of value has remained steady at 71 per cent average from a previous fall from 73 per cent in 1991 and 75 per cent in 1990. The average price margin over base rate or LIBOR a borrower will have to pay is 1.9 per cent; this is slightly less than 1993 (2 per cent), but close to the 1992 figure (1.8 per cent). These figures have generally been stable between 1.8 and 2 per cent. The lenders increased their average maximum advance from £18.5 million in 1991 to £25 million in 1992; this fell to £15 million in 1993 and has recovered to £18 million in 1994.

Development

54 per cent of the lenders provided development finance in 1994; this compares with 48 per cent in 1993, 63 per cent in 1992, 74 per cent in 1991 and 94 per cent in 1990. Only 19 per cent undertook loans for speculative developments in 1994, up from 12 per cent in 1993 but lower than 1992 (23 per cent) and 1991 (44 per cent), although the major reduction in lenders had been from 1990 when 77 per cent would provide monies. Even using a sample based on development lenders only rather than the total sample, only 31 per cent would lend on speculative property. The term of loans was on average eight years in 1994, the same as 1993 but up from 1992 (six years).

Only 15 per cent provided mezzanine finance and 27 per cent generally provided finance on a limited recourse basis in 1994; these figures are up from 1993 but in the last survey they had fallen from the previous years. In terms of interest capitalisation over the period of the loan, 58 per cent of lenders responding in 1994 will provide this and as a protection, 35 per cent will use mortgage indemnity policies. These compare to 69 per cent and 26 per cent in 1993, 79 per cent and 41 per cent in 1992 and 87 per cent and 46 per cent respectively in 1991.

The range of advances in 1994 was identical to that in 1993; the average minimum/maximum loan was £2 million/£16 million but the range maximum had increased to £100 million. Loan:cost ratios remained steady at 77 per cent for construction costs and an average of 67 per cent for land costs (this is lower than surveys before 1993). Loan:value ratios in development property were also steady at 71 per cent in 1994, down from 73 per cent in 1991 and 75 per cent in 1990.

The sectors in which lenders were interested to lend in 1994 were in commercial properties (51 per cent), rather than leisure, residential or mixed development and this mirrors feelings from 1993. There did however appear to be an increased interest in the residential sector for the second year running.

Location

The location preferences for development lending in 1992 were different from those for investment lending. For the two years 1993 and 1994, the preferences were broadly similar and this reflected the experience in the surveys prior to 1992. The main aspect noted in 1994 was that there is a broad range of interest for investment and development lending locations, whereas in 1992, for development lending, Central London took precedence, see Table 8.1.

Overseas investment loans as a percentage of the total portfolio averaged 25 per cent in 1994, down from 15 per cent in 1993 and the same as 1992, but note that only 22 per cent of lenders responded to this question.

Table 8.1 *Location preferences for investment and development lending, 1994*

	Investment (%)	Development (%)
Central London	20	19
Outer London	20	17
South East	22	24
Rest of England	22	23
Scotland	14	15
Europe	2	2

Future

In the 1994 survey, 5 per cent were more cautious about property lending than they had been six months previously. 43 per cent said that their criteria for lending was unchanged from six months ago. However 52 per cent were thus more 'bullish' about property, and this is an increase on the 38 per cent in 1993.

15 per cent of the total respondents in the 1994 survey appeared ready to lend on speculative developments in the future given certain conditions whilst a further 20 per cent would lend on speculative property only in exceptional situations. These figures are an increase on the 1993 figures and show some return of confidence in the development lending market. Many organisations expressed an opinion that this sort of lending was not their policy and would be unlikely to be so in the foreseeable future.

In the 1994 survey, 73 per cent of the respondents to this question were expecting to increase their loan book in the forthcoming year, a marked increase from 1993 and 1992 (both 53 per cent) and even up on the 69 per cent in 1991. The typical increase based on a limited return is £85 million.

The main criteria for judging a loan have remained the same according to the sample. The most important factors are quality of the property and cash flow, the quality of the tenant, the financial status of the borrower, the location and finally the track record and experience of the borrower.

Additional topical questions

Additional questions were asked as part of the 1994 survey, the first question asked 'How satisfied are you with the way the government is handling the economy?' In response 52 per cent were satisfied, 44 per cent were dissatisfied and 4 per cent very dissatisfied. This is a marked improvement for the government from 1993 where the response indicated that only 8 per cent were satisfied, 59 per cent were dissatisfied and 33 per cent very dissatisfied. Predictably no one in both years admitted being very satisfied.

In the debate on property valuations 82 per cent of respondents said they were generally happy with the quality of valuations they received; this should give comfort to valuers at a particularly difficult time for them. A number of suggestions were listed to elicit a response as to how valuations might be improved. The improvements suggested and ranked in order were:

- more yield and rental comparables;
- more realistic assumptions;
- more analysis of tenant's covenants;
- greater appreciation of the wider business view;
- greater use of forecasting;
- more accountability; and
- more experienced valuers.

In the 1994 survey, lenders were also asked :'Would you consider lending on a property (limited or non-recourse) with the following continuous lease length (i.e. without a break clause) assuming a good covenant?' Various lease lengths were then set out for the different sectors. On this issue a majority were prepared to lend on leases with limited- or non-recourse facilities for a lease exceeding 10 years (79 per cent of the respondents for retail property, 70 per cent for industrial and 73 per cent for office). These percentages were higher than in 1993. The retail sector fared slightly better than the others.

Lenders were also asked 'Following the launch of the government's private finance initiative, how has your attitude to public sector lending changed?' Respondents decided that this would have no impact (88 per cent) although 11 per cent thought they would be more likely to lend to the public sector.

On the issue of the outstanding debt to the property sector the respondents were asked, 'Which of the following would you expect to have the most impact in reducing the £35 billion of property debt? (rank in order)'. Increased institutional investment was a clear winner with rights issues second, the full list in order was:

- increased institutional investment;
- rights issues;
- write offs;
- debt to equity swaps;
- securitisation;
- increased overseas investment.

On the issue of a secondary debt market, 17 per cent thought that such a market would not develop, 22 per cent thought it would develop over the coming year and 41 per cent in one–two years. 20 per cent thought it would take longer than two years. On the question of the size of the secondary debt market, there was little response, 69 per cent had no opinion on this, of the remainder 13 per cent thought it would be small (less than £0.5 billion) and another 12 per cent thought it would be between £0.5 and £2 billion. 6 per cent, however, thought it might be more than £3 billion, up to £5 billion.

8.5   CORPORATE FINANCE

The two areas of corporate finance relate to debt capital (or loans) and equity capital (or shares). Equity finance is capital paid into or kept in the business by the shareholders, the owners of the business. It is long-term capital and carries the greatest risk and attracts the highest returns. Debt finance is money invested in the business by third parties, usually for a shorter period of time than equity and carrying a lower risk and lower return.

Corporate finance is related to the financial structure of the company itself. Choosing the right mix of debt and equity capital that meets the investment requirement of a business is a key financial management decision. There are 4 strategic issues here:

- *Risk*: There is enormous uncertainty in the business environment. Considerations about risk will consider how the firm would deal with a downturn in business or the economy.
- *Ownership*: The ownership of the firm is critical; it is important to know who exercises the current control over the company as a desire to retain control will affect financing decisions. The desire to retain control may mean that borrowing is preferred to raising equity capital.
- *Duration*: Finance should match the use to which it is put. Finance for investments with no returns in the early years should be raised so there are no payments in these years. One should not raise long-term finance for a short life programme, the firm will be over-capitalised and won't generate sufficient returns to repay the finance.
- *Debt capacity*: The ability to borrow more depends on the existing level of borrowing; this also depends on the type of business and the sector of operation (Pike and Neale 1993, p. 274)

Sources of cash for the firm

The balance sheet model of the firm, which is discussed in more detail in Chapter 10, can be used to analyse the sources of cash available to the corporate structure. There are three basic sources of cash for the firm.

Shareholders' funds

The largest proportion of long-term finance is usually provided by share-holders and is termed equity capital. Share ownership lies at the heart of modern capitalism. By purchasing a portion of or share in a company, almost anyone can become a shareholder with some degree of control over a company. Ordinary share capital is the main source of new money from shareholders. They are entitled to participate in the business through voting in a general meeting of the shareholders and also to receive dividends out of the profits. As owners of the business, the ordinary shareholders bear the greatest risk but enjoy the main fruits of success in the form of higher dividends and capital gains.

Retained profits

For an established business, the main source of equity funds will be internally generated from successful trading. Any profits remaining after all operating costs, interest payments, taxation and dividends are reinvested in the business (i.e. ploughed back) and regarded as part of the equity capital.

Loan capital

Money lent to the business by third parties is debt finance or loan capital. Most companies borrow money on a long-term basis by issuing stocks or debentures. The supplier of the loan will specify the amount of loan, rate of interest, date of payment and method of repayment. The finance manager will monitor the long-term financial structure by examining the relationship between loan capital, where interest and loan repayment are contractually obligatory, and ordinary share capital, where dividend payment is at the discretion of the directors. This relationship between debt and equity is called gearing (known in the USA as leverage). Strictly, gearing is the proportion of debt capital to total capital in the firm.

The three sources of cash previously described are matched by three uses of cash in the firm:

(i)   Cash is used to service (pay returns to) the main sources of finance. Dividends are paid to shareholders, interest is paid to lenders along with any repayment of the loan due. Tax is paid on the profits earned.

(ii)   Cash is invested in long-term assets such as buildings and plant, to produce goods or services. The investment decisions made in respect of these long term assets are critical for the success of the company.

(iii)   Cash is also used to pay for materials, labour, overheads and costs incurred in producing the goods or services offered to customers. It is also used to purchase stocks of raw materials, work in progress, finished goods and debtors. In a property trading company these current assets would also include properties and developments in the process of completion held for trading. Current assets in a firm are offset by the current liabilities which are amounts owing to suppliers of goods and services (Pike and Neale 1993, pp. 8–9).

The main ways in which a property company could increase its capital include:

(i)   the issue of debenture stock;
(ii) the issue of loan stock;
(iii) preference shares;
(iv) ordinary shares.

These instruments are described later on in this chapter; as a general introduction it is important first to look at issues relating to the difference between debt and equity. Equity investments in a company usually come in the form of share ownership and in this chapter, types of share including their issue arrangements are discussed; in addition there is a summary of debt approaches related to corporate finance. The use of different types of corporate finance can be gauged from the Savills Indicator which relates to the amount of loans, bonds and rights issues over the period 1986–1993, as shown in Figure 8.2.

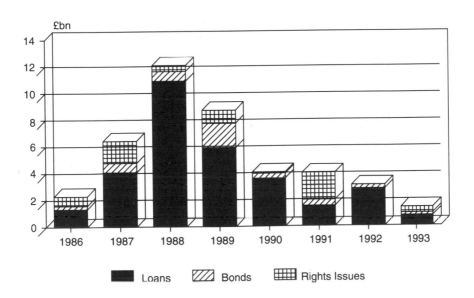

Source: Savills (1993a): 1993 to April only
Figure 8.2   *Savills indicator of Loans, Bonds and Rights Issues, 1986–93*

Equity finance

Equity finance can be in the form of direct investment or partnership arrangements. The distinction between debt and equity is hazy when considered in the context of loans with conversion rights to shares and mezzanine finance, a halfway house between debt and equity. In this chapter when dealing with corporate finance, the distinction is:

Equity	*Debt*
Ordinary shares	Debentures
Preference shares	Loan stock
Warrants	Bonds
Options	General facilities
Converted stock ⟵———	Convertible stock

Ordinary and preference shares

The equity of a company consists of ordinary shares, and shareholders participate in the profits of a company once prior demands have been met; these prior demands for payment will include creditors (trade creditors), holders of debt and preference shareholders. If a company finds that the total of accumulated and retained profits in the company's reserves has grown in relation to issued capital, then a scrip or capitalisation issue can be made.

Preference shares rank after debentures and loan stock but before ordinary shares in terms of a charge to the company. If profits are insufficient to pay the fixed rate dividend then arrears can be carried forward if the preference share is a cumulative type. Conversion rights may be available to convert the shares to ordinary capital. This sort of share may be set up if the company is a new company and thus there may be a risk attached to the ordinary shares. If, for instance, the company is a management buy-out or start-up company then it may attract 'venture' capital, that is risk-taking capital used to finance new business opportunities. In this case the investor may wait some years for the company and its cash flow to stabilise before converting the fixed return preference share to an ordinary share. Preference shares are unsecured so if no profits are made no dividend will be paid but if they are cumulative, they can carry forward the payment due as indicated above. The characteristics of preference shares are thus:

(i)   more secure than ordinary shares;
(ii)   less secure than debentures or loan stock;
(iii) return is from a fixed rate dividend payable from profits;
(iv)   unsecured;
(v)   can be cumulative or non-cumulative;

(vi)   can be voting or non-voting shares but rarely are voting;
(vii) can be convertible or not convertible into ordinary shares.

The priority of charge against the profits of the company are simply:

(i)   debentures and loan stock;
(ii)   preference shares;
(iii) ordinary shares.

Issues and options

Company shares together with other securities such as government bonds and stocks and the loan stock of public authorities are traded on the Stock Exchange. The Stock Exchange arose out of the need to deal in the shares of joint-stock companies which originated in the seventeenth century. By pooling of risk, combination of resources and the development of limited liability, these companies expanded and created the requirement of transferability of capital. Owners of shares or loan capital in the companies required a market to sell their holdings otherwise the original investment would not have been attractive. The Stock Market is thus a secondary market for investment in the sense of reselling shares and securities, but it is also a primary market as a source of new funds.

The primary market operates for new issues and where a company is seeking a listing on the Stock Exchange it will need to be represented by a broking firm. The broking firm will advise on the company's prospectus and the issue price. The Bank of England controls large issues to programme the timing of such issues. Underwriting is arranged so that if the stock is advertised but not fully taken up, the underwriters take up the under-subscription. This new issue procedure is called a prospectus issue, but other methods exist such as an offer for sale, a placing and a rights issue. In 1983, more than 100 property companies were listed on the London Stock Exchange and at the beginning of 1983 the market value of the 42 major property companies monitored by brokers Rowe and Pitman exceeded £4.27 billion. By the end of 1993, 118 companies were listed by the *Financial Times* in their property section; the Datastream analysis of property companies in their sample had a total market capitalisation in excess of £13 billion and this figure appears to be at the same level as quoted by Millman in 1988 (Millman 1988, p. 169), although the sample may be different. The main features of a property company which would be considered by an investor would be: the quality of assets; the quality of management; sources of income; capital structure and financing. The quality of assets is dependent on the portfolio composition and the location, age and tenure of individual properties within the portfolio. The quality of management is very much a subjective judgement and may in fact be related to the persona of the founder or managing director of the company. Sources of income to property companies vary greatly between investment companies reliant on rent and development companies reliant on the capital gains from the sale of completed developments. Capital structure is important from the point of view of the investor, as a highly geared financial structure is more appropriate for established companies deriving a large proportion of revenue from rental income than for development companies dependent on less secure trading profits.

New public property companies created since the 1960s have rarely gone through the expensive process of obtaining a full listing on the Stock Market. A quoted property company may emerge from an existing company whose manufacturing or trading activities have declined or been sold off, or a company may be bought as a shell into which property assets are transferred. Another alternative which was popular was to obtain a quotation on the Unlisted Securities Market (USM); this however has been suspended at the time of writing.

The advantages of property shares over direct investment lie in two general areas. First, equity investments generally provide a means of investing in very small units and denominations and thus risk can be spread. Equity investments can also be traded easily in the Stock Market at low costs of transfer. Thus, beside the liquidity advantage, trading takes place in a market characterised by almost perfect knowledge where share prices are known. The second area of advantage relates to the nature of property itself. The advantages of durability and its effectiveness as a hedge against inflation are clearly seen. As the shares of property companies are based on income arising from rents, then these companies are perceived as providing a higher degree of income security than other equities (Debenham, Tewson and Chinnocks 1984, p. 45).

8.6   CORPORATE FINANCE INSTRUMENTS: A SUMMARY

Major instruments used in the national financial system comprise first, share capital which can consist of preference capital and equity capital; secondly, loan capital; thirdly, bills of exchange and fourthly, treasury bills. Comments on these different instruments follow. Although there are other instruments, these are the key ones to understand.

Share capital

As indicated previously, share capital consists of preference shares and equity shares. The suppliers of this form of capital accept a greater risk than other contributors to funding the company. In return for this greater risk, the providers of share capital are able to participate in the sharing of the earnings of the company. On the other hand, if the company goes into liquidation, they are the last to be repaid.

Preference shares

Preference shares of a company get a priority over ordinary shares for a fixed dividend, out of the after-tax earnings. If there is liquidation of the company, again the owners of share capital have a priority for repayment over the equity share owners. However, the owners of preference shares have little control over the company. For instance, for shareholders meetings, the owners of preference capital rarely have the opportunity to vote. However, there are different types of preference shareholders and the rights of these preference shareholders are contained in the Articles of Association of the company. There may be variations in preference share capital including the rights to vote and the rights of a cumulative payment. Cumulative payment means that, in the event of there being no profit in one particular financial year, the right to the appropriate fixed dividend will carry on to the next, and thus the return to the preference capital shareholder will accumulate over time.

In the past few years, the use of preference shares has declined because of tax reasons. Loan capital has been more attractive because the interest charges paid to the owners of the loan capital was tax deductible. There are four types of preference share:

1. *Non-cumulative preference shares*
   These shares are entitled to a fixed dividend before any dividend is paid to the ordinary shareholders. If the company decide not to pay any dividends in a particular year, then the owners of the non-cumulative preference shares do not have a dividend and have no right to carry this claim forward to subsequent years.

2. *Cumulative preference shares*
   The owners of these shares have a fixed dividend in priority over the ordinary shareholders and they also have the right to carry forward any arrears of dividend owing from previous years. They have the right to have these debts from previous years made good before the payment of any dividend to the ordinary shareholders.

3. *Redeemable preference shares*
   These preference shares can be redeemed by the company on a specified date. The conditions under which a company may issue and redeem preference shares are very strict indeed and usually it is a rule that the company cannot pay back share capital previously invested.

4.   *Convertible preference shares*
These shares can be converted into ordinary shares on a specified date, under certain conditions.

Equity capital

This is the risk capital in the company. The suppliers of equity rank last in receiving their return from the annual profits and, in the event of a company going into liquidation, are the last to have a charge over the remaining invested funds. They have rights to vote and can control the company by appointing and dismissing directors. Ordinary shares usually have a single vote. The vote relates to the share. The classes of equity shares are:

1.   *Ordinary shares*
The owners of these shares are the residual owners of the company. They rank last in payment of dividend and repayment of capital if the company is liquidated but they have the largest say in the control of the company, exercising their rights through voting at meetings.

2.   *Non-voting or restricted voting shares*
These are similar to ordinary shares but their holders have no or less voting rights. They are sometimes called 'A' shares.

3.   *Deferred shares*
The holder of these types of shares usually has the same rights as the ordinary shareholders but his/her entitlement to a dividend is restricted until the earnings of the company have reached an agreed level.

4.   *'B' shares*
The holders of these types of share usually have the same rights as the ordinary shareholders but they have the entitlement to receive fully paid shares instead of dividend.

Loan capital

People who provide loan capital to the company have no rights in the company in the way that the suppliers of share capital have. They are basically creditors of the company. The difference between the providers of loan capital and other trade creditors is that providers of loan capital are involved in the long term with the company; they have a financial contract under which they are supplying funds to the company. Also providers of loans have their debt listed, on the balance sheet of the company, as a liability of that company. The interest payments on the loan are set out in the profit and loss account of the company and are an expense of the company. There is usually a trust deed which is administered by independent trustees and this trust deed specifies the terms relating to future borrowings of the company, any provision for repayment, etc. From the company's viewpoint loan capital has several attractions. Interest is deductible from profits as an expense. The loan has a fixed interest repayment and this will be despite any changes in inflation which might occur. The company can deal in its own loan stock so the company can reduce or increase its liability depending on the nature of interest rates in the market. However, the problem about loan stock relates to the fact that the company usually has to meet the interest payments and loan repayments on the dates agreed. If the income to the company is low this may be extremely difficult and may force the company into liquidation.

The types of loan capital are:

1. *Debentures*
A debenture is a loan which has been issued by a company under its seal. The debenture, thus, is one in which a return is specified by the company as well as the date of repayment. The debenture is usually secured by a floating charge over the assets of the company. The charge gives the debenture holders the rights to appoint a receiver who will sell assets and repay the debenture holders should certain circumstances arise. The usual one is that the company is made insolvent. The debenture holders are also protected in a number of ways against additional loans raised by the company.

2. *Perpetual debentures*
These are debentures where there is no liability on the company to effect a repayment of the principal at any date unless the company goes into liquidation.

3. *Mortgage debentures*
These are debentures secured upon specific assets of the company, usually property. They give the holder greater security than the ordinary debenture which has a floating charge over assets. In this case the company is unable to dispose of the asset on which the charge is secured without the agreement of the mortgage debenture holder.

4. *Naked debentures*
These are totally unsecured loans and in the event of liquidation they rank with the trade creditors for repayment.

5. *Loan stocks*
There are varied types of loan stock issued by companies. The general practice is for the loan stockholders to be protected in the same way as

the debenture holders previously mentioned. There are a number of types of loan stock. These can be guaranteed loan stocks which are guaranteed by someone outside of the company. There are convertible loan stocks which give the holders a right to exchange loan stock for the equity of the company at specified prices on specified dates. They are thus secure to begin with but can be transferred into equity as the company improves its trading position. Other types of loan stocks are bonds and notes of a short-term nature which are not secured and share warrants which are sometimes issued in conjunction with an issue of loan stock. These are contracts issued by the company giving the holders the right to buy shares at specified prices on specified future dates. The purpose in issuing them is to reduce the rate of interest that would otherwise be necessary to pay on the loan stocks to which they originally relate.

Bills of exchange

Bills of exchange are not commonly used in property but relate to trading transactions. The bill of exchange is defined as an unconditional order, in writing, addressed from one person to another and signed by the person giving it. The bill of exchange requires the person to whom it is addressed to pay on demand (or at a fixed or determinable future time) a sum in money to the specified person or to the bearer. In the past the bill of exchange was very important in the commercial life of the UK. There has been a relative decline in the use of bills used within the UK over the last 50 years or so. The major cause for this has been the growth in the bank overdraft as a source of short-term finance. Foreign bills of exchange are still important for the export trade.

Treasury bills

Treasury bills are used as a method of short-term finance. These are issued by the British government and the history of their use goes back to the late nineteenth century. The Treasury bill issue is basically made up of tender bills which are made available to financial institutions who are invited to tender for them. Institutions offer the highest price they can for the bills and thereby receive the right to purchase. Discount houses specialise in this field and these are banking institutions.

REFERENCES

Baring, Houston and Saunders (1991) *Property Report*, Baring, Houston and Saunders, London, November.

Barter, S. L. (1988) 'Introduction', in S. L. Barter (ed.), *Real Estate Finance*, Butterworths, London.

Berkley, R. (1991) 'Raising Commercial Property Finance in a Difficult Market', *Journal of Property Finance*, vol. 1, no. 4, pp. 523–9.

Beveridge, J. A. (1991) 'New Methods of Financing', in P. Venmore-Rowland, P. Brandon and T. Mole (eds), *Investment, Procurement and Performance in Construction*, RICS, London.

Brett, M. (1983) 'Indirect Investment in Property', in C. Darlow (ed.), *Valuation and Investment Appraisal*, Estates Gazette, London.

Brett, M. (1990), *Property and Money*, Estates Gazette, London

Brett, M. (1991), 'Property and Money: Mortgages which convert into property', *Estates Gazette*, 17 August.

Cadman, D. and Austin-Crowe, L. (1991) *Property Development*, E. & F. N. Spon, London.

Chesterton Financial (1991) *Property Lending Survey*, Chesterton Financial, London, February.

Chesterton Financial (1992) *Property Lending Survey*, Chesterton Financial, London, February.

Chesterton Financial (1993) *Property Lending Survey*, Chesterton Financial, London, February.

Chesterton Financial (1994) *Property Lending Survey*, Chesterton Financial, London, February.

Chesterton Financial (1995) *Property Lending Survey*, Chesterton Financial, London, February.

Chesterton Financial/CSW (1993) *Property Confidence Barometer*, Chesterton Financial, London, July.

Clarke, R. J. (1990) 'Refinancing', *Journal of Property Finance*, vol. 1, no. 3, pp. 435–9.

Cohen, P. (1992) 'Non-recourse Property Funding', *Journal of Property Finance*, vol. 3, no. 3, pp. 319–24.

Darlow, C. (1988a) 'Direct Project Funding', in C. Darlow (ed.), *Valuation and Development Appraisal*, Estates Gazette, London.

Darlow, C. (1988b) 'Corporate and Share Capital Funding', in C. Darlow (ed.), *Valuation and Development Appraisal*, Estates Gazette, London.

Darlow, C. (1988c) 'The Supply and Sources of Finance', in C. Darlow (ed.), *Valuation and Development Appraisal*, Estates Gazette, London.

Debenham, Tewson and Chinnocks (1984) *Property Investment in Britain*, Debenham, Tewson and Chinnocks, London.

DTZ Debenham Thorpe (1993) *Money into Property*, DTZ Debenham Thorpe, London, August.

Evans, P. H. (1993) 'Statistical Review', *Journal of Property Finance*, vol. 4, no. 2, pp. 75–82.

Fielding, M. and Besser, A. (1991) 'Syndicated Loans – caveat Borrower', *Estates Gazette*, 15 June, pp. 78 and 103.

Fox, J. W. W. (1993) 'Sale and Leasebacks: A Case Study', *Journal of Property Finance*, vol. 4, no. 1, pp. 9–12.

Fraser, W. D. (1993) *Principles of Property Investment and Pricing*, 2nd edition Macmillan Press, London.

Freed, N. (1992) 'Bridging Finance', *Journal of Property Finance*, vol. 3, no. 2, pp. 187–90.

Gibbs, R. (1987) 'Raising Finance for New Development', *Journal of Valuation*, vol. 5, no. 4, pp. 343–53.

Graham, J. (1985) 'New Sources of Finance for the Property Industry', *Estates Gazette*, 6 July.

Jennings, R. B. (1993) 'The Resurgence of Real Estate Investment Trusts (REITs)' *Journal of Property Finance*, vol. 4, no. 1, pp. 13–19.

Journal of Valuation (1989) 'Market Data', *Journal of Valuation*, vol. 8, no. 1, pp. 87–9.

Mallinson, M. (1988) 'Equity Finance' in S. L. Barter (ed.), *Real Estate Finance*, Butterworths, London.

Millman, S (1988) 'Property, Property Companies and Public Securities', in S. L. Barter (ed.), *Real Estate Finance*, Butterworths, London.

Orchard-Lisle, P. (1987) 'Financing Property Development', *Journal of Valuation*, vol. 5, no. 4, pp. 343–53.

Pike, R. and Neale, B. (1993) *Corporate Finance and Investment*, Prentice-Hall, London.

Ratcliffe, J. (1984) 'Development Financing: Drawing up the Agreement', *Architects Journal*, 22 and 29 August p. 63.

Ratcliffe, J. and Scott G. (1985) 'Funding', *Estates Gazette*, 24 August.

Riley, M. and Isaac, D. (1991) 'Property Lending Survey 1991', *Journal of Property Finance*, vol. 2, no. 1, pp. 74–7.

Riley, M. and Isaac, D. (1992) 'Property Lending Survey 1992', *Journal of Property Finance*, vol. 2, no. 4, pp. 38–41.

Riley, M. and Isaac, D. (1993a) 'Property Lending Survey 1993', *Journal of Property Finance*, vol. 4, no. 1, pp. 43–48.

Riley, M. and Isaac, D. (1993b) 'Commercial Property Lending: Confidence Survey', *Journal of Property Finance*, vol. 4, no. 3.

Riley, M. and Isaac, D. (1994) 'Property Lending Survey 1994', *Journal of Property Finance*, vol. 5, no. 1, pp. 45–51.

Ross, S. A., Westerfield, R. W. and Jaffe, J. F. (1993) *Corporate Finance*, Irwin, Boston.

Ryland, D. (1991) 'Authorised Property Unit Trusts', *Estates Gazette*, 9 November, pp. 163–4.

Savills (1989) *Financing Property 1989*, Savills, London.

Savills (1993a) *Financing Property 1993*, Savills, London.

Savills (1993b) *Investment and Economic Outlook*, Savills, London, issue 3, October.

Scott, I. P. (1992) 'Debt, Liquidity and Secondary Trading in Property Debt', *Journal of Property Finance*, vol. 3, no. 3, pp. 347–55.

Scrimgeor Vickers & Co. (1986) *UK Research, Annual Property Report*, Scrimgeor Vickers & Co, London.

Sexton, P. and Laxton, C. (1992) 'Authorised Property Unit Trusts' *Journal of Property Finance*, vol. 2, no. 4, pp. 468–75.

Shale, A. (1991) 'The Use of Deep Discount and Zero Coupon Bonds in the UK Property Market', *Journal of Property Finance*, vol. 2, no. 1, pp. 11–17.

Venmore-Rowland, P. (1991) 'Vehicles for Property Investment' in P. Venmore-Rowland, P. Brandon and T. Mole (eds), *Investment, Procurement and Performance in Construction*, RICS, London.

Wolfe, R. (1988) 'Debt Finance', in S. L. Barter (ed.), *Real Estate Finance*, Butterworths, London.

9 Structure of Property Finance

9.1 INSTITUTIONAL INVESTMENT

The financial institutions consist of the insurance companies and pension funds, the two principal channels for the nation's savings. Because of the nature and risks of the real property market and because of the larger lot size, individual investors have generally withdrawn from the market; also the channelling or collectivisation of saving into financial institutions is more tax effective than direct investment.

The financial institutions dominated the funding of development properties in the late 1970s and early 1980s. The traditional approach adopted for development finance was to obtain short-term finance to complete a development and then arrange a buy-out by an institutional investor. The dominance of the financial institutions has since declined. Since 1985, the important new money into commercial property has been from banks, property companies and through overseas investors (Evans 1992, p. 116). Thus the growth of financial institutions, evident from the expansion of their development activity in the post-war period, has now abated and resulted in a significant move away from property investment and funding by institutions (Woodroffe and Isaac 1987, p. 12). The decline of the institutions in the commercial property market has been matched by an increase in indirect investment in property companies by way of bank advances. Outstanding bank loans to property companies increased from £5 billion in 1985 to just over £40 billion in the second quarter of 1991 and have declined only slightly since to £36.8 billion at the beginning of 1993; by the second quarter of 1994 they had declined to £32.5 billion (CSO 1994). Over the period between 1986 and 1992 institutions' purchases have generally exceeded their sales but their net property investment has been a declining share of the total. Institutional net property investment is shown in Table 9.1 and Figure 9.1.

From 1984 there was thus a noticeable fall in the availability of long-term institutional funding, and the reaction of the City to the shortfall was to turn to innovative financing methods. Out of necessity developers turned to alternative finance sources to complement institutional finance (Richard Ellis,1986). Money flowing into property from investors during the early 1980s increased from £2 billion to £4 billion in the period from 1980/1986. Between 1986 and 1989 there was a rapid increase to £14 billion. It then tailed off to £8 billion, £4 billion and finally £0.5 billion in 1992. Of the financial institutions, the pension funds' involvement had been relatively static but decreased in the late 1980s. The insurance companies have been more stable investors with an increase in investment in the period 1989–91. The Stock Exchange has not been a significant contributor except in 1987, 1989 and 1991. Banks rapidly increased their involvement between 1986 and 1991, but this has since decreased quite dramatically (see Figure 9.2).

Table 9.1   *Institutional net property investment, 1986–94, £ million*

	1986	1987	1988	1989	1990	1991	1992	1993	1994[a]
Insurance companies:									
Life funds	789	726	1008	1090	946	1493	668	452	2024
General insurance	32	29	94	420	134	−10	−68	−220	−156
	821	755	1102	1510	1080	1483	600	232	1868
Pension funds	434	240	312	92	−491	467	349	299	−282
Property unit trusts	−101	−516	99	31	−61	19	−12	92	89
Total	1154	479	1513	1633	528	1969	937	623	1675

Note: [a] First 2 quarters 1994 only.
Sources: Evans (1993), p. 79; CSO (1994).

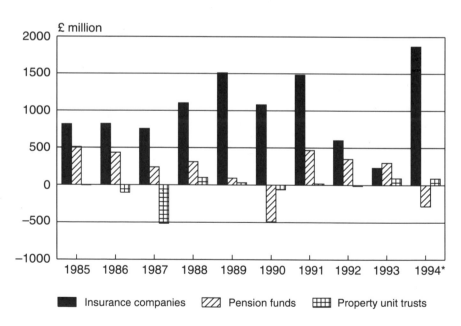

Note: First 2 quarters 1994 only.

Sources: Evans (1993), p. 79; CSO (1994).
Figure 9.1   *Institutional net investment in property, 1985–94*

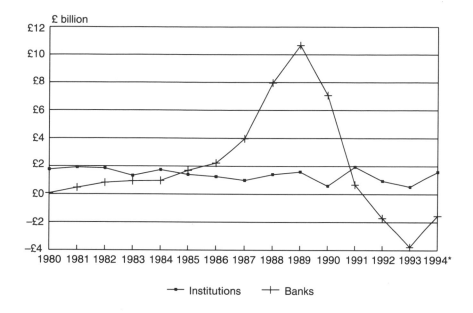

Note: First 2 quarters 1994 only.

Sources: Evans (1993), p. 76; CSO (1994).

Figure 9.2   *Institutional investment and bank finance in property, 1980–94*

Property as a proportion of overall institutional investment has been falling in recent years. The Investment Property Databank Annual Review for 1993 suggests that the best end of year figures for the proportion of property in institutional portfolios as at December 1992 showed a fall to 7 per cent from the figure in December 1991 which was 9 per cent. The bulk of the drop can be explained, however, in terms of the differential price movements between the different asset classes held in the portfolio. Net property investment by institutions is still positive, but as at the end of 1992 was the lowest recorded level since 1980 (Investment Property Databank 1992).

History

In the early post-war period the insurance companies in particular played an important role in property financing by lending long-term fixed interest funds. This approach was useful immediately after the Second World War when inflation was low and thus the returns were not eroded. Financial arrangements between developers and property companies were encouraged because of the shortage of supply of commercial space, the heavy demand and the resultant rental growth and capital value gain. When inflation established itself, the fixed interest approach was no longer attractive to the institutions, and insurance companies which had previously had financial arrangements with major developers broke these arrangements and moved into providing funds for sale and leaseback or situations where they could obtain some share in growth. Eventually the institutions carried out their own direct development, funding the developer on an arrangement whereby the developer received a project management fee with some additional incentives.

The good performance of equities in the 1980s was matched by a poor performance in property. The demand for development sites by the institutional funds increased land values and capital values of completed developments; the levels of income arising from the developments in terms of rentals were over-exaggerated and thus the yield was poor. The insurance companies had been more firmly established in the development markets and the decline in activity affected them less. The pension funds, except for a few larger ones, cut back their portfolios quite drastically. As has been said, new purchases were still made but marginal or poor performing properties were removed from portfolios. In 1990 the property holdings of the insurance companies (life and general companies combined) reached £42 billion, with pension funds having holdings of £22 billion (Brett 1990, p. 242).

Partnership arrangements

The larger insurance companies and the very large pension funds have extensive property departments, capable in many cases of actually carrying out development as well as advising on the purchase and management of completed investment properties. Smaller funds may choose alternative approaches to investment in property, by indirect investment in unauthorised property unit trusts, for instance.

Conventional mortgage finance was replaced by direct development by institutions in the 1980s as mentioned previously; alternatively the institution would fund a sale and leaseback. This involved the sale of the freehold of the property to the institution and the taking back of a long lease by the developer who then sublet the development to occupying tenants on conventional 25-year occupational leases. Early deals had no provision for rent reviews but in the late 1960s and early 1970s as shorter and shorter review periods became the norm so these interests provided an appropriate inflation-proofed equity investment at the same time minimising any management problems (which were taken on by the developer). Equity sharing sale and leaseback arrangements are extremely complex and relate to the balance of risk and return of the parties involved. They have been discussed in Chapter 5 when considering ground rents and partnership schemes.

Direct versus indirect funding

Long-term savings institutions, the pension funds and insurance companies are the main sources of equity finance. The history of the involvement of institutions has been a move towards direct funding of property development and property investments. Smaller institutions wanting to take a stake in commercial property but lacking the size of resources to invest direct can use indirect routes into property (see Figure 9.3). The main indirect routes are:

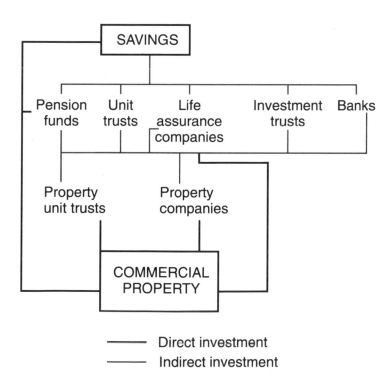

Figure 9.3   *Direct and indirect investment in property*

(i)   Property company shares
(ii)   Property bonds – unit linked life assurance schemes
(iii)   Exempt unit trusts and managed funds
(iv)   Mortgages and debentures (Brett 1983, p. 107).

The property company differs from the other indirect routes in that it is a corporate body whose shares can be quoted on the Stock Exchange. The value of its shares will bear some relation to the underlying property assets held in the portfolio of the company, but the link is not a direct one. Property bonds and unit trusts work on a different principle. The value of the unit is directly determined by the value of the properties in the fund. Funds which operate on the unit principle are 'open-ended' in the sense that the number of units can increase or decrease with the purchase or sale of assets, whereas the share capital of a company is fixed apart from new issues of shares or capital reductions requiring legal permission.

9.2   JOINT VENTURES

There are a number of different types of joint venture arrangements but basically they involve the joining together of two or more parties to undertake a transaction. These parties may include institutions, banks, contractors, overseas investors, local authorities and public sector bodies.

The reasons for forming a joint venture may be numerous but essentially are about two areas – finance and expertise. A property company may not have sufficient finances to enable it to complete a transaction and find the development costs; in this case financial advisers may market the scheme to attract a third party investor. Developers may also form joint ventures and other forms of partnership with owners of land or a development where the latter do not have the expertise to develop; this may be the case where the landowner may be unused to the process of development and engaged essentially in non-property oriented activities. In recent years other factors have influenced the formation of joint ventures and these relate to the reduction of debt in the arrangements for development and, allied to this, the reduction in risk.

Thus additional reasons for forming joint ventures could be listed as:

(i)   the increased risk in property development;
(ii)   the lack of equity in the property market and property companies unable to raise new funds on their own accord in the market;
(iii)   pressure to reduce debt in the property sector, by the Bank of England and lenders; and
(iv)   demands of overseas investors who have a preference for joint venture arrangements in their dealings.

Criteria for the choice of joint venture structure

The main types of joint venture structure are the partnership and the joint venture company (JVC). The decision to choose between the two will rest on a number of criteria, which include:

(i)   favourable tax treatment;
(ii)   tax benefits;
(iii)   limitations of liability;
(iv)   control mechanisms;
(v)   the number of participants;
(vi)   the timescale for the development, its disposal and whether this is a one-off or one of a number of schemes;
(vii)   proposed methods of financing the development.

In the analysis it is generally assumed that the joint venture has been formed for trading purposes, that is to develop a property, let it and sell on the investment created to a third party. The factors to be considered in negotiating a joint venture are summarised in Box 9.1.

The formal joint venture agreement

The participants in a joint venture need to ensure that there is proper documentation between them. The nature of the agreement needs to look at the overall control of the projects, the day to day operation and the final exit or separation of the parties. The detailed agreement governing the activities of a joint company will be embodied in its Articles of Association. In the joint venture arrangement it is important to distinguish between the overall control and day to day management. The important point is to avoid destructive deadlocks.

The formal agreement should clearly indicate elements such as:

(i)   the level of funding proposed;
(ii)   the development period;
(iii)   the control mechanism for decision-making;
(iv)   provision for dissolution; and
(v)   arrangements for settlement of disputes.

If things go wrong in a joint venture then dissolution of the joint venture may be the only option. This could be done by one party buying out the other parties at an agreed valuation. The formula for the valuation could be previously agreed; it may well be that the triggering of such dissolution may be at an inappropriate time for one or other of the joint venture partners, especially in respect of the valuation of any work in progress. One approach suggested

---

JOINT VENTURES

FORMS OF JOINT VENTURE
Limited liability companies
Partnership
Partnership arrangements for profit division

PURPOSES OF JOINT VENTURE
One off, or for a number of projects
Tax advantages
Attract financial investment
Attract development expertise
Reduce debt/risk
Buy into an existing development programme

JOINT VENTURE AGREEMENTS
Should contain details of:

- funding level
- development period
- control
- profit distribution
- dissolution
- disputes

CLIENTS FOR JOINT VENTURES
Landowners without development expertise or finance
Developers without finance or land
Owner occupiers with land banks
Banks and other lending institutions.

Box 9.1   *Summary of joint venture arrangements*

is that if there is a deadlock, either party may offer to purchase the other's interest within a given timescale and at a figure quoted by the offeror. The offeree then has the option of either accepting the offer or buying the offeror's interest at the same price. If interests are not equal then this will need to be done on a pro-rata basis. This approach is known as the 'Texas Option', amongst other things (Bramson 1988, p. 148).

9.3   PROPERTY COMPANIES

Property business is defined as extraction of value from land and buildings such that the landlord takes a creditor's view rather than an equity holder's view of the occupiers. In March 1988 the quoted property company sector (this refers to quoted property companies, that is ones that are listed on the Stock Exchange) owned property valued at £17 billion, had a market capitalisation of shares worth £13 billion and net assets of £14 billion. This could have been compared at the time with the market capitalisation of BP (£15 billion) and the commercial banking sector (£16 billion)). 70 percent of the shares at that time were owned by institutions (Millman 1988, p. 169). The total book assets of the sector increased up to 1990 when they reached a peak of nearly £30 billion but subsequently decreased in 1992 to £25 billion. (S. G. Warburg Securities 1993, p. 17) Debt has continued to rise in the balance sheets of the property sector, although less rapidly than the period to 1992. Table 9.2 sets out a summary of asset values and borrowings in the balance sheets of property companies.

In 1993 there was a dramatic rerating of property companies because of a major shift in confidence. In the first half of 1993, equity and convertible issues raised by property companies totalled around £1.3 billion. Capital issues raised subsequently showed a rapid expansion (see Figure 9.4). To the end of 1993, share prices rose so strongly that they no longer traded at a discount to net asset value. Property companies were, at the end of 1993, in the rare position of being able to raise money without significant dilution of net asset value or earnings. However the situation in 1993 was marred by a continued fallout from the consequences of over-lending, over-development and much reduced property values (Evans 1993, p. 77). A number of property companies had huge write offs. For example London & Edinburgh Trust (LET), the subsidiary of the Swedish Company SPP, had a 1992 pre-tax loss of £449m against a loss of £138m in the previous year. SPP bought LET in 1990 for £491m. By 1994

Table 9.2 *Quoted property companies: balance sheets, gearing and financing, 1986–92*

	Total book assets (£m)	Total borrowings (£m)*	Cash (£m)	Debt† as % of book assets	Short-term borrowings (£m)	Short-term‡ borrowings as % total
1986	11 298	3 087	437	24.4	1 075	34.8
1987	15 172	4 254	722	24.4	1 506	35.4
1988	19 862	4 988	1 407	19.4	1 748	35.0
1989	27 055	6 939	1 716	20.6	2 648	38.2
1990	30 933	8 590	1 453	24.2	3 642	42.4
1991	27 992	10 132	1 223	32.7	4 374	43.2
1992	25 462	11 130	1 278	38.7	5 218	46.9

Notes: * Total borrowings include convertible loan stocks and bonds.
†Debt is net of cash.
‡ Short-term borrowings are less then five years and also include convertible loan stocks and bonds.
Source: S. G. Warburg Securities (1993), p. 17.

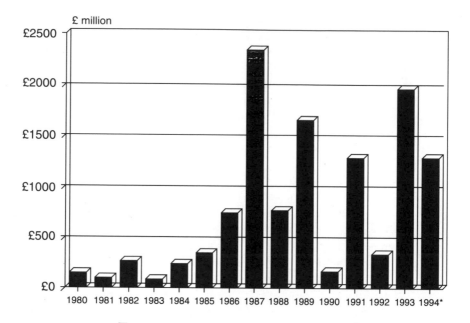

£ million

Note: 1994 To September only.

Sources: Bank of England; Evans (1993), p. 82; CSO (1994).
Figure 9.4   *New capital issues by property companies*

property companies shares were again being traded at a discount to net asset value. Table 9.3 gives a sample of the main quoted property companies on the Stock Exchange and their market capitalisation.

Features of property companies considered by an investor

The property companies listed on the Stock Exchange offer potential investors a range of different opportunities. The main features of a property company to be considered by an investor are:

(i)   *The quality of assets in the portfolio:* the age, location and tenure of individual properties will be important, as well as the investment's relative importance in the portfolio. The different types of property and the proportion of overseas investment in the portfolio, should also be considered.

(ii)   *The perceived quality of management in the company:* this perception is very subjective and is often restricted to the market's view about single individuals in the company.

Table 9.3 *Major quoted property companies: company ranking by market capitalisation, UK property sector, January 1995*

Company	Share price (p)	Market capitalisation (£m)
Land Securities	572	2915.8
MEPC	384	1560.8
British Land	359	1100.6
Hammerson	323	913.7
Slough Estates	220	858.1
Capital Shopping	190	691.6
Great Portland	177	572.7
Brixton Estate	176	409.7
Bradford	178	260.0
Chelsfield	158	247.1
Burford	83	245.3
London Merchant (Ord)	94	228.2
London Merchant (Def'd)	53	40.9
Bilton	241	211.5

Source: UBS 1995, as at 19 January; only those in FT-SE 100 Index and FT-SE Mid 250 quoted.

(iii) *The sources of income of the company*: these will vary between well established property investment companies relying on rents for income and property trading companies whose income arises from selling on completed developments.

(iv) *The capital structure and gearing of the company*: A highly geared financial structure is more appropriate for established companies deriving a large proportion of revenue from rental income rather than for trading companies dependent on less secure trading profits. The nature of debt is also important.

Property shares

Property companies hold all or most of their assets in property, shares are thus a surrogate for property. There should be a close correlation between share prices and property values. Shares are more favoured than direct property because of the general rising share market; because of gearing which can increase returns to equity; because of the benefits of stock selection and because of the perceived dynamic management of property companies (Barter 1988, p. 70). The drawback of share ownership against direct property investment is the incidence of tax; this affects the returns compared to direct property investment as the shareholder is in effect double taxed (see Box 9.2).

Thus property company shares offer the investor four main features.

**CAPITAL GAINS TAX: DISADVANTAGE OF OWNERSHIP
THROUGH A CORPORATE ENTITY**

A property was purchased in 1965 for £4m, had £6m spent on it and was sold in 1982 for £40m. Consider the different tax position of direct ownership against purchase by a UK holding company, which was sold after sale of the property to put its shareholders in funds:

	£m
Sale proceeds	40
Cost	(10)
Gain	30

	Holding company	Direct ownership
Gross gain	30	30
Tax on capital gain	(9)	
Available to shareholders	21	

	Tax on capital gain	Net proceeds	Tax on capital gain	Net proceeds
UK gross funds	–	21	–	30
Non-resident	–	21	–	30
UK tax-payer	6.3	14.7	9	21

Source: Millman (1988), p. 174.

Box 9.2   *Capital tax disadvantages of the corporate structure*

Management

This takes away the direct problems of management and offers specialist management and entrepreneurial skills.

Gearing

Gearing (debt/equity as a percentage is used here, which is common in the market, but as mentioned earlier debt/total capital is usually used in economic texts) of the larger quoted companies at January 1993 varied quite dramatically, for instance, Speyhawk (before its demise) had a negative equity of £105m, Stanhope had a gearing of 600 per cent whilst Bradford and Warnford had no borrowing. Land Securities had a gearing of 54 per cent (S. G. Warburg Securities 1993, p. 36). As well as the level of debt, the type of debt is important, whether it is fixed or variable rate, short- or long-term is important. Gearing can increase the equity return but can lead to problems of insolvency if overall returns fall.

Liquidity

The market in shares has a central price and there is a speed of entry and exit in and out of the market.

Other participants

Liquidity exists because there are other participants in the share market, institutional investors hold a high percentage of shares. Usually the shares are held as part of an equity rather than a property portfolio and thus are managed in the more market-led style of equity shares rather than the more asset-led style of direct property (Mallinson 1988, p. 71).

Discount on net asset value

Property investment companies as opposed to property trading companies are valued on the basis of their net assets rather than the income produced. A feature of the market in property investment shares is that they are traded at a discount to the net assets held. This may not be in cases of a very bullish market and for exceptional performers, but generally over longer periods this discount appears to be around 20 per cent. The average discounts on net asset value for property investment companies 1977–94, as analysed by S. G. Warburg Research, are shown in Figure 9.5.

The discount is measured as:

$$\frac{\text{Net asset value per share (NAV/share)} - \text{Share price}}{\text{NAV/Share}} \times 100\%$$

This means that the underlying assets are undervalued because of this discount. Three reasons are commonly given for the existence of the discount:

(i)   the problems of possible loss on the forced sale of the company's assets;
(ii) tax liabilities, being the capital gains tax liability on disposal of the properties in the company's portfolio and the tax inefficiencies of holding shares as opposed to direct investment;
(iii) disquiet over the quality of valuations carried out by surveyors on the underlying property assets.

Recent research is inconclusive as to the precise reasons for the discount but this situation has an effect on financing and activity in the sector. Assets

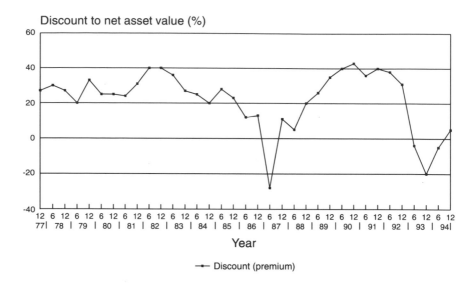

Discount to net asset value (%)

Year

—•— Discount (premium)

Note: * Figures are as at December and June. Projected figures for December 1993 and 1994.
Source: S. G. Warburg Research (1993), p. 5.
Figure 9.5   *Property Share Price: Average discount on net asset value, 1977–94*

are under-valued because of the discount and this discourages the growth of property companies through equity expansion and forces them into borrowing to expand. This leads to companies being highly geared (having a high ratio of borrowed capital to total capital). It discourages takeovers within the sector because takeover situations raise share prices and narrow the discount. Subsequently, following takeovers, the share price will tend to fall to a realistic discount as perceived by the Stock Market. On the other hand property investment companies could be vulnerable to takeover by firms from other sectors where discounts do not exist (Woodroffe and Isaac 1987 p. 1026).

Contingent capital gains tax on property investment companies prior to the 1988 budget (which moved the base date for capital gains tax forward from 1965 to 1982) probably amounted to about 20 per cent of net asset value but subsequently this has fallen to probably 10 per cent. There is an argument for valuing property investment companies by net net asset value (NNAV) which takes into account the contingent liability for capital gains tax. On this basis the discount would be narrowed (Millman 1988, p. 188). Investment trusts are companies which hold their investments in shares and they also suffer from discount on net asset value in respect of their ownership of property investment company shares, but investment trusts are not liable to capital gains tax.

1994 turned out to be a poor year for the property sector. The FT Property Share Index fell by 21.5 per cent mainly due to rising interest rates, and the projected forecast for premiums on share prices in the sector relative to net asset values was dashed. The majority of companies by the end of 1994 were again standing at a share price discount to net asset value. Examples of discounts in January 1995 were British Land at 18.3 per cent, Greycoat at 23.5 per cent and Land Securities at 16.3 per cent (Paribas Capital Markets 1995a). These examples remained static to March 1995 (see Table 9.4).

Corporate capital structure

The question of an optimal capital structure for a particular company is a question which has aroused much debate, and this is especially important in property companies where there may be high levels of debt. The problem is the choice of the best mix of debt (loans, debentures) and equity (ordinary shares, reserves and retained profits). Five following factors ought to be considered, but assessing the weight to be given to each one is a matter of judgement.

Cost

The current and future costs of each potential source of capital should be estimated and compared: the costs of each source are not independent of one another. It is generally desirable to minimise the average overall cost of capital to the company.

Table 9.4 *Net asset values and discount on major quoted property companies: UK property sector, March 1995*

Company	Share price (p)	Current net asset value (NAV) (p)	Discount to current NAV (%)
British Land *	363	424	14
Brixton Estates	179	214	16
Burford Group	94	92	(2)
Capital SC	193	221	13
Great Portland	170	215	21
Hammerson	319	390	18
Land Securities	586	689	15
MEPC	387	489	21
Slough Estates	227	289	21

Source: Paribas Capital Markets (1995b), as at 8 March; * adjusted for current open offer.

Risk

It is unwise to place a company in a position where it may be unable, if profits fall, to pay interest as it falls due or to meet redemptions. It is equally undesirable to be forced to cut or omit the ordinary dividend to shareholders.

Control

Except where there is no alternative, a company should not make any issue of shares which would have the effect of removing or diluting control by the existing shareholders.

Acceptability

A company can only borrow if investors are willing to lend to it. Few listed companies can afford the luxury of a capital structure which is unacceptable to the main institutional investors. A company with readily mortgageable assets will find it easier to raise debt.

Transferability

Shares may be listed or unlisted. Many private companies have made issues to the public so as to obtain a listing on the Stock Exchange and improve the transferability of their shares (Isaac and Steley 1991, pp. 154–5).

International investment

Over the past decade UK investors have continued investing abroad; this expansion has been encouraged by the need to increase the performance of the property portfolio and reduce market risk through diversification. Hedging techniques are available to these companies through foreign exchange futures, options and swap contracts but a recent study (Dawson 1995, p46) found that 72 per cent of property companies, institutions and fund management groups with overseas property exposure did not avail themselves of this protection, thus leading to lower returns on the portfolio. The extent of the dispersion of the top five quoted companies who invest abroad: Hammerson, MEPC, Slough Estates, Brixton Estates and British Land is shown in Figure 9.6.

9.4   SECURITISATION AND UNITISATION

Securitisation is the creating of tradable securities from a property asset.
    Unitisation is also the creation of a tradable security, but the aim in this case is to produce a return comparable to direct ownership.

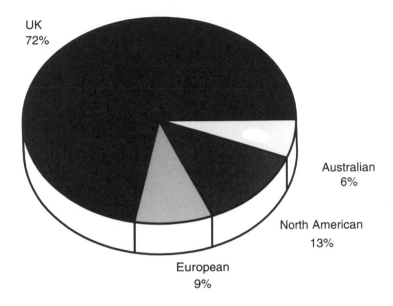

UK
72%

Australian
6%

North American
13%

European
9%

Source: Dawson (1995), p. 46.
Figure 9.6   *Top five investors' overseas portfolios: breakdown of 1994 property assets by country*

This distinction may sound confusing but an analysis of the difference of debt and equity should clarify this. To begin with one must consider a single property rather than a portfolio. For a single property, if we divide the interest into a number of holdings, then we divide the equity and this is unitisation. If we divide the interest and add debt securities, in the way a company may have shares and loan stock, this is securitisation. In fact securitisation is rather like imposing a corporate finance structure on a property, that is a single asset property company, but this approach simplifies matters because it is important to understand the objectives of securitisation and unitisation which will differ from the objectives of operation of a property company. From the above, securitisation thus includes unitisation and can be used as a general term incorporating unitisation, and this will done here except when discussing securitisation historically or when the securitisation of the equity alone is considered. The distinction between securitisation and unitisation is shown in Figure 9.7.

The distinction of a single property is important to this analysis; if a portfolio of properties is considered then unitisation is basically akin to property units as in an authorised property unit trust, whilst securitisation of a portfolio would be a property company's shares and loanstock/debentures. A matrix of options to clarify this is shown in Figure 9.8.

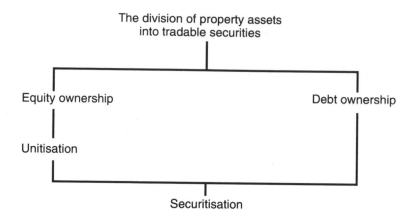

Figure 9.7   *Securitisation and unitisation*

Securitisation

	Equity	Debt
One property asset	Unitisation Securitisation	Securitisation
Portfolio of assets	Unit trusts Shares in a property company	Mortgage backed securities Loan stock/debentures in a property company

Figure 9.8   *Securitisation matrix*

A further analysis has been used in the past by the Barkshire Committee (Barkshire,1986) related to the distinction between the unitised property market in which the investor gets a percentage interest in the ownership of the property investment and property income certificates where an investor gets a percentage income that the investment produces. This distinction of structure is not very useful and confuses the elements of debt and equity. Nevertheless so that the clarification can be exaggerated, the framework is outlined in Table 9.5.

Table 9.5 *Unitisation and securitisation vehicles*

Vehicle	Ownership		*Securitisation of equity (unitisation)*	*Securitisation of debt (total securitisation)*
SPOTS	Direct	} Unitised Property	Yes	No
SAPCO	Direct	} Market	Yes	Yes
PINCS	Income owned		Yes	Possible
	(PINCS were initially unitised but debt securities could be added)			

The vehicles for unitisation and/or securitisation are:

- Single Property Ownership Trusts (SPOTs)
- Single Asset Property Companies (SAPCOs)
- Property Income Certificates (PINCS).

Thus SPOTS, because they only deal with equity, are vehicles for *unitisation* whereas SAPCOs and PINCS can be *securitised*. To summarise, securitisation in general is the conversion of an asset into tradable securities (these are certificates of ownership or rights to income). In the property context used here, securitisation is the conversion of a single property and the tradable securities may be debt or equity based. Unitisation is included in securitisation but specifically refers to the securitisation of the equity interest. In its simplest form this unitisation will provide a share of the rental and capital growth with no obligation of management. This approach contrasts to property share ownership in the sense that with unitisation, the investor selects specific property assets in which ownership is held rather than having to accept an existing managed portfolio. In this respect Barter, writing in 1988, suggested that the income yield which could arise from unitisation (which, because of its tax transparency, will be the equivalent of investing directly in property) may be twice the dividend yield from property company shares (Barter 1988, p. 213). Aspects of tax transparency were discussed earlier in this chapter.

History of the development of securitisation

The pattern of investment in commercial property has changed substantially over the post-war period. There has been a collectivisation of savings and the property investment market has become dominated by the major institutions: the insurance companies and the larger pension funds. This has reduced in recent years from the late 1980s when property investment and development has attracted more funding by banks and by the raising of equity by property companies.

The drive toward securitisation and unitisation arose because of problems with the ownership of large property investments; this in turn has arisen because of the lack of liquidity in the market. There are difficulties in transferability of these ownerships; extended negotiations may be necessary to achieve matched deals. Other investment media such as quoted shares have a centralised market and do not experience these problems. Further problems with illiquidity have been experienced in terms of the increasing size of investments available. A number of recent property developments are too large to fit neatly within the portfolio of existing institutions. Institutions would not commit a large proportion of their available funds to a single property investment where this may be contrary to existing policy or where over-commitment to one project may increase risk within the portfolio related to the balance of the investments.

The number of potential purchasers for a larger investment (say, more than £20 million) is thus limited and this will affect the price of the asset. The problem of illiquidity will affect the demand, supply and value of large projects because of the way the asset is traded.

Other problems with large investments may relate to situations where a developer or investor wishes to organise a partial disposal, for instance, or where developers may wish to retain the investment but recoup some of the project cost. There is also a lack of opportunity to spread the risk of investment portfolios because the incorporation of larger buildings in the portfolio, which may be attractive assets because of location and prestige, will mean that they dominate the portfolio in terms of value. Finally, there will be problems associated with the valuation of such large properties by traditional methods of valuation where comparable evidence is lacking and a bulk discount relating to size or a discount reflecting the lack of ease of transferability, especially important in the event of a forced sale, will need to be incorporated.

Indirect investment in property shares and unit trusts has been readily available to investors and to some extent has addressed the problems of illiquidity. For a long period; until recently, property unit trusts (PUTs) where they were unauthorised had not been able to invest in real property. Exempt unauthorised unit trusts could not under previous law (the Prevention of Fraud (Investment) Act 1958) be openly offered for sale to the public. The result is that only the main institutions were originally involved in this form of investment. Property bonds also suffer from illiquidity problems and some contain provisions which may delay repayment of investments. Property share investment has been popular since the Second World War and the growth of property investment companies over this period has been a major factor in the property market. Company share ownership suffers from three major difficulties. First, there is a tax problem relating to double taxation of income (the shares are not tax transparent). Secondly, there is not purity of investment in the sense that the portfolio of properties can be large, varied and changing and it is therefore difficult for the investor to identify the asset ownership related to share ownership. Finally, net asset values of property investment companies are discounted on the Stock Market relative to share price as discussed earlier, whilst property trading companies are valued on the assessment of future profitability which may not readily be related to existing asset values.

Three unitisation vehicles were originally suggested to deal with this problem. For simplicity these structures have been considered here as single asset property companies (SAPCOS); single property ownership trusts (SPOTS) and property income certificates (PINCS). In the first two cases, the single property vehicles are divided up on the basis of ownership of the asset. In the case of SPOTS, the interest is divided up into equity units which are identical whilst, in the case of SAPCOS, the division is by securitisation, the layering of negotiable interests in the investment on a risk/reward basis and including debt as well as equity interests. In SAPCOS, different interests are thus created in relation to the assets in much the same way as companies are financed through a variety of corporate funding techniques. Finally, PINCS differ from the previous two vehicles in that they provide ownership rights to the income arising from the investment rather than direct investment in the asset. Other vehicles which were considered were property unit trusts (PUTs) and mortgage backed securities (MBSs) which were common in the USA and have now established themselves in the UK. Mortgage backed securities were originally developed in the residential market enabling Building Societies or specialist mortgage lenders to raise funds using a portfolio of mortgage debt as collateral. The strength of such collateral meant that the issue received a high credit rating. MBSs allow the issuer to repackage their mortgage assets for sale in capital markets, thus freeing up their capital to make additional loans. The Building Societies Act 1986 has now meant that the Building Societies have been able to commit funds to commercial property as well as the residential sector. The presence of Building Societies in the market may accelerate the take up of MBS issues (Savills 1989, p. 10).

Objectives of securitisation: a summary

Securitisation:

(i)   Provides for liquidity in the market and this can sustain the level of values, increase the size of the market and speed up transfer transactions.

(ii)   Assists in the diversification of risk. Securitisation provides a range of opportunities for a mixed portfolio and to invest in different development proposals more precisely with regard to the investor's risk/reward profile. Securitisation offers the ability to invest in debt and equity securities which, in themselves, have different risk profiles.

(iii)   Provides the opportunity to avoid the responsibility of managing the property which occurs with direct ownership and to leave the task to the more skilled and experienced.

(iv)   Provides tax transparency and avoids the double taxation which exists with property company shares.

(v)   Provides a more flexible financial structure to encourage the sale of debt instruments and thus develop gearing situations, allowing more flexibility for the sale of the developer's interest or part interest and providing better opportunities for refinancing short-term development funds with long-term investment funds.

9.5   CASE STUDY: RESEARCH STUDY INTO THE UNITISATION OF PROPERTY IN HONG KONG (from Yuen, McKinnell and Isaac 1988)

This is a summary of joint research carried out in 1988 jointly sponsored by the Department of Surveying at Hong Kong University and the School of Land and Construction Management at the University of Greenwich in the interests of widening international comparative research into real estate issues. The research was carried out with the assistance and comments provided by professional practices and other bodies operating in the Hong Kong financial and property markets and also with information provided by various bodies sponsoring various Single Property Vehicles. The research is intended to provide an overview of the Hong Kong property market as a suitable environment for the introduction of unitised vehicles. The market comments and political situation relate to the 1988 situation.

The Hong Kong investment market

It should initially be noted that-long term investment in the Hong Kong Market is overshadowed by the implications of the 1997 treaty with the Peoples Republic of China (PRC). The Basic Law to be introduced states that property ownership rights shall correspond to the real value of property. The system looks set to be stabilised but further monitoring of the market closer to 1997 and some analysis of capital movements in and out of the market, especially from the PRC, will be required.

The nature of the market in Hong Kong is different from that in the UK. Collectivisation of savings has led to the institutional investors being the major investors in the UK. In Hong Kong individuals have enormous interests associated with trading and manufacturing as well as investment. Looking at the market from the demand side, the market is dominated by individual investors at different investment levels. The main objective and the over-riding motivator in the market is short-term capital gain rather than long-term growth. Property is traded more as a commodity than held as a long-term investment. There is also a view held that property is attractive to certain investors when held directly because the physical existence of the asset is comforting; indirect investment through unitisation and shares does not provide the same function.

Thus the problems of the Hong Kong market relate to its relative lack of maturity. Speculation in the property markets is evidenced in the sale of all types of accommodation especially in the residential sector; in some instances speculators are in a majority in purchasing new residential units. Speculative activities reached a peak in 1980–1 and reappeared in 1985–6 after the collapse of the market in 1982. Speculative finance of property development through pre-sales is an attractive alternative to bank financing at times of high interest rates. Speculation produces distortion in the markets and generates price cycles of extreme amplitudes associated with wild movements in building completions. Developers thus misread the market signals and exaggerate the problems. Speculative activities in a small unitised property market could lead to extreme movements in unit prices. The lack of institutional participation in the market is also a problem of this immaturity. Insurance companies and pension funds do not have the established position they have in the markets of Japan and the UK. Sources of finance for property development are raised in the Stock Market where players are a mixture of large corporations, small companies and individuals. Lack of institutional participation suggests a more volatile market with a larger proportion of investors realising short-term gains. The long-term commitment necessary for the successful operation of a unitised property market is thus missing in Hong Kong. A further problem of the immaturity of the market may relate to problems of unit size; suggestions of the size of unit discussed in the UK may not be applicable to the Hong Kong market which experience suggests may need to be smaller to tempt the investors and compete with alternative investments. A final point relating to the problems of the market was shown by the relative failure of the PUTs, which proved unsuccessful following a lack of interest subsequent to their launch.

The Hong Kong market suffered as badly as other world markets in the crash of October 1987; in a controversial four-day closure the market fell by 45 per cent. Since this time the local property market has quietened down although vacancy rates remain low especially in the prime office market. The Stock Market crash has resulted in investors holding liquid investments and decreasing portfolio acquisitions, and this it is not an ideal scenario to launch a new property investment vehicle. However, against this, the property market in 1987–88 looked sound with two significant features emerging. First, developers looked more toward the Stock Market to finance their projects rather than the banks and secondly, there was evidence of a movement of international institutional investment into the Hong Kong property market. It may also be the case that with the problems related to the crash, investors might now be willing to consider new investment vehicles. It still remains the case that the usual way of investing in property in Hong Kong is by way of property shares or direct investment. Unitisation would be less popular in the Hong Kong investment market because a large proportion of the shares traded relate to activities in the property sector. Investors, if you like, have adapted to this type of 'package'. Direct involvement is also common, especially in the residential sector, where purchase costs are less and the transaction simpler than in the UK. Transactions costs are obviously higher for direct involvement and certainly a vehicle with similar characteristics but with lower transactions costs may prove popular.

Looking at the supply side of the property market there appeared to be few properties in 1988 which might be available for unitisation. There are a number of issues here. First, the stock of prime properties is small; secondly, the supply of sites and building completions is limited; finally, when available, the capital cost is such that potential purchasers/investors are not available and often the assets are held in the developer's portfolio and not disposed of. If only prime and large commercial properties are unitised initially, the total number may not be adequate to set up an efficient unitised market. Such buildings can be found in Central, Queensway, Causeway Bay and Tsim Sha Tsui but the supply is much more limited than in the UK. It may also be evident that the market conditions are more volatile in Hong Kong and thus changes may undermine the status of the asset.

Having looked at supply and demand we may test the structure of the market and the determination of price. Valuation problems of large investment properties was one issue previously mentioned relating to the need for unitisation in the UK. Valuation methods vary in Hong Kong with valuations being more related to short-term views, for instance dealing with payback periods, rather than long-term yields. The valuation argument is thus confused in terms of the Hong Kong market. The small size of the Hong Kong market is another problem that unitisation would need to face. The Hong Kong Stock Market is small compared to New York, Tokyo and London. Supervision of such a small market would be a key issue. Two problems spring to mind, first, a major investor could dominate the market, secondly there could be problems of matching supply and demand. In the case of market domination, it may be possible to manipulate the market through ownership of a large proportion of the shares or units depriving the minority shareholders of a realistic secondary market; this problem is accentuated if the market is small. Regulations would need to be enforced to ensure holdings in any asset do not exceed a maximum percentage. In respect of the matching of supply and demand, if the market is too small it may not be able to achieve matched deals because of the lack of variety and number of players in the market. The consequences of this mismatch would be that prices may swing widely according to the prevailing view.

Finally, in order to examine the potential role of unitisation in the Hong Kong market, one needs to be aware of competing financial arrangements. Division of property is more common in the Hong Kong market in terms of the ownership of residential flats, the ownership of floors and part floors of commercial areas. This is a product of the physical nature of Hong Kong and the shortage of land giving rise to multi-storey development, but it also reflects a need for owner occupation and the desire to hold real property as a capital asset. Dealings in shares are common in the Hong Kong market with easy access for all because of the different tax structure. Here the tax transparency arguments are not so strong.

The application of unitised property vehicles

The nature of the market is such that at first glance the concept of unitisation would appear not to have much appeal. There appear to be other negotiable securities on the market which would compete with the issue of units. Property shares are popular in the Hong Kong market and although companies appear to have problems of discount on net asset value, this is not as evident as in the UK Stock Market. (Note that this was the evidence at the time of the study). Also the problems related to the tax transparency are less evident in Hong Kong as there is no capital gains tax and the levels of income tax are less. Thus the attraction of unitised property vehicles appear less in the Hong Kong market. The short-term nature of the Hong Kong market also militates against the introduction of unitised property as the Hong Kong market is looking for short-term gains rather than long-term investment.

Preconditions for a successful market

For single property vehicles to be of interest to the market, the structure of the market will need to change. The report commissioned by the Hong Kong Government and chaired by Ian Hay Davison suggested that self-regulation and market discipline had failed to develop in the Hong Kong Stock Market. Even allowing for this problem it appears that the major problem of the market place relates to the lack of players; for a successful market to develop in single property vehicles there must be a greater number of institutional investors looking for long-term investment and in sufficient numbers to ensure that the market operates properly. From the supply point of view there have to be sufficient properties to provide an ongoing number of suitable investments for unitisation.

Conclusion

Single property vehicles are not usefully applicable to the Hong Kong market unless the preconditions outlined in the previous paragraph are fulfilled. This requires that the nature of the market or the vehicles themselves change. Two possible areas of improvement may assist the introduction of such schemes.

Firstly. if the market demand for property expands with new capital inflows, for instance from China or Japan, the provision of new investment could widen and deepen the demand and make the single property vehicle market more attractive. The evidence of increased international institutional investment in the Hong Kong property market is perhaps an indication that this is happening.

Secondly, the vehicle could be changed to a more attractive vehicle, such as an Investment Trust containing a mixed portfolio of interest to overseas institutional investors. The portfolios may be SE Asia or Far East based or may include Pacific Rim properties like attractive West Coast investments in the USA. Real Estate Investment Trusts (REITs) in the USA are possible examples of such an approach. Real Estate Investment Trusts have institutional investors but most, especially the smaller ones, are dominated by private individuals.

REFERENCES

Albert, D. and Watson, J. (1990) 'An Approach to Property Joint Ventures', *Journal of Property Finance*, vol. 1, no. 2, pp. 189–95.

Bank of England (1994a) *Quarterly Bulletin*, vol. 34, no. 3, August.

Bank of England (1994b) *Quarterly Bulletin*, vol. 34, no. 4, November.

Barkshire, R. (1986) *The Unitised Property Market*, Working Party of the Unitised Property Market, London, February.

Barter, S. L. (1988) 'Introduction', in S. L. Barter (ed.), *Real Estate Finance*, Butterworths, London.

Barter, S. and Sinclair, N. (1988) 'Securitisation', in S. L. Barter (ed.), *Real Estate Finance*, Butterworths, London.

Baum, A. E. and Schofield, A. (1991) 'Property as a Global Asset', in P. Venmore-Rowland, P. Brandon and T. Mole (eds), *Investment, Procurement and Performance in Construction*, RICS, London.

Beveridge, J. (1988) 'The Needs of the Property Company', in S. L. Barter (ed.), *Real Estate Finance*, Butterworths, London.

Bramson, D. (1988) 'The Mechanics of Joint Ventures', in S. L. Barter (ed.), *Real Estate Finance*, Butterworths, London.

Brett, M. (1983) 'Indirect Investment in Property', in C. Darlow (ed.), *Valuation and Investment Appraisal*, Estates Gazette, London.

Brett, M. (1990) *Property and Money*, Estates Gazette, London.

Central Statistical Office(CSO) (1994) *Financial Statistics*, CSO, November.

Chesterton Financial *Internal Uncirculated Reports*, Chesterton Financial, London.

Colliers (1987) 'Unitisation: elaborate experiment or worthwhile and much needed solution?', *International Review*, no. 20, Colliers International Property Consultants, London.

Dawson, A. (1995) 'Finance: Picking a path through the hedges', *Estates Gazette*, 11 March, pp. 46–7.

Evans, P. H. (1992) 'Statistical Review', *Journal of Property Finance*, vol. 3, no. 1, pp. 115–20.

Evans, P. H. (1993) 'Statistical Review', *Journal of Property Finance*, vol. 4, no. 2, pp. 75–82.

Fraser, W. D. (1993) *Principles of Property Investment and Pricing*, 2nd edition, Macmillan Press, London.

Gibbs, R. (1987) 'Raising Finance for New Development', *Journal of Valuation*, vol. 5, no. 4, pp. 343–53.

Investment Property Databank (1992) *Annual Review 1993*, IPD, London, December.

Isaac, D. (1986) *Corporate Finance and Property Development Funding: An analysis of property companies' capital structures with special reference to the relationship between asset value and share price*, unpublished thesis, Faculty of the Built Environment, South Bank Polytechnic, London.

Isaac, D. and Steley, T. (1991) *Property Valuation Techniques*, Macmillan Press, London.

Isaac, D. and Woodroffe, N. (1987) 'Are Property Company Assets Undervalued?', *Estates Gazette*, 5 September, pp. 1024–6.

Isaac, D. and Woodroffe, N. (1995) *Property Companies: Share Price and Net Asset Value*, Greenwich University Press, London.

Mallinson, M. (1988) 'Equity Finance', in S. L. Barter (ed.), *Real Estate Finance*, Butterworths, London.

Maxted, B. (1988) *Unitisation of Property*, College of Estate Management, Reading.

McIntosh A. and Sykes S. (1985) *A Guide to Institutional Property Investment*, Macmillan Press, London.

Millman, S. (1988) 'Property, Property Companies and Public Securities', in S. L. Barter (ed.), *Real Estate Finance*, Butterworths, London.

Orchard-Lisle, P. (1987) 'Financing Property Development', *Journal of Valuation*, vol. 5, no. 4, pp. 343–53.

Paribas Capital Markets (1993) *Monthly Property Share Statistics*, Banque Paribas, November.

Paribas Capital Markets (1995a) *Prospects for the Property Sector*, Banque Paribas, January.

Paribas Capital Markets (1995b) *UK Property Sector Review 1*, Banque Paribas, March.

Peat, M. (1988) 'The Accounting Issues', in S. L. Barter (ed.), *Real Estate Finance*, Butterworths, London.

Pike, R. and Neale, B. (1993) *Corporate Finance and Investment*, Prentice-Hall, London.

Richard Ellis (1986) 'Development Finance', *Property Investment Quarterly Bulletin*, Richard Ellis, London, April.

Royal Institution of Chartered Surveyors (RICS) (1985) *The Unitisation of Real Property*, RICS, London.

Rydin, Y., Rodney, W. and Orr, C. (1990) 'Why Do Institutions Invest in Property?', *Journal of Property Finance* vol.1, no.2, pp. 250–8

S. G. Warburg Research (1993) *UK Property: Monthly Review*, S. G. Warburg, London, November.

S. G. Warburg Securities (1993) *UK Property: Review of 1992 and Prospects for 1993*, S. G. Warburg, London.

Savills (1989) *Financing Property 1989*, Savills, London.

Savills (1993) *Investment and Economic Outlook*, Savills, London, issue 3, October.

Temple, P. (1992) 'How to Beat a Hostile Takeover', *Journal of Property Finance*, vol. 2, no. 4, pp. 476–83.

UBS Global Research (1995) *UK Property Service: company ranking by market capitalisation*, UBS, London, January.

Woodroffe, N. and Isaac, D. (1987) 'Corporate Finance and Property Development Funding', *Working Paper* of the School of Applied Economics and Social Studies, Faculty of the Built Environment, South Bank Polytechnic, London.

Yuen Ka Yin, McKinnell, K. and Isaac, D. (1988) 'The Unitisation of Real Property in Hong Kong', unpublished research paper, Hong Kong University and University of Greenwich.

10 Financial Management in Property Development

10.1 FINANCIAL STRUCTURES

It has already been stressed that property finance is important in the property investment market. The costs and availability of finance will affect the cost of the provision of new investment property and therefore its supply. It is through finance that the structure of the investment interest in property may be created, so finance has an effect on the form of the interest. Whilst the costs and availability of funding are obvious in the case of the funding of development property it is important to realise that it is critical to the investment market also. The value of an investment may be driven by the opportunities or lack of opportunities to fund it and this was the main impetus of the move into the securitisation of property, a repacking of the property asset into appropriate financial packages which provide added value.

There are a number of basic principles related to the financial structure which have been identified by Fraser amongst others:

(i) A company must maintain a balance between equity and debt capital. Traditionally property companies are highly geared; this means that these companies carry a high level of debt capital relative to equity or total capital. The security of property and the growth in rental values and capital value have provided an appropriate environment for increasing debt capital. Apart from the balance of equity and debt, the nature and composition of equity and debt in themselves are important.

(ii) There should be a balance of maturity dates of the debt, with the majority of the debt being long-term. Redemptions should be spread evenly to avoid the risk of a major refinancing operation occurring at a time of adverse financial conditions. The needs of a major refinancing could have an adverse effect on the market, making available monies scarce and putting up the costs. A proportion of the money should be flexible so that it can be repaid without cost or penalty at any time during the duration of the term.

(iii) A company should match short-term assets with short-term liabilities and long-term assets with long-term liabilities; this is called asset matching. If long-term property investment is funded

213

through short-term borrowing, for instance overdraft or short-term debt then there could be major problems for refinancing as an appropriate stock of new capital may not be available at the crucial time of refinancing. This in turn may mean that the property asset will have to be disposed of at an inappropriate time leading to a collapse in its market value.

(iv)   Companies should maintain a balance between fixed interest money and variable interest money. Fixed interest rates protect the company in a period of rising interest rates but obviously they are expensive if rates fall, so they are a hedge against future risk. A hedge is a means of avoiding financial risks, associated in this case with changes in interest rates. Variable rate monies need to be available if interest rates fall so that the benefits of the reduced cost of money can be obtained. Excessively high fixed interest money could have a disastrous effect on a property company in a period of low inflation.

(v)   Debt should be structured so that interest repayments are spread over the year so as to even out the cash flow for the company, or better still to coincide with income received.

(vi)   To avoid foreign currency risk, companies with operations overseas should reduce their exposure to this risk by matching overseas assets and debts in the same currency.

(vii) The financial structure should aim to maximise its tax shield, that is the avoidance of tax payments to maximise the after-tax cash flow. Thus, where appropriate, the interest repayments should have tax relief and be available to offset against income.

(viii) Apart from interest rates, the arranging costs should be minimised. The price of capital includes not just the interest rates, but also commitment and arrangement fees, penalties for early repayment, frequency of repayment and how interest is calculated on the outstanding amount (Fraser 1993, p. 267).

The finance function

Management and finance theory tells us that in a well organised business, each section of the business should arrange its activities to contribute to the attainment of corporate goals. Central to this function in a corporate entity is the maximisation of shareholders' wealth. This is basically done by the generation and management of cash. This is the fundamental concern of finance. Pike and Neale suggest the simple cash flow diagram shown in Figure 10.1.

The sorts of questions which may be critical in our understanding of what finance strategy to undertake in a generalised corporate context are:

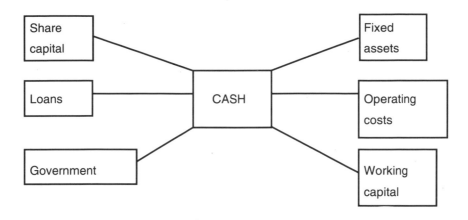

Source: Adapted from Pike and Neale (1993), p. 8.
Figure 10.1   *The importance of cash in the business*

- what long-term investment strategy should a company take on?
- how can cash be raised for the required investments?
- how much short-term cash flow does a company need to pay its bills?

These are strategic decisions which will determine the strategy for generating cash and at the same time ensure that the company is liquid.

One way that companies raise cash to finance their investment activities is by selling or issuing securities. These securities are also called financial instruments or claims, as they are claims on the cash and assets of the company. These securities may be roughly classified as equity or debt and are loosely called respectively stock or bonds in the US and shares and loan stock in the UK. The differences in terminology do make this a problem when dealing with finance literature from the US. Sometimes the basic concepts behind a security or its operation may differ, as in the operation of financial options which are discussed later.

The difference between equity and debt is a basic distinction of the modern theory of finance. To summarise, all the securities of a firm are claims that depend on or are contingent on the value of the firm. Maximising shareholders' wealth is the primary goal of the company and thus financial decisions are made to increase value for shareholders. A company raises cash by issuing securities to the financial markets. There are two basic types of financial markets, the money markets and the capital markets. Money markets deal with debt securities that pay off in the short term, usually less than one year. Capital markets are the markets for long-term debt and equity shares.

The balance sheet model of the firm

The concept of the finance function as a corporate activity can be seen easily in the use of a balance sheet model of the firm shown in Figure 10.2 (Ross *et al.* 1993). The balance sheet is a yearly snapshot of the assets and liabilities of the firm.

The assets of the firm are shown on the left side of the balance sheet, these are current or fixed. Fixed assets are those which last a long time and are durable, such as buildings and plant. Some fixed assets are tangible such as machinery and equipment, others are intangible such as patents, goodwill and trademarks. The other category of assets are current assets which have short lives and are intended to be turned in to cash. For a property company the distinction may be between properties held for investment and those which it intends to trade in the short term.

In order to invest in these assets, the company must raise the cash to pay for the assets, and this is shown on the right side of the balance sheet. The firm will sell claims to its assets in the form of debt (loan agreements) or equity shares. Just as assets are classified as long or short-term, so are liabilities. Short-term debt is a current liability and consists of loans and other obligations which must be repaid in one year. Long-term debt is thus that debt

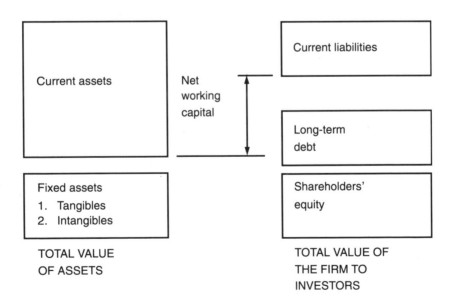

Source: Ross *et al.* (1993), p. 5.
Figure 10.2   *Balance sheet model of the firm*

whose repayment date is more than one year from issue. Shareholders' equity is the difference in value between the assets and debt of the firm and is thus a residual claim .

The balance sheet model highlights the questions that have already been mentioned and provides an appropriate response.

- In what long-term assets should the company invest? This is a question about the left side of the balance sheet. The type and proportions of the assets invested in will depend on the nature of the business. Making and managing expenditure on long-term assets is called **capital budgeting**.
- How can a firm raise cash for the required capital expenditures? This question concerns the right side of the balance sheet, and the answer involves the firm's **capital structure**, which represents the proportions of the firm's financing from current and long-term debt and equity.
- How should the short-term operating cash flow be managed? There is a mismatch between the timing of cash inflows and outflows during operating activities; financial managers must manage these gaps in cash flow by managing the firm's net working capital (current assets *less* current liabilities). This is the subject of **short-term finance.**

From a property perspective we may see these activities as, respectively, the areas of property investment, finance and operational financial management. This chapter is essentially about finance but seen in the context of property investment and the financial management aspects of property development.

10.2   PROPERTY ACCOUNTS

Company financial statements

A company's financial statements are contained in the reports sent to their shareholders. The reports provide details of the operations of the company. They contain a Chairman's review which looks at the preceding year and prospects for the future. There is also a Director's Report which comments on such matters as profits, dividends, fixed assets and finance, and includes the report of the auditors and a summary of the accounting policies of the company which can be useful in the analysis of the position of the firm. Accounting policies are important in the property sector in respect of asset valuation, and there will be different bases according to whether a property company is an investment or a trading company. Attached to the report are the financial statements; these financial statements would be:

- The profit and loss account;
- The balance sheet;
- Notes to the accounts;
- Current cost accounts;
- A statement of source and applications of funds;
- A statement of value added.

The balance sheet and the profit and loss account are the main statements of the financial situation of the company. The balance sheet would be for an individual or group of companies but if there were a parent company then this might be included in addition. The main accounts would be in accordance with historic cost conventions but current cost accounts would attempt to take into account inflation of asset values. It is useful to remind ourselves, at this stage, of those particular groups who need to use published accounts, because it is their needs for information which will have to be satisfied. These are set out in Box 10.1.

WHO ARE THE USERS OF PUBLISHED ACCOUNTS?

The equity investor group, including existing and potential shareholders and holders of convertible securities, options or warrants.

The loan creditor group, including existing and potential holders of debentures and loan stock, and providers of short-term secured and unsecured loans and finance.

The employee group, including existing, potential and past employees.

The analyst – adviser group, including financial analysts and journalists, economists, statisticians, researchers, trade unions, stockbrokers and other providers of advisory services such as credit rating agencies.

The business contact group, including customers, trade creditors and suppliers and in a different sense competitors, business rivals, and those interested in mergers, amalgamations and takeovers.

The government, including tax authorities, departments and agencies concerned with the supervision of commerce and industry, and local authorities.

The public, including taxpayers, ratepayers, consumers, and other community and special interest groups such as political parties, consumer and environmental protection societies and regional pressure groups.

Source: Westwick (1980), p. 4.

Box 10.1   *The users of published accounts*

The balance sheet

The balance sheet lists the balances of assets and liabilities as at the accounting date. As a result of the EEC's Fourth Directive on company accounts, balance sheets are now in a standardised form. The balance sheets are built up from three categories of entry: assets, liabilities and shareholders' funds. Thus total assets are equal to the sum of shareholders' funds plus liabilities if one looks at the balance sheet from the point of view of the company; alternatively from a shareholder's view one can see that the difference between assets and liabilities is the shareholders' funds.

> *Business view:*   Assets = Shareholders' funds + Liabilities
>
> *Shareholders' view:*   Assets − Liabilities = Shareholders' funds.

Fixed assets + Net current assets (current assets *less* current liabilities) = Capital employed (shareholders' funds + long-term liabilities). This is a modification of the business view, taking current liabilities to the asset side of the equation.

Profit and loss account

Whilst the balance sheet is for a particular moment a profit and loss account is for a year ending on the accounting date − it is the result of the year's activities. The profit is shown before and after tax; profit attributable to minority interests arises from investment in other companies amounting to 50 per cent or less of ownership, and these profits are now allowed to be consolidated in the balance sheet. The accounts also show the proportion of profit distributed and retained. To grow, a company will need to increase its assets. The balance sheet shows that assets = liabilities plus shareholders' funds, so that the ways to grow would be to increase liabilities (borrow more) or increase shareholders' funds. There are two ways of increasing the shareholders' funds, by issuing more shares or ploughing back profits. Ploughing back profits is not necessarily the cheapest source of long-term funds for the company and it also restricts the payment of dividends.

Example 10.1: A balance sheet

Balance sheet as at 31 March 1993

	£000	£000
Fixed assets		
(Investment properties for property companies)		3000
Land and buildings for occupation		400
Plant and machinery		200
Fixtures and fittings		200
		3800
Current assets		
Stocks (trading properties for property companies)	3000	
Debtors	100	
Cash	100	
	3200	
Current liabilities		
Bank overdraft	400	
Trade creditors	600	
	1000	
Net current assets		2200
Total assets less current liabilities		6000
Capital and reserves		
Issued share capital		2000
Revenue reserves		1000
Capital reserves		1000
Shareholders' interest		4000
Long-term liabilities (over one year)		
Loans		2000
Total long term capital		6000

Source: Adapted from Asch and Kaye (1989) p. 25.

Notes to balance sheet

The notes to these accounts refer to an ordinary trading company. Notes relating to the peculiarities of property companies are in brackets.

Fixed assets

Assets were normally valued at historic cost for an ordinary company. Land and buildings were shown at original cost less depreciation in normal accounts but because this does not reflect worth, companies now revalue to market value. Depreciation is an annual allowance for wear and tear and reduces the balance sheet valuation, it is deducted from profit as a cost. (For a property company the valuation should be market value for an investment property or the lower of cost and realisable value for a property in the course of development, but intended as an investment property – that is, intended as a fixed asset.) Fixed assets are intended to be permanent features of the company's assets, current assets are turned into cash usually within one year. Plant and machinery and fixtures and fittings are shown at cost *less* depreciation.

Current assets

Stocks are valued at cost. (For a property company, properties to be traded are stocks and are valued at the lower of realisable value or cost. Cost includes the expenses paid out on a property since purchase and interest.)

Current liabilities

These are the amounts due to creditors within one year. The balance of current assets *less* current liabilities is called the net working capital.

Capital and reserves

Issued share capital is the amount paid in by the shareholders when they originally bought the shares in the company. Reserves arise because profits are not distributed to share-holders but ploughed back in the company; these are called revenue reserves. Revenue reserves have to be distinguished from capital reserves which arise on the revaluation of assets and which then may give rise to a surplus. Capital reserves are especially important in property companies arising from revaluation of the assets rather than profits from rents or trading.

Long-term liabilities

These are amounts owed by the company at a future date, longer than one year.

Example 10.2: A profit and loss account

Profit and loss account for the year ended 31 March 1993		£000	£000
Turnover			10000
less cost of sales (direct costs)			6500
Gross profit			3500
less (indirect costs)	Administration expenses	1000	
	Selling and distribution costs	200	
	Interest on loans	150	
			1350
Net profit before tax			2150
Corporation tax			750
Profit on ordinary activities after tax			1400
Extraordinary item after taxation			200
Profit for the year			1200
Dividends			600
Transfer to reserves			600

Source:　Asch and Kaye (1989) p. 28.　　　　　　　　　　　*Notes overleaf*

Notes to profit and loss account

Whereas the balance sheet reveals the state of affairs of the company at one point in time, the profit and loss account shows how much net cash has been generated by activities over the accounting period by matching the expenditure of the year against the revenues. The cost of sales are the cost of raw materials, production or direct labour, power and other factory costs. An extraordinary item is unusual in terms of size and frequency. They are infrequent and thus need to be omitted when considering profit trends over a period of years; for instance, a large profit may have been made from disposal of part of the business, an event which is unlikely to occur again and which distorts the profit figure for that year.

Basic accounting concepts

The financial statements are produced and based on accounting concepts. Four rules or concepts are observed in all published accounts unless it is otherwise stated. These rules are:

- The going concern concept;
- The accruals concept;
- The consistency concept;
- The prudence concept.

The going concern concept assumes that the business will be continuing its activities for the foreseeable future on a similar scale. Thus the values attaching to assets and liabilities in the balance sheet reflect going concern values. This concept is important in property asset valuation for accounts purposes. The accruals concept says that it is vital for an accurate assessment of profit and loss for the accounting period to compare costs and benefits accurately. It is important to assign costs and financial returns to the period incurred which may not be the same time period when money costs are incurred or financial returns received. For instance, if a sale has legally taken place, whether or not cash has been received from the customer for the goods delivered, the transaction will be taken as a sale and included as part of the sales revenue appearing in the profit and loss account. The consistency concept is necessary so that approaches to the formulation of the accounts remain the same and so valid comparisons and analysis can be made against previous results and with other companies. The prudence concept covers the attitudes to dealing with costs and revenues; it is the cautious way an accountant approaches the problem unless it is certain. Based on the above concepts, the Companies Acts makes it a legal requirement that a company's balance sheet should show a true and fair view.

Techniques for analysis

The analysis of company accounts involves the initial consideration of three problems:

(i)   Is the company making a satisfactory profit?
(ii)   Is the company short of cash or cash rich?
(iii)   What should be the source of long-term funds?

    These problems relate to profitability, liquidity and capital structure and are as applicable to individual property projects as they as are to property companies or any firm. The techniques applied are based on relationships between the elements in the financial statements (financial ratios) and rates of return (yields). The area of capital structure is of major interest to financing arrangements, which also has parallels in the financial structure of property projects.

Profitability measures

The key ratios used to analyse the profitability of an enterprise are:

(i)   Trading profit as a percentage of turnover.
(ii)   Profit before interest and tax as a percentage of average capital employed.
(iii)   Earnings per share either basic (based on issued share capital) or fully diluted (based on authorised share capital, which is the total share capital that can be issued).
(iv)   Dividend per share.
(v)   Number of times covered – that is, the number of times a dividend is covered by earnings. This is also a measure used by property managers to access the security of a tenant by testing the number of times the rent is covered by the net profit of the tenant company.
(vi)   Assets per share – the asset backing of shares based on the value of the net assets divided by the number of shares. There has been much discussion in this area in relation to the share price of property investment companies as one would expect the asset value per share to relate to the market price of the share. However,

traditionally, the market has discounted the net asset values of property investment companies historically by an average of approximately 20 per cent. The discount is measured by:

$$\frac{\text{Net asset value per share} - \text{Share price}}{\text{Net asset value per share}} \times 100\%$$

(Isaac and Woodroffe, 1986, p. 1024)

Return on investment

This is defined as

$$\frac{\text{Profit}}{\text{Assets}} \times 100\%$$

Thus profit is looked at as a percentage of capital and this is further influenced by two further ratios comprising the profit margin (profit as a percentage of sales) and the rate of asset turnover (sales divided by assets):

$$\frac{\text{Profit}}{\text{Assets}} = \frac{\text{Profit}}{\text{Sales}} \times \frac{\text{Sales}}{\text{Assets}}$$

or:

$$\text{Return on capital} = \text{Profit margin} \times \text{Turnover}$$

The return on capital may vary from one industry to another but wider variations may be found in the profit margin and rates of turnover. For instance, a return of 20 per cent could be achieved by a high profit margin and a low turnover (the corner shop) or low profit margin and high turnover (the supermarket piling the goods high and selling cheap).

A sector comparison should show that the capital intensive industries with long production cycles would have a low rate of turnover but a high profit margin. From the key ratios above a number of subsidiary ratios relating costs or assets to sales can be formulated. Depending on the use to which the ratio is put, the definition of profit and assets will differ. Generally a wider view of company performance is taken:

$$\text{Return on capital} = \frac{\text{Profit before tax, interest and dividends}}{\text{Total capital employed}}$$

The comparison of profitable ratios enables firms within a sector to be compared against one another and for the various sectors to be compared.

Liquidity and cash flows

As well as being profitable, it is also important that a company should be liquid. A profitable and fast expanding company may find that it has tied up its profits in fixed assets, stocks and debtors and that is has difficulty paying its debts as they fall due. There are two main ratios to examine the liquidity of a company, the liquidity ratio and the current ratio.

The liquidity ratio is also called the acid test ratio because it is a most important test. It is the ratio of liquid assets to current liabilities and a 1:1 ratio means that a company has sufficient cash to pay its immediate debts. Liquid assets are defined as current assets excluding stocks of goods which cannot be quickly turned into cash. In effect liquid assets are debtors, cash and any short-term investments like bank deposits or government securities. A company can survive with a liquid ratio of less than 1:1 if it has an unused bank overdraft facility.

The other test of a company's liquidity is the current ratio which includes stocks and work in progress on the grounds that stocks eventually turn into debtors and then into cash itself. It is calculated by relating all current assets to current liabilities. A norm of 2:1 is generally regarded as being satisfactory but this will depend on the average for a particular industry.

Thus:

Liquidity ratio = Liquid assets : Current liabilities

Current ratio = Current assets : Current liabilities.

Gearing ratio and interest cover

Two important measures of financial analysis are the gearing ratio and interest cover.

The gearing (or leverage) ratio is the ratio of debt to shareholders' funds. This could be expressed as the ratio of debt to net operating assets and this is the approach used in most economic texts, but normally in the market it is stated as:

$$\text{Gearing ratio} = \frac{\text{Debt (borrowings)}}{\text{Shareholders' funds}}$$

also known as the debt : equity ratio.

Interest cover is the profit available to pay interest charges.

$$\text{Interest cover} = \frac{\text{Profit before interest and tax}}{\text{net interest}}$$

Example 10.3: Financial analysis

	Co. A	Co. B
Balance Sheet	£m	£m
Net operating assets	100	100
Financed by: Debt	20	80
Shareholders	80	20
	100	100
Profit and loss account		
Operating profit	15.0	15.0
Less interest payable @ 10%	(2.0)	(8.0)
Profit before tax	13.0	7.0
Tax @ 35%	(4.55)	(2.5)
Net profit	8.45	4.5

$$\text{Gearing ratio} \qquad \frac{20}{80} = 25\% \qquad \frac{80}{20} = 400\%$$

$$\text{Interest cover} \qquad \frac{15}{2} = 7.5 \text{ times} \qquad \frac{15}{8} = 1.88 \text{ times}$$

The gearing ratio is used to compare levels of debt between companies. Interest cover indicates the safety margin before profits become inadequate to cover the interest charge. Gearing and interest cover are used by lenders to determine whether a company's borrowings are at a reasonable level, and whether it is prudent to lend more.

Investors are concerned with the company's capacity to absorb a downturn in profit without having to sell assets in possibly unfavourable market conditions. Also, gearing is a measure of the potential to finance expansion without recourse to the shareholders which would depress share price. If a company requires additional debt to fund a new project the resultant gearing effect may depress share price and restrict flexibility to respond to future opportunities. Thus there is pressure to record the project, the asset and debt off balance sheet.

REFERENCES

Accounting Standards Committee (ASC) (1990) *Exposure Draft 51, Accounting for Fixed Assets and Revaluations*, ASC, London, May.

Asch, D. and Kaye, G. R. (1989) *Financial Planning: Modelling methods and techniques*, Kogan Paul, London.

Barkham, R. J. and Purdy, D. E. (1992) 'Financial Company Reporting: Potential weaknesses', *Journal of Property Valuation and Investment*, vol. 11, no. 2, pp. 133–44.

Brett, M. (1990a) *Property and Money*, Estates Gazette, London.

Brett, M. (1990b) *How to Read the Financial pages*, Hutchinson, London.

Calachi, R. and Rosenburg, S. (eds)(1992) *Property Finance, An International Perspective*, Euromoney Books, London.

Isaac, D. and Woodroffe N. (1987) 'Are Property Company Assets Undervalued?', *Estates Gazette*, 5 September, pp. 1024–6.

Peat, M. (1988) 'The Accounting Issues' in S. L. Barter (ed.), *Real Estate Finance*, Butterworths, London.

Pike, R. and Neale, B. (1993) *Corporate Finance and Investment*, Prentice-Hall, London.

Purdy, D. E. (1992) 'Provoking Awareness Through the Provision of Relevant Information in Property Company Accounts', *Journal of Property Finance*, vol. 3, no. 3, pp. 337–46.

Ross, S. A., Westerfield, R. W. and Jaffe, J. F. (1993) *Corporate Finance*, Irwin, Boston.

Ryland, D. S. (1992) 'Changes in Accounting Rules', *Journal of Property Finance*, vol. 3, no. 1, pp. 28–37.

Smee, R. (1992) 'Capitalisation of Interest for Property Companies', *Journal of Property Finance*, vol. 3, no. 1, pp. 13–22.

Westwick, C. A. (1980) *Property Valuation and Accounts*, Institute of Chartered Accountants in England and Wales, London.

11 Design and Construction

11.1 DESIGN IMPLICATIONS AND COST

This chapter covers two important stages of the property development process, the design and construction phases. These are areas where there are a number of specialist texts. This chapter will only attempt an overview of what the project manager may need to know about aspects of design and construction.

Design and layout are very important both from an aesthetic, economic, functional and qualitative point of view. The economic viewpoint would consider that a high quality building of good design would be both more efficient and innately more valuable, this would add to the value of the completed development. An efficient building may be economic relative to the cost of construction but also economic in terms of minimising costs-in-use over the life of the building. The principal constraints on the layout and design of the building are:

(i)   the site and its surroundings;
(ii)   the budget or economic limits on construction;
(iii) planning permission, building and fire regulations and layout standards laid down by the planning authorities;
(iv)   the users' requirements.

The designer/architect has to seek a solution to satisfy both the client and the local authority. The client has to be satisfied in respect of the budget, the space and layout, finishes, services, appearance, access and open space and daylighting. The local authority will have to be satisfied as to planning and highway considerations, building regulations and fire precautions. Finally, the architect designer may have to convince other consultants within the development process that the design is appropriate. This includes the financier who is providing the funding for the scheme. Some of the aspects relating to these constraints are now considered.

The site

The designer of the development will need to know the load-bearing capacity of the subsoil to determine the substructure. The designer or design team will also need to know if there are any restrictions on the legal ownership of the site which might affect the design, including easements and restrictive covenants. Planning authorities are sensitive to the effect of height, mass and materials on the street scene, particularly in areas of historic character.

Project or economic limits

The designer should aim to increase the value of the completed development by reducing the costs in the design. The value on completion can be increased by enlarging the floor space but this obviously adds to cost as well. The capital value of the completed development can also be improved by a more economic layout defined by the efficiency ratio and also by low costs-in-use and high quality finishes.

The shape of a building is an important consideration and, from analysis, it is evident that the shape closest to a cube gives the greatest economy in terms of external surface but there are difficulties in dealing with this shape. First, the site and aesthetic considerations, secondly, lighting and ventilation would be difficult in such a shape, as permanent artificial lighting and air conditioning may need to be considered.

The efficiency ratio is the relationship between gross internal floor area and net usable space. The difference between the two is the space used for internal access areas in terms of stairs, lifts and passageways, toilets and plant rooms. Open plan offices reduce the space used by internal divisions. A fairly optimum efficiency ratio for an office is about 80 per cent, but shops should give at least 90 per cent. In covered shopping centres, non-retail space will need to be allowed for malls and arcades and for servicing, plant rooms, offices for the manager and communal toilets.

The type of construction will also affect the budget and cost considerations include the structural frame, for instance, a steel frame and precast concrete floors may be more expensive than a cast *in-situ* reinforced concrete frame. Column spacings vary according to the use to which the property is put. For shops a 6 metre grid is conventional; offices are built to 12 metres with factory and warehouse construction at 18 metres. Large clear spaces can be achieved but at a cost in terms of roof members, roof depth and loadings on the columns and foundation pads. External cladding can directly affect the costs of construction, the cladding will also need to satisfy thermal insulation and noise insulation requirements. In terms of internal finishes, suspended ceilings are now frequently installed for concealing service runs and also suspended flooring. Often commercial space is let in a shell form in which the tenants set out the space and other fittings to their particular requirements.

Town planning and layout criteria

The planning authority may inhibit the amount of development that can be carried out on a site. These inhibitions can be categorised as follows.

Plot ratio

This is a device used by planning authorities to determine the maximum gross area of building space to be allowed on a site to be developed. It is used for commercial or industrial purposes. The ratio is a ratio of the area of the built space to the gross area of the site. Office schemes seldom exceed a plot ratio of 3 ½:1 and warehouse/industrial developments are usually 1:2 or a coverage of half the site.

Daylight

For traditional buildings, simple daylight angling tests used to be used for planning considerations. Modern daylighting standards now apply tests based on percentage of total light from an unobstructed sky.

Car parking

Local authorities are generally concerned about the extent of car parking. However, owner-occupiers generally require on-site car parking and lack of provision may prevent sale or letting. One car parking space per 50–100 m^2 of gross built space may be a typical provision but this will depend on circumstances. The need for parking spaces for shopping facilities is very important, This may amount to three spaces per 100 m^2 of gross retail floor space.

The users' requirements

Users' requirements relate to the future tenants' requirements but sight should not be lost of the need to accord with the requirements of future owners, investors and financiers. If institutional investors are going to buy the development, they will have certain criteria for design, including floor loadings, ceiling or eaves heights, plot density and size of units. For industrial and warehousing premises, the location may need to be close to the transport infrastructure. Manufacturing premises will need to be convenient for a workforce including transport and community facilities. A developer will usually provide various sizes of buildings in a typical commercial estate to cater for different demands. The site layout of industrial and warehouse estates is also important. The units can be terraced to achieve economies in cost and maintenance. Adequate turning spaces need to be required for the manoeuvring of heavy goods vehicles. Car parking requirements may vary considerably depending on the numbers of staff employed and the customers and visitors calling at the premises. In terms of eaves height, for warehousing, an economic height is usually about 6 metres. For manufacturing, this is generally 4 metres. Ancillary offices for industrial and warehouse premises are generally provided at no more than 10 per cent of total space but with high-tech premises this proportion could be much higher. Offices should have some form of central heating and be insulated from noise from the manufacturing areas. In terms of construction, with a minimum floor loading of 2500 kilograms per m^2, the cost could be £400/m^2 in 1995.

For business parks and science parks the location is very important with good access to road, rail and air transport. These developments should be low density and of higher quality with good landscaping and good car parking. In addition, for science parks, the use of the unit should include research and development and exclude conventional production uses. A dynamic relationship between the entrepreneurs on the site and researchers and staff of an academic institution is useful for science park developments. In practice, there are few differences between business park and science park developments and both uses are classified as B1 under the Town and Country Planning (Use Classes Order) 1987. Buildings defined as high-tech normally cater for advanced technology companies. Car park standards for business and science parks are much higher than for traditional industrial estates. Most schemes will want to provide car parking space at the ratio of one space per 20m^2 of lettable industrial space.

Specific types of property

In shopping centres the chief design criterion is to achieve concentrated pedestrian flows in the malls and arcades. The selection of key tenants and the overall tenant mix is a second important ingredient of success. To attract shoppers, the magnet or anchor stores should be located where they will draw people along the malls. Careful siting and management of car parks is essential. Tenant mix should include a balance of trades to meet shoppers' requirements. Restaurants, play space and seating help towards the attractiveness of the shopping centre. Malls and arcades should be wide enough for pedestrian traffic, but not too wide to lose the window shoppers' attention (15 metres for the mall but 6 metres for the arcades with a height of 4.5 metres).

Shopping units will vary in size from the department store (up to 25 000 m^2) to specialist stores (6000 m^2), supermarkets (around 2000 m^2), and the majority in the 100–400 m^2 metres range. These areas are all measured in gross internal floor areas (between the internal surfaces of the external walls, see Chapter 4).

Retail warehousing is a recent introduction to the retail scene. A number of such warehouses, either individually or in a communal park, have been developed since the mid-1980s. Location is the most important criterion; they can be located in or out of town but need to be close to centres of population and major road networks. In many cases, in order to provide economic buildings, the retailers deliberately avoid high specifications. A range of units within a retail park may be from 500 to 5000 m^2. The frontage to depth ratio is at least 1:2. Surface parking is essential for a non-food store, ideally at a ratio of one space to 20 m^2.

For offices, there are a number of considerations that need to be made including the lettable area, column spacing and ceiling height, access, including the approach and entrance halls, the quality of finish and the services. Column spacing at 6 metres is reasonably economic, ceiling height minimum should be about 2.8 metres. Floor loading should be based on an institutional requirement of 3 kN per m^2.

Summary

The architectural design of buildings is influenced by a number of basic factors which the designer needs to be aware of in providing a design solution. These factors can generally apply to all buildings but in this summary focus on office buildings.

(i)   geographical location;
(ii) occupier or user requirements – from corporate requirement to individual office employee;
(iii) economics of development – for the owner-occupier and speculative developer;
(iv) legislative control – town planning, Building Regulations and similar legislation;
(v)   construction – constructional techniques, materials, components and the use of sophisticated equipment;
(vi) aesthetic or architectural design – the 'creative ingredient' : local characteristics, climate, materials, sense of identification, architectural 'fashion'.

Geographical location

- Determined by economic/organisational factors (i.e. decentralisation of organisations has thrown up demands for building in the suburbs or in regional towns and cities where previously office buildings were rare).
- Existing character of the town, may be a significant factor in architectural design (i.e. positive style in an industrial town to enliven environment/low key building in traditional materials in historic town centre).
- Siting within town. A self-contained office on its own detached site poses a different architectural and planning problem from one that is an element of a comprehensive development with shopping and car parking. Problems of precedence of office v. retail use (entrances, layout, etc.).

User requirements

- Of paramount importance are the needs of users, not the prestige/ whim of the architect/developer.

- Owner-occupied buildings with specific occupiers' requirements; there is a need here to establish user requirements before design is commenced (involvement of design team at an early stage in conception of project).
- Important that the architect's brief is drawn up in response to client's requirements, not written in isolation. Generally, the user/developer should write the brief.

Clients' brief

- number of people to be accommodated;
- what activities will be carried out in the building;
- where activities will be carried out and how they will be organised;
- working conditions and environment required;
- welfare and amenity facilities required;
- special technical requirements (computer systems, etc.);
- budget cost;
- date for completion.

Legislative controls

Maintaining town planning and Building Regulations.

Planning control:

- plot ratio (ratio of gross built floor area to actual site area, i.e. 1:1);
- daylighting angles;
- car parking requirements;
- planning agreements;
- height massing and aesthetic design.

Constructional techniques, materials and equipment

Design of structure will have an effect on:

- method of construction;
- time;
- aesthetic appearance.

Choice of external materials will depend on:

- cost;
- ease of construction and manufacture;
- ability to be weatherproof;

- weathering;
- maintenance costs;
- appearance.

Internal materials:

- durability, ease of cleaning, appearance;
- the provision of equipment depends on the developer's provision as against actual tenant need.

Other factors:

- air conditioning an integral part of structure and layout;
- flexibility of layout for changing office arrangements;
- floor loadings to take office machinery;
- spacing of columns, flexibility v. cost.

Aesthetic design

- most appropriate and suitable design given client's brief;
- relationship and scale to adjoining buildings important;
- materials sympathetic but not necessarily the same as surroundings.

11.2   COST OF CONSTRUCTION

The objectives of development are to maximise the value or income from the investment. The key facts in terms of construction are completion on time, within the budget and to the required standard. In order to improve the time element, sometimes system building is employed, but here there is a trade-off between the cost/time and the actual quality of the building. There is an overlap in the design and construction stage.

In terms of the construction costs, the budget estimates are drawn up for the development appraisal and these are initially drawn up prior to the preparation of detailed drawings and specification. Building costs have already been discussed in Chapter 4; building costs can be estimated on the basis of per square metre rates on a gross internal floor area basis. BCIS (1994, p. 30) define this as:

> The total of all enclosed spaces fulfilling the functional requirements of the building measured to the internal face of the enclosing walls. It includes areas occupied by partition columns, chimney breasts, internal structural or party walls, stairwells, lift wells and the like. Also included are lift, plant and tank rooms and the like above the main roof slab.

The initial estimates of cost are based on average costs per square metre, assessed from comparable historical data on previous contracts. The costs can be based on a number of factors which will influence the out-turn costs. These are (i) location, (ii) site characteristics, (iii) design and specification criteria, (iv) form of contract and (v) market conditions.

Location

Location will affect the cost of building because the basic resources of labour, material and plant will differ according to the geographical location in which they are employed. Labour is dependent on local availability, materials are dependent on local supplies, the size of load and delivery costs and the general level of construction activity. Market conditions can also affect costs.

Example 11.1: Regional index of building cost

Regional and county factors which are used in assessing building cost can be indexed according to location.

UK mean	*1.00*
South East excluding Greater London	1.00
Essex	0.98
North West	1.02
South West	0.95
Scotland	1.08
Greater London	1.14
London postal districts	1.16
Outer London	1.09

(*Source*: BCIS (1994), pp. 13–16).

Site

A site can be affected by the soil conditions, the water table, site access, etc. which will affect the cost of works. The cost of piling in situations where the soil conditions are bad can add perhaps 10 per cent or more to the cost of works. Also basements are expensive to construct especially if there is a high water table. Underground car parking, for instance, is expensive and not economical unless there are severe restrictions on the building height or site area. Demolition costs can be affected by the ability to obtain income from salvageable items.

Design and specification

The form, height and width of the building will affect the cost. The lower the height of the property, the lower will be the construction costs per m^2 generally. In terms of value, a higher net lettable area to the gross area will increase the value of the completed building but may also increase cost per m^2. Gross internal floor area, as indicated earlier, is measured to the internal face of the external walls including internal voids, partitions, stairs, etc.

Building costs and tender prices

The contract arrangements are very important in determining the building costs. To safeguard the developer in any particular building contract, the project manager where appointed should firstly set objectives encouraging the selection of a competitive contract and the completion of the development within the programme time. Secondly, introduce a contractor into the design and building team at the most appropriate time. Thirdly, secure value for money in terms of the time, cost and quality elements of the project and finally, ensure genuine competition and equal information to each tenderer. The regional tender price index gives an indication of how tender prices are changing on a quarterly basis (see BCIS, 1994, p. 5).

Example 11.2: Regional tender price index
1985 mean = 100

Year	Quarter	South East	Rest of UK
1992	1	105	116
	2	102	111
	3	99	109
	4	100	110
1993	1	98	112
	2	107	109
	3	104	115
	4	103	112
1994	1	102	116
	2	114	122

Contract arrangements

These can be grouped into specific categories. First, management contracts and costs reimbursement contracts, secondly, lump sum and remeasurement contracts. Management contracts involve the execution of work by subcontractors under the supervision and co-ordination of the management contractor who may not carry out the actual building work. Cost reimbursement contracts involve reimbursement to contractors, the actual costs of materials, plant and labour with the addition of a fee for profit and overheads. Traditionally, fees have been around 6 per cent for management contracts and around 8 per cent for cost reimbursement contracts. On the other hand, there are lump sum and remeasurement contracts. These contracts can be based on bills of quantities. In the former, firm bills are used while the latter involves bills which are approximate at the tender stage but which reflect the character of the work by way of accurately weighting the quantities. As construction proceeds, the work is remeasured and priced using the rate in the approximate bill of quantities. The lump sum approach encourages competition. The remeasurement contracts have an advantage in the sense that not all the design information needs to be available at the time of tendering. A comparison of contract arrangements is shown in Table 11.1, with the relative suitability of each contract to the criteria listed set out on a scale of 1–4 (highest being the most suitable).

11.3   MANAGING THE CONSTRUCTION PHASE

In assessing the approach to contract management in the building phase and in the selection of contracts and contractors outlined later in the chapter, one should be aware of the key variables in the organisation of this phase which may lead to success or failure in the construction process. Essentially, these relate to:

- the integration of the client with the project team;
- the organisation of the design team;
- the integration of the construction team into the design and management process.

Table 11.1   *Comparison of contract arrangements*

Criteria	Lump-sum contract based on bills of quantity	Remeasurement contracts based on approximate bills of quantity	Cost reimbursement contract based on cost plus	Cost reimbursement contract based on target cost	Management contract
Time economy	2	4	4	4	4
Cost economy	4	4	1	2	2
Financial commitment	4	2	1	2	2
Post-contract cost control	4	4	1	2	2

The client's role is important in this process and it is important to differentiate between a client who has no construction expertise and an organisation where there are in-house staff to liaise closely with the project team and thus be able to integrate effectively into the construction process.

The organisation of the design team is important because the attitude toward construction management will differ according to whether there is an overall project manager overseeing the project. The design team will differ according to whether the architect acts as head of the design team and as project manager or whether a separate project manager is appointed. The project manager in this role may play an executive role (as in project management and construction management) or a non-executive role (this occurs in the BPF system which is discussed later). It is clearly important for the client to be represented on the design team so that the client can be better integrated into project design. Management systems also enable this to happen.

The integration of the contractor into the design and management process is facilitated by systems which allow management and design functions to be provided by a contractor, as these more closely involve the expertise of the building contractor in the design process.

Building contracts may be tendered for in competition or by individual negotiation; the choice between these options will depend on a number of factors including:

(i)   the size and complexity of the project;
(ii)   the building type, i.e. office or housing;
(iii)   the likely method of construction, e.g. traditional or system built;
(iv)   time available before a start on site is required;
(v)   likely involvement of the contractor in the design process;
(vi)   availability of contractor and professional team (Hancock 1984, p. 27).

JCT standard form of contract

The contractual arrangements normally entered into by the developer can broadly be divided into three main categories; these use contracts evolved by the building industry and provided generally by the Joint Contracts Tribunal (JCT). The first is the traditional standard form of contract which provides for a main contractor to carry out the construction in accordance with the design and specification prepared by the developer's own team of professional advisers and upon which they must rely for the quality of design, adequate supervision of contract and suitability of the building for the purpose for which it is designed. The second area is the design and build or design and manage contract and the third area is management contracting or construction management. This section will deal in detail with the standard form of JCT contract. The JCT contract is widely used although management contracting as an alternative is becoming more widespread. The two basic forms of standard contract are with quantities and without quantities and there are also private and local authority editions in each case. The developer, or the employer, as referred to in the contract documents, will employ his own team of professional advisers who are responsible for the design of the building to meet his requirements, for supervising the carrying out of the works and generally administering the contract. The architect or project manager leads the project team and calls in specialist advisers as necessary, for instance, there may be structural engineers and mechanical and electrical engineers required. Quantity surveyors are appointed at the outset so that the full benefit of their cost control services are available. The architect is responsible for obtaining planning permission unless a planning consultant is used. The architect is responsible for the design of the building in terms of aesthetics, functions and economic viability in accordance with the developer's brief. The architect is also principally responsible for the management of the contract although supervised by the project manager, if one is appointed.

The quantity surveyor is responsible for preparing estimates of building costs, preparing tender documentation and, during construction, for preparing the valuations of work upon which the architect issues the interim and final certificates. The quantity surveyor should be appointed early in the development process to advise on cost and alternative forms of construction. The quantity surveyor reports on the cost of construction and measures payments against the estimated cash flow. The quantity surveyor is also responsible for estimating the cost of variations in design so that the development team can decide on whether or not to agree these variations. Other specialists may include mechanical and electrical engineers and structural engineers. Provided that the contractor executes the building work in a good and workmanlike manner and in accordance with the architect's drawings, the specification often contained in the bill of quantities and with any subsequent instructions from the architect, the contractor will not normally have responsibility if the building is not suitable for the purpose it was designed. Developers must turn to their architect and other professional advisers for any remedy. Developers will require the design team to enter into deeds of collateral warranty. These warranties extend the benefit of the developer's contract with the professionals to investors, financiers and tenants. They require the professional advisers to warrant that all reasonable skill, care and attention has been exercised in their professional responsibilities. The length of the building contract may be subject to extension for a number of reasons. Some extensions also entitle contractors to recover additional expenses. Thus the developer might not only find that the completion of works is delayed, but also that increased costs are involved. Reasons for the extension of contract time, which entitle the contractor to recover additional expenses, are firstly inadequacy of the contract documents, secondly delay by the architect in issuing drawings and instructions, thirdly delays caused by tradesman directly employed by the developer. In addition, there are reasons which may entitle the contractor to an extension of time but not additional expense and these would include failure of nominated subcontractors, that is subcontractors nominated by the architect. Other reasons would include bad weather, strikes and lockouts, shortage of labour or materials, damage by fire and force majeure (acts out of the control of those involved in the contracts—acts of God).

The choice of contractor when using the JCT standard form of contract is by means of an invitation to contractors to submit tenders for carrying out the work usually based on a selected list. They price the work from the bill of quantities. Usually, the number of contractors asked to tender is limited to (say) six to eight. Reliability and financial stability are important considerations in the choice of contractor. Because of the financial problems within the industry, contractors may be asked to take out a performance bond with an insurance company which guarantees to reimburse the employer for any loss incurred up to an agreed amount as a result of the contractor failing to complete the contract. The contractor sets out the arrangements for payment for the building works. This obviously has serious repercussions for the cash flow of the builder. Under the JCT standard form of contract, the architect authorises monthly payments based on the value of work as certified by the quantity surveyor. Usually, a percentage of total value is retained until the end of the defects liability period under the contract and the completion of all defective work.

In the standard form of contract, the contractor usually submits bids on either a firm price or a fluctuation basis. The firm price means that the cost of labour and materials will not vary the price in the contract although in the market it may fluctuate. On the fluctuation contract the contract may adjust for an increase or decrease in labour and materials. The benefits of the JCT standard form of contract are its flexibility with the way that the price for the project is fixed and the type or quantity of work within the contract can be varied. These changes create uncertainty especially in terms of the financial appraisal on which the developer is dependent for his profit.

Monitoring construction progress

The project manager, where appointed, will report to the developer on the construction progress and cost. Any delays in completion will affect the profitability of the development. The developer will need to update the cash flow appraisal. Every project manager will have an individual way of reporting, but the best methods use charts and graphs to compare actual progress and cost against the original forecasts. Typical reporting methods may include the bar chart which is a calendar of the development programme. The programme is divided into various tasks and the period during which each of these is to be carried out is shown on the chart. The bar chart can be used to indicate when information or decisions are required by the architect/project manager from the developer and contractor. The contractor's bar chart may be substituted once a contractor is on site and the contractor's bar chart identifies the timescale for each trade involved on site and is usually accompanied by a method statement showing the way in which the work will be carried out. Cash flows, tables and graphs should be prepared by the project manager. The purpose of the cash flow is to estimate the developer's flow of cash payments throughout the development period. The project manager will also prepare financial reports. These will be based on the quantity surveyor's cost reports and the payments already made to the contractor as certified by the architect. It enables the developer to identify variations in costs throughout the contract. The project manager should advise a developer of the reasons for any cost variation based on data supplied by the quantity surveyor.

11.4   CASE STUDY: SELECTION OF THE BUILDING CONTRACT

The choice of building contract for a project is driven by a specific selection process; this includes details of the client's brief for the building project, the nature of the building project, the method of selection of the building contract, the types of building contract (procurement) available and the constraints on procurement because of the nature of the project. The client's objectives, the assessment of alternatives and the final selection are three key inputs into this process. The approach used in this case study is the selection of a building contract for the erection of a supermarket in the south east of England and this provides the context in which to carry out the elementary analysis.

Client's brief

The brief here is to assess possible forms of procurement of building and management contracts for the erection of a supermarket. The different methods of organising and managing the project have to be looked at in the context of the nature of the project and the client's requirements. The choice of contracts in this case needs to take into account the client's needs for flexibility in the contractual arrangements and in the programme to allow for variations in design. These requirements are necessary in the rapidly changing environment of retail food sales.

Nature of the project

The development of the supermarket involves the construction of the supermarket itself and two upper floors of car parking. The construction method is a reinforced *in-situ* concrete frame with brick cladding. The building has high quality finishes and includes complex service installations including air conditioning and a lift. The construction period has been assumed to be 18 months. The building contract excluding profit but including preliminaries and subcontractor payments is £5 million and a substantial amount of the work is associated with service installations and fitting carried out by subcontractors. The structure may be relatively straightforward in terms of design but the extent of the services and finishes in the contract require strict management control of a complex programme.

Selection of method of building procurement

The selection of the procurement method is made by looking first at the nature of the project and its implied management and contractual relationships which assist in selecting the appropriate arrangement. Subsequently the needs and objectives of the client can be related both to the building programme and the specific needs of this project. From this analysis a suitable approach can be assessed.

Types of building procurement available

This section will look at a number of types of procurement. Some approaches are purely contractual but others may involve both management and design input. The traditional form of competitive tender, for instance, involves appointed consultants agreeing a form of contract with a builder, whereas in a management contract, the management contractor takes on the role of selection of works contractors which may not occur in competition. This procurement has three dimensions: contract, management and design. A summary of the main types of procurement is shown in Table 11.2.

Estimates of the use of procurement systems as indicated in various surveys (Masterman 1992, p 16) are shown in Table 11.3; the 1990 estimates are from Turner (1990), p. 59:

Masterman (1992, p. 3) suggests that procurement systems can be grouped together in three categories:

- *Separated and co-operative procurement systems*, where responsibilities for the design and construction aspects of the project are the responsibility of separate organisations, e.g. design consultants and contractors.
- *Integrated procurement systems*, where design and construction become the responsibility of one organisation, usually a contractor.
- *Management oriented procurement systems*, where the emphasis is placed on the overall management of the design and construction of the project, with the latter element usually being carried out by works or package contractors and the management contractor having the status and responsibilities of a consultant.

Table 11.2   *Types of procurement*

Contracts to build

- Competitive tender
- Separate trades contract

Contracts to manage

- Management contracting*
- Construction management
- Project management

Contracts to design, manage and build

- Design and Build
- Design and manage
- Package deal

* Management contracting may include design.

Table 11.3   *Use of procurement systems*

Year	Traditional and variants (%)	Design and Build and variants (%)	Management contracts and variants (%)
1984	83	5	12
1985	78	8	14
1987	79	12	9
1989	67	11	22
1990 (est)	50–65	15–25	15–20

There may be a number of different approaches to building procurement although the same methods of tendering (competitive, two stage, negotiated, etc.) and the same contractual arrangements (fixed price, cost plus or cost reimbursement) may be used in each approach.

The traditional system

This involves a contractual relationship between the parties as set out in the standard form of contract (with quantities) which has been discussed earlier. The client briefs an architect who provides outline schemes for costing by a quantity surveyor and the client selects a proposal. Following this selection, the architect then consults with other specialists (structural and services engineers, etc.) and detailed drawings and specifications are prepared. The quantity surveyor assesses the quantities of construction work required in a bill of quantities, usually in accordance with the Standard Method of Measurement of Building Works (SMM7). The drawings, bill of quantities and other tender documents are sent to selected contractors who submit tenders. The building contractor estimates the costs involved in the project and calculates the duration of the project, if not already determined by the client. A profit and overheads figure is added to the costs. If a tender is accepted, then the builder concerned becomes the main contractor and enters into a contract. The contractor establishes the site management and building programme and subcontractor's work where required, for both subcontractors engaged directly by the contractor and those nominated by the architect.

The management structure is shown in Figure 11.1. In this system the client appoints consultants to act on its behalf to produce the design and supervise the construction phase. Each consultant acts in an independent role and has to produce the best design solution as well as be an efficient manager of the process. The increasing complexity of buildings, the need for efficient financial planning, the need to reduce design and construction periods and more complex contract administration combined to encourage different forms of management and these are discussed subsequently.

Construction management for a fee

There are a number of variations in this approach but essentially the management contractor offers to undertake the management of works for a fee. The management contractor takes on the relationship that consultants have with

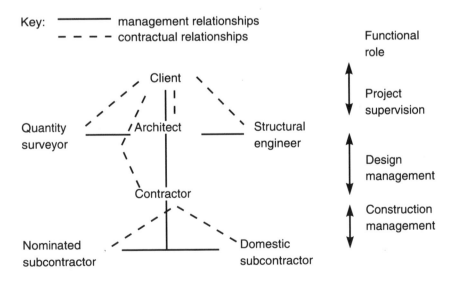

Source: Adapted from Walker (1989).
Figure 11.1   *Traditional management structure for construction*

the client in the traditional system. The management contractor thus lets the contracts to specialist contractors who actually carry out the work.

Thus, the management contractor is involved in the project at an early stage, he can contribute his experience to the design process and integrate the client into the design and building process. The design and building process can proceed at the same time and there is room for adjustment and changes in design. The problem associated with this approach is that the contractor does not take the risk if things go wrong but is only liable to the extent of the percentage fee which may reduce under these circumstances. This form of arrangement is generally good for performance but poor on cost.

In construction management, the contractual relationship is directly between the client and subcontractor (see Figure 11.2). All parties in a construction management arrangement are employed on an equal basis with the client providing overall management. The client employs a construction manager who takes responsibility for the project. The construction manager thus provides a service of management for a fee but all contractors deliver the project and each enter into a direct contract with the client (Turner 1990, p. 55).

Design and build

In this section I have grouped together design and build systems, package deals and turnkey operations. In the design and build system, the client engages an agent (usually an architect) to set out his 'Employer's Requirements'. These requirements are passed to a number of design and build contractors who prepare a design and submit a tender together with their time and cost proposals. The client accepts one proposal and the contractor designs and completes the work using his own staff or subcontractors (see

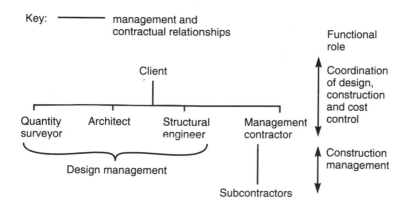

Source: Adapted from Walker (1989).

Figure 11.2   *Management structure for management contracting*

Figure 11.3). In this situation, the construction process is integrated with the design process. The client often employs a professional team to monitor progress and ensure that the 'Employer's Requirements' are complied with. The package deal is a similar situation to design and build except that the former usually deals with semi-standardised buildings, package deals provide buildings rather than designs and land and planning permissions may be included in the deal. When the deal also includes finance for the project it is referred to as a turnkey contract.

Separate contracts

In this system, the architect designs the works to meet the client's needs and arranges contracts, on the client's behalf, with a number of separate contractors. Thus the client briefs the architect, who with other consultants prepare a design. The architect and quantity surveyor arrange contracts with specialist contractors and the design work proceeds in parallel with a programme of let contracts. In this case the design team provides the design and construction management functions.

Project management

This system operates as follows: the client engages a project manager who co-ordinates a team of consultants to produce alternative schemes and advise

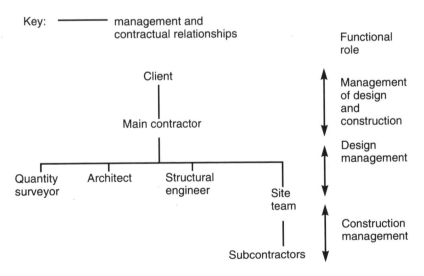

Source: Adapted from Walker (1989).
Figure 11.3   *Management structure for design and build*

the client. If the client decides to proceed, the project manager will assemble a design team and agree with the client the appropriate contract system. The procedure will then be determined by the contract adopted (e.g. management fee or traditional competitive tender, etc). Thus project management is a system of planning, control and management of a project to be used in conjunction with other systems rather than instead of them.

British Property Federation System (BPF)

This system is an amalgam of previous approaches and is based on a manual setting out procedures and responsibilities. It is a system of project management which utilises a 'Client's Representative' to manage the project and who develops an outline design and cost with the client. A design leader is then appointed with overall responsibility for pre-tender design and sanctioning the contractor's design. The design team develops the design and the client's representative monitors progress and lets the contract. The management structure is similar to that of project management, with the client's representative standing in place of the executive project manager.

Constraints on procurement because of the nature of the project

The alternatives having been listed, it is important to distinguish the criteria by which to judge them. In this section the nature of the building work, problems of the size and complexity of the contract and the purpose of the building are dealt with. The next section considers the general nature of client's objectives; cost, quality and time. The next section will also deal with more specific objectives related to risk, flexibility and the type of client. This analysis is summarised in Table 11.4.

The contract to be used in the case study has been previously analysed; it is a relatively large contract of straightforward design but with expensive services and finishes. The complexity of the subcontract work, where a number of variations may occur and where the programme of work would need to be closely followed, does not appear suitable for a traditional contract. The purpose of the building is important in determining the type of contract; here

Table 11.4   *Constraints on building procurement*

Nature of project	*Client's objectives*	
	General	*Specific*
Size and complexity	Time	Type of client
Purpose of building	Quality	Risk
	Cost	Flexibility

a well finished building is required with close liaison between client, design team and contractor on design; this would appear to count against adoption of a traditional contract. The complexity and high quality of finish required may reject a design and build solution.

Client's objectives

Using a matrix of objectives based on time, cost and quality a hierarchy of priorities can be devised. Cost is obviously an important priority but must be weighed against other objectives. In selecting an approach, it should be remembered that the management contracting approach, along with other management approaches, may well offer a more expensive solution than the traditional method. A design and build method may be cheaper, but provides a solution using standardised products which may be of lesser quality. Quality is important in this case study as a supermarket development requires good quality finishes and service provision. A supermarket is essentially based on a high functional and technical standard rather than an aesthetic one. The traditional method of building procurement scores well on quality provision, but most other systems, including design and build, could also provide a quality building in most circumstances. The design team may be under greater pressure in management contracts than in the traditional ones, and this may lessen the quality in the finished product. Time is important in this situation, not only because of financial implications, but also because of trading implications, the necessity to establish a business in an area and defeat business competition. Plans to establish a market dominance might well change if a competitor completed a store during the building contract. In relation to the criterion of time, the traditional system fares badly, it has a construction process which follows after the design period and thus has none of the advantages of other procurement methods where fast-tracking techniques of running design and construction processes in parallel exist.

Of the specific criteria, the type of client is important in this case, as the client may be able to provide in-house expertise to monitor the various management approaches to contracting. In essence, the provision of in-house expertise means that management contracting could be a more favourable option whereas a form of executive project management may be less applicable. In terms of decision-making, it is assumed that the company has a flexible approach to contracts and can proceed with alternatives to a fixed price contract.

Risk is not considered an important factor in this case as the uncertainty of a contract sum is unlikely to affect the building decision once a site has been located and the market research carried out. However, systems like separate contracts and management contracting put more risk on the client than the contractually 'safe' methods of competitive tender or design and build. Risk in these cases is often dependent on the quality of professional advice. Flexibility is a key variable in this project and it is important to remember that traditional systems have less flexibility than some management systems. Package deals, in providing a set format for buildings are also less flexible but management contracting, construction management and separate contracts score well on this variable.

Assessment of alternatives

In order to assess the alternatives, a matrix can be established which relates the client's requirements of the project to the different systems. Using a score of 1 to 5 one can compare the requirements with a score for each of the systems. This approach is subjective but should at least allow differentiation of those systems which are unlikely to fit.

The client and project requirements may be assessed as in Table 11.5.

Table 11.5   *Client requirements matrix*

Requirement	*Score* (1 to 5) (1 = unimportant, 5 - important)
Time	4
Quality	5
Cost	3
Risk	0
Flexibility	5
Complexity	3

The systems may therefore be analysed in the approach set out in Table 11.6.

Table 11.6

Management system Performance requirements	Traditional	Management fee	Package deal	Design and build separate contracts	Project management
Time economy	1	4	4	4	4
Cost economy	3	4	4	4	5
Quality	4	3	1	3	3
Complexity	3	3	3	4	4
Flexibility	2	5	2	4	4

Note: Risk has been omitted because of its relative unimportance in this particular case study.
Source: Adapted from Franks (1984a).

The key areas of requirement in flexibility and quality are best met by a systems other than the package deal system and the traditional method. The conventional method also scores badly on the time requirement. If the requirement of size of contract is now examined, a separate contracts system could lead to a complex system of contracts and perhaps conflicts. Because of the importance of the design of the interior, finishes and services, a specialist design team may need to be appointed. It is may be that this form of design work would not be dealt with by the in-house staff of design and build contractors or management contractors.

The above assessment may leave two options, project management and management contracting using a separate design team. Because of the expertise of the developer, it may be suggested that a project management solution might be unwieldy. The process could be better integrated using an in-house non-executive project manager with a management contractor and a separate design team. It is important to monitor progress and costs through the project management appointment. This solution integrates both client and contractor into the design process and allows for flexibility and quality of finish.

Recommendations

The case study involves a simplistic approach to deciding on contractual arrangements for the construction phase; however it is useful in comparing the alternatives. In this analysis, a system of management contracting would appear to be the most appropriate system. A design team would be separate and a non-executive project manager (from 'in-house' staff) could represent the client. The project manager would need to monitor closely the costs and progress of the project. This solution deals with the major objectives of flexibility, quality and time but its major weakness lies in cost as it is unlikely to be cheaper than the traditional method.

Postscript

A number of recent events have had influence on the environment in which building procurement arrangements are made. The dramatic growth of joint venture vehicles for construction projects has had the effect of confusing the industry's understanding of the responsibilities and procedures within procurement arrangements (see Yates 1991, p. 225). The Latham report *Constructing the Team*, which was published in 1994 suggested a number of new proposals on procurement to be contained in a Construction Contract Bill. The report recommends the greater use of the 'New Engineering Contract' (NEC) which is essentially non-adversarial in nature. The NEC requires that disputes be solved by adjudication and that a mediator is named before the project begins. The proposed Government Bill would ensure that the contract was used without amendment (*Building Engineer*, 1994, p. 10), but the outcome as of 1995 was not certain.

The Construction (Design and Management) Regulations, generally known as the CDM Regulations, applied from 31 March 1995; these regulations place new responsibilities on clients and designers as well as creating new legal appointments, those of Planning Supervisor and Principal Contractor. The Planning Supervisor is required amongst other responsibilities to ensure that a number of Health and Safety measures are complied with (Design and Construction Safety Ltd, 1995).

REFERENCES

Aqua Group (1990) *Tenders and Contracts for Building*, Blackwell Scientific Publications, Oxford.

Building Cost Information Service (BCIS) (1994) *Quarterly Review of Building Prices*, BCIS, issue no. 55, September.

Building Engineer (1994), 'Sir Michael's Cure for Construction Conflict', *Building Engineer*, October, pp. 10–11.

Cadman, D. and Austin-Crowe, L. (1991) *Property Development*, E. & F. N. Spon, London.

Chartered Institute of Building (CIOB) (1982) *Project Management in Building*, *Occasional Paper*, no. 20, CIOB. London.

Design and Construction Safety Ltd (1995) 'Construction (Design and Management) Regulations 1994', *DCS News*, issue 1, March.

Franks, J. (1984a) *Building Procurement Systems*, Chartered Institute of Building, London.

Franks, J. (1984b) 'Building Procurement Systems', Royal Institution of Chartered Surveyors seminar, *Project Management – prospects, procedures and pitfalls*, November.

Franks, J. (1989) *Building Procurement Systems*, Chartered Institute of Building, London.

Franks, J. (1991) *Building Contract Administration and Practice*, Batsford/Chartered Institute of Building, London.

Franks, J. (1993) 'The Design-and-Build Approach to Procurement', *Construction Papers*, no. 27, Chartered Institute of Building, London.

Hancock, P. (1984) *Building Costs and Contracts*, Centre of Advanced Land Use Studies, College of Estate Management, Reading.

Latham, M. (1994) *Constructing the Team*, HMSO, London.

Masterman, J.W. E (1992) *An Introduction to Building Procurement Systems*, E. & F. N. Spon, London.

McKinney, J. (1983) *Management Contracting*, Chartered Institute of Building, *Occasional Paper*, no. 30, CIOB, London.

Rogers Chapman, *Project Management: a client's guide*, Rogers Chapman, London.

Seeley I. H. (1984) *Quantity Surveying Practice*, Macmillan Press, London.

Turner, A. (1990) *Building Procurement*, Macmillan Press, London.

Walker, A. (1989) *Project Management in Construction*, BSP Professional Books, Oxford.

Yates, A. (1991) 'Procurement and Construction Management' in P. Venmore-Rowland, P. Brandon and T. Mole (eds), *Investment, Procurement and Performance in Construction*, RICS, London.

12 Marketing and Disposal

12.1 INTRODUCTION

Marketing is an important part of business strategy; Ansoff (1986) suggests that firms need a well defined scope and growth direction; the product market scope specifies the particular sector to which the firm confines its position, the growth sector indicates the direction in which the firm is moving with respect to its current market posture. Besides objectives relating to growth of turnover, market share and earnings growth, the firm needs to have additional decision rules if it is to have orderly and profitable growth. These rules and guidelines comprise a strategy, and the concept of strategy involves:

(i)   a broad concept of the firm's business;
(ii)   guidelines for the search for direction and new opportunities;
(iii)   decision rules which narrow firms' selection process to the most attractive opportunities (Ansoff 1986, p. 94).

These principles can apply equally to a firm marketing its own services as well as to firms marketing a product. Firms operating in the market can be defined in terms of their market share and the potential growth of that market; this is shown in the Business Portfolio Matrix in Figure 12.1. The stars are firms in high growth markets and these may eventually become cash cows which are the main income business units of the company. Problem children require serious consideration by management and often require heavy financial support to maintain market shares.

Property is a buyer's market, even more so with the demise of the boom times of the 1980s in residential and commercial property, and marketing is an activity which can convert the customer's purchasing power into effective demand. Thus marketing is the skill of matching the needs of a buyer with the product of a seller for a profit. Two distinct areas need to be considered in property marketing:

(i)   The function of agency, both commercial and residential estate agency; the types of agents and their roles in property and the market functions they provide.
(ii)   The marketing tools to be used, that is:

•   market research and information;
•   advertising;

Each strategic business unit is located in the matrix according to its relative market share and the growth of that market.

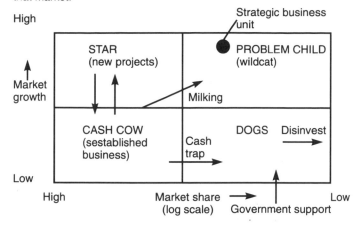

Source: Cleaveley (1984), p. 20.

Figure 12.1 *Business Portfolio Matrix (Boston Consulting Group)*

- promotions, exhibitions;
- public relations 'to create a favourable atmosphere' for marketing.

The range of marketing tools to be applied in any situation is termed the marketing mix; these are the set of controllable market variables which the firm will blend to produce the response in the market. These variables, to be discussed later, may be product, price, place and promotion. Marketing management is a deliberate process designed to mix the resources applied to the controllable variables. In the property world, for instance, estate agents would concentrate on promotion (Bevan 1991, p. 4). The determination of the target market is the key to this management process, whereas the market is the set of actual and potential buyers of a product, the target market identifies the subject group at which a particular marketing strategy may be directed.

The marketing strategy involves a number of steps and procedures. A simplified approach to property marketing would be:

(i)   Market Research (specify information required, assemble research team);
      ↓

(ii) Market Strategy (select team, get the right message, get the message across);
      ↓

(iii)   Methods of Selling (private treaty, auction, etc.);
↓
(iv)   Market Segmentation (shops, offices, etc.);
↓
(v)   Selling Techniques (brochures, mail shots, press advertising, site boards, demonstrations).

The market strategy can be thought of in two summaries:

The 4 Ps:

- **P**roduct
- **P**rice
- **P**lace (where the transaction takes place)
- **P**romotion.

Another useful summary, particularly for property marketing, is taken from Ratcliffe (1984):

DRAMA:

- **D**emonstration (brochures, viewings);
- **R**ecommendation (from satisfied tenants);
- **A**rithmetic (rents);
- **M**easurement (size information);
- **A**ssurance (give guarantees).

Property marketing in perspective

A useful definition of marketing as used by the Institute of Marketing is:

> Marketing is the management process responsible for identifying, anticipating and satisfying customer requirements profitably.

There are important considerations with regard to property which may be peculiar to the property sector: first, the property agent does not sell a product but advises clients and facilitates transfer of ownership. Note that the definition outlined above does not mention a product being marketed but specifies customer requirements. Thus the requirements of a customer can be either a product or a service. A key point of being able to fill the client's requirements is that the needs and expectations of client or property user have to be identified and agreed before the product or service is provided. A second point is that markets can be stimulated to accept products or services, but generally markets are developed from needs which are not being fulfilled, that is from a *market gap*. Some key conclusion drawn by Cleaveley (1984) about marketing property are outlined in Box 12.1.

SOME CONCLUSIONS FROM E. S. CLEAVELEY, ON THE MARKETING OF INDUSTRIAL AND COMMERCIAL PROPERTY

There are key areas of mismatch or interest in the property market in relation to marketing:

- The designation of land for development in the UK is undertaken by local authority planners and is not driven directly by user requirements nor demand.

- The amount of empty property on market (1½m+sq ft of offices in Croydon at the time he wrote) may not be due just to a recession in the market but a mismatch with user requirements

- Because of the long lead-in and the time taken for developments to be completed, it is easy to be wrong in anticipating user requirements.

- The provision of certain buildings in the property sector are established with no real market research into user requirements nor assessment of scale or timing of supply. The provision of high-tech buildings is an example. These units were sometimes developed as merely traditional premises with different headroom, finishes and landscaping, providing a higher rent to the landlord for nothing more than superficial finishes.

Box 12.1 *Conclusions from Cleaveley (1984).*

Principles of marketing

Selling

Selling needs to be distinguished from marketing, it is one specific technique of marketing. Selling is a component of promotion and is described as a channel of persuasion. Marketing is the overall function of a practice, the aim being to increase profits. The sales force, advertising campaign and mail-shots are methods of communication and persuasion.

Marketing mix

The marketing mix is a set of controlled market variables which a firm will blend to produce the response it wants in the market place. The controllable variables are the 4 Ps indicated earlier: product, price, place and promotion. The management of the marketing process is the deliberate process designed to mix the resources applied to the controllable variables. Estate agents will tend to concentrate on promotion. Market segmentation is the dividing up of the market into distinct groups of buyers who might merit separate products or marketing mixes (Bevan 1991, pp. 4 and 10).

Marketing planning

The potential market is divided into segments based on consumer requirements and thus there is a need to target each segment accurately. Whereas the market is a set of actual and potential buyers of a product, the target market is the identification of a subset of the overall market for the product for whom the marketing is planned. A segment is thus a defined group of possible users; as an example, Texas Instruments identified four market segments with different requirements and therefore produced four products (Cleaveley 1984):

Segment		Requirement
General public	⟶	Cheapness
Scientific use	⟶	Functions
Business use	⟶	Reliability
Education use	⟶	Durability

These market segments may therefore merit separate products or marketing mixes. Such segmentation is looked at in detail in the next section.

Product pricing

The approach used in the property profession to value land can be compared against a procedure used with marketing techniques; these comparisons are set out in Table 12.1.

Whilst many of the stages may be implicitly examined in the property valuation process, the comparison, using a marketing approach, shows the explicit stages of consideration required.

Summary: The marketing plan

The marketing plan is a selling document, an encapsulation of thought about markets, pricing and promotion (Bevan 1991, p. 217). The presentation of a marketing plan should thus include:

- *Market research findings*
  - end user requirements
  - competition
  - demand

Table 12.1   *Approaches to product pricing*

Valuer's approach:
The valuation is based on prices previously paid but they must be adjusted for changes since previous transactions took place, the market will then determine the accuracy of the estimate.

Marketing approach:

Step 1   *Set price policy objectives* (limits, timescales, fall-back position)
↓
Step 2   *Identify influencing factors* (presentation, location, economic factors, etc)
↓
Step 3   *Review market information* (demand, market profile, segmentation)
↓
Step 4   *Review competitive information* (competitive schemes, empty properties, activities of agents, selling prices)

↓
Step 5   *Review costs* (grants, incentives)
↓
Step 6   *Establish pricing strategy* (special offers, rent-free periods, leaseback, reverse premiums)

↓
Step 7   *Set price and negotiating level* (asking price, fall-back price)
↓
Step 8   *Review price performance* (regular monitoring).

- *Marketing strategy*
  - objectives
  - target
  - promotional plan
  - timescale
- *Pricing strategy*
  - objectives
  - rents
  - special deals
  - competitive positioning
- *Construction costs/timescale*
- *Monitoring and management arrangements*

12.2   MARKET RESEARCH

The increasing fragmentation of the property market means that a higher level of skill is required in discovering and exploiting the profitable location. Research is necessary into the likely scale, design, layout, occupancy, tenure and service requirements of prospective purchasers. Market research is an important area which would aim to establish the current demand and supply of property within the area to ensure that the property could be sold or let. The estimation of current demand may include the estimation of the current total market potential, which is the maximum amount of sales that might be available to all competing firms during a given period in a given market segment under a given level of marketing asset.

Basically the seller wants to know if the market is large enough to justify the company's participation. Cleaveley (1984, p. 36) quotes a formula for this estimate which is

$$m = n \times q \times p$$

where m is the total market potential, n is the number of buyers in the specific market, q is the quantity purchased by an average buyer and p is the price of the average product. If we apply this to the property field, for instance in the area of the provision of high technology units, then, if there were for instance 200 high-technology companies buying a new production facility every five years and the average price is (say) £200 000 for an average 500m^2 of space then the total market potential is approximately £40 000 000 over a five-year period. The most difficult element of this calculation is to assess the number of buyers in that particular market in a given time period.

A variation on the above approach to assess current demand can be worked out by the 'chain method'; this is based on the premise that it is easier to look at each component of magnitude than at the overall magnitude itself. So again, the current demand for high-technology building would equal the number of high technology companies in the UK times the average percentage of those without spare capacity on site times the average percentage of those companies who need specialised premises times the average percentage of those companies who would pay current market rent for high-tech buildings. This 'chain method' appears a lot more complex but in fact the elements of the calculation may be easier to assess.

Market research procedure

Cleaveley (1984, p. 87) suggests that there are five steps in the setting up in the operation of a market research project and these are applicable to the property industry. The first step is the defining of objectives. Here the research objectives or the subject to be investigated is defined. A clear direction of research activities is required to ensure that the results come from the right target market and that sufficient valid data is obtained.

(i)   Designing the research methodology: Decisions must be taken about the appropriate method of obtaining data. These may be, for instance, desk research, the study of published information or in-house information from appropriate agents. It may come from observation or finally by survey research which may consist of face to face interviews, self-completing questionnaires, interviewing by telephone, or group discussion where opinion leaders are drawn together to discuss markets under the direction of the trained group leader, this latter approach can be very effective in finding out a general consensus of view points.

(ii) *Sampling*: Because of the costs of analysing the total target market, most research programmes will focus upon samples of that market. Larger samples obviously give more reliable data but the degree of accuracy required must be related to the amount of funds available to be spent on the research project. Most research projects begin with a pilot survey which will evaluate the procedure intended to be used and also the design of the research method and the level of response likely. Random sampling is effective and easy to administer but structured sampling and non-random methods have also been designed to achieve maximum statistical reliability from the results.

(iii) *Fieldwork*: Trained interviewers or executives can be employed to carry out the fieldwork to provide the information on the research project. The supervisor to the project will need to monitor closely what is happening in terms of the fieldwork and to ensure that it is completed accurately without bias and on time.

(iv) *Data analysis*: The analytical techniques used in the data analysis can vary from simple statistical techniques to a very complex regression analysis. The extent of the analysis should be agreed with the client before the research is entered into.

(v) *Presentation of report*: The results of research and any conclusions are shown in a comprehensive report which should have clear recommendations so that the findings of the research can be translated into action by the client.

12.3 THE MARKETING OF PROPERTY

To summarise the main concepts dealt with so far, marketing has been defined as the management process responsible for identifying, anticipating and satisfying customer requirements profitably. The requirements can relate to a service or a product and, in the case of property development, the product will be a development property or the service provided by professional agencies in the development process. The term 'identifying' recognises the needs and expectations of the end user and that these expectations and needs must be established before the product or services are provided. It is often possible to stimulate demand for new products, but certainly in the property market and generally in other markets, most profitable new markets are developed from the recognition of a need and this is termed a market gap. As an example of the need for a market gap, the production of high-tech industrial units in the 1980s and the science parks, which were being built at the same time, probably did not have any clear market requirement identified. In most high-tech developments, architects and developers were providing traditional premises differing only in terms of headroom, finishes and landscaping from traditional types of property which would have been provided. High-tech became associated with high rents and did not provide any technological base to the space provided. Critics have said that they are traditional units with painted red doors.

What does the client want?

The client's usual requirement is an early choice of agent to work up the marketing strategy. There is a need to decide the type of agent whether large, small, local, national, specialist, a firm or an individual consultant. For the marketing campaign, the client will need to make a budget allowance in the initial appraisal, this may need 1 per cent of the gross development value. The strategy of the campaign may require 'a number of nudges rather than one blast', that is developed over a period of time. The client will also need to be able to monitor progress (Ratcliffe and Butler 1985).

Marketing differentiated from sales

Selling is a tactical weapon in the marketing armoury. Other weapons, such as advertising join with selling to enable the marketer to achieve the objective of satisfying consumer requirements profitably in a particular market. Selling is a component of promotion. In other product areas, salesmen are usually employed as the most important means of obtaining information on products and services and these are regarded as being much more important than advertising or mailshots. However, mailshots and advertising are the commonly used approaches in the property industry. There are a number of channels of persuasion which will encourage a potential consumer to purchase the product. Besides selling, other approaches that could be used in property include video and films, straight advertising, sign-boards, exhibitions, conferences and seminars, mailshots, and other approaches such as references in literature or the press. The development of a marketing campaign for a development property needs to be planned effectively. The stages of a marketing campaign are summarised in Figure 12.2 showing the management and marketing process used in property development. These stages of the campaign would include:

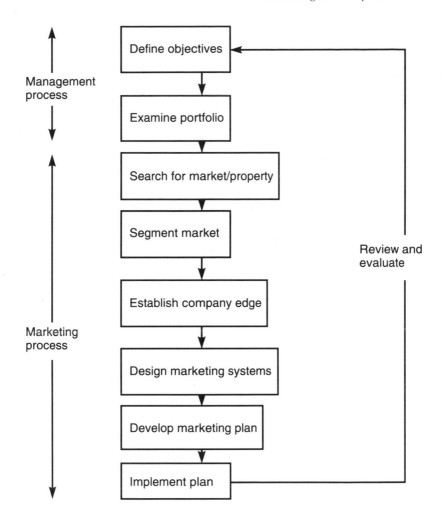

Source: Simplified from Cleaveley (1984), p. 22.
Figure 12.2 *The management and marketing process*

(i)   The definition of the objectives of the campaign.
(ii)   The examination of the property to see how it fits within these objectives.
(iii)   The examination of the market segment for the property itself.
(iv)   The segmentation of the market into different user groups.
(v)   The establishment of a competitive edge in the promotional campaign.

(vi)   The design of marketing systems appropriate for the promotion which is going to be carried out.
(vii)   The development of a marketing plan.
(viii) The implementation of the plan, at which stage there is a review and evaluation which may feed back to the definition of objectives and the examination of the property itself.

Market segmentation

The task of segmentation is described as the identification of groups of consumers inside a market who share a common need. Segmentation identifies those variables which are used in the purchase decision and can rank them in order of importance by means of market research. A term commonly used in the segmentation activity is 'gap analysis', which describes the gap in the market which potential products can fill. Most markets break down into what is termed preference segments. There are three of these and, although fairly wide, do represent the first step in segmentation analysis.

(i)   *Homogeneous preferences*: where all consumers in the market have roughly the same preferences. Most companies will position their product in the middle.
(ii)   *Diffused preferences*: consumer preferences here are scattered with each requiring something different from the product. Companies often decide to position in the middle to minimise consumer dissatisfaction.
(iii)   *Clustered preferences*: distinct clusters are evident suggesting further segmentation. A company must decide which course of action to follow. For instance to position in the centre to appeal to most groups, position in the biggest cluster to try to become market leader, or develop several brands to cover each cluster.

Bevan (1991, p. 10) suggests an approach to market segmentation involving classification on the following basis:

- *Geographic*;
- *Demographic*;
- *Pyschographic*, based on social class;
- *Behaviouristic*, involving aspects such as: occasion of purchase, benefits sought, user stature, usage rate, loyalty status, readiness stage (for product) and attitudes to the product.
- *Conceptual*, the differential advantage of the product in the market and its positioning relative to other products.

For segmentation to be successful there must be differences among consumers or else mass marketing would be the appropriate strategy; however, within each consumer group there must be enough consumer similarities to develop an appropriate marketing plan for the entire segment (Evans and Berman 1988, p. 144)

Promotion

Promotion is the art of communicating with prospective customers. It is a vital component of the marketing mix used to market a product. The purpose of promotion is to bring a product or service to the attention of a buyer or group of buyers in the target market. Promotion includes selling as one of its constituent parts, but is an activity under the marketing umbrella. The timing of the promotion will be based upon the anticipation of that need. Promotion could include a number of communication channels which may include advertising through press, television, radio and signboards, publications through press, public relations and sponsorship, direct selling, direct mail, exhibitions, literature, film and audio visual material, conferences and seminars, packaging and presentation and special events. Different types of promotional activity are related to the stage of the potential consumer or buyer. Thus the activity can be defined by the stage which the buyer is in. This is summarised in Box 12.2.

PROMOTION	
BUYER STAGE	**PROMOTIONAL ACTIVITY**
AWARENESS	Advertising and press editorial
COMPREHENSION	Literature, exhibitions and special events
CONVICTION	Direct selling, signboards and advertising site visits
PURCHASE	Direct selling, public relations.

Box 12.2 *Promotional activity*

Selling

Marketing is obviously an essential tool in letting and selling a development and it is assisted by the public relations exercise to promote, communicate and reinforce the corporate image of the development company. Developers need to realise that their image plays an important part in the success of their development schemes (Cadman and Austin-Crowe 1991, p. 142). Until recently property developers did not employ the professional advisers in the advertising world, but this did develop during the boom years of the 1980s. The agent's role is to persuade the purchaser or tenant to purchase or rent a property at the right price and terms. It is obviously important, as discussed earlier, for the developer to identify the target market which is referred to as the market segmentation.

Especially within the activity of selling property, the agent's role is particularly important. Agents have advantages because of their better position in a market, perhaps knowing local contacts and having detailed knowledge of the local market. Agents' fees may amount to something like 10 per cent of the rental value as a fee for letting or 2 per cent of the value for sale. However, in most cases, joint agencies are set up where there are two or more agents acting often with a central London agent and a local agent knowing the local markets being used . In situations like this, a developer will pay a larger fee, say 15 per cent or 3 per cent on the capital value. Agents may share the fee 50:50, or on an agreed basis. The agents should undertake to contribute to the planning, design and evaluation of the project and should be brought in at an early stage. The benefit of this is that the agents will become familiar with the product they are selling. It is important not to get too many agents involved. In some cases, agents may be retained by clients and therefore will not seek a fee. When agents refer applicants they will expect a commission if a sale results from one of their introductions.

Methods of promotion

The methods of promotion that can be used in letting and selling development properties include advertising, mailshots, particulars in brochures, site boards and site hoardings, launching ceremonies and show suites in offices. The need, as indicated earlier, is to ensure that the target market has been assessed early in the development process when evaluating the scheme and developing the design. There is a need to 'brand' the building by naming it and providing an appropriate logo or concept so that this theme can be recognised by the market and perhaps reflect the strategy of the advertising campaign. The target market, it should be remembered, is not just the potential occupier but also the potential purchaser and funders. The property should promote the space but also the amenities and location of the area. The component activities of promotion are shown in Figure 12.3.

Advertising

Advertising is aimed at potential occupiers or agents. This can be done in national or local newspapers or in property journals. The advertisement

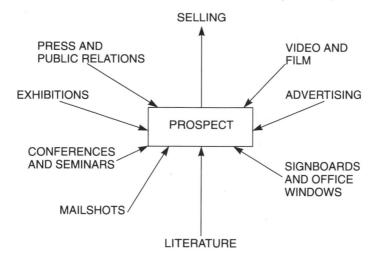

Figure 12.3   *Components of promotion*

should contain details of the design and layout of the property but it also needs to create an appropriate impression according to how the property has been targeted. The cost of a one-off advertisement needs to be compared to a programme of smaller advertisements over a period of time. Information should be readily available in the advertisement as to the type of property, the approximate size, the location and whether the premises are for sale or to let.

Mailshots

These can be very effective specially from a cost point of view. A selected list of potential occupiers would need to be used. These can be provided by specialist direct mail order firms. The mailshots need a short sharp message. Often gimmicks are used such as free gifts which are sent with the mailshots.

Particulars and Brochures

Particulars and brochures are sent to potential occupiers and agents, they describe the location of the premises, the accommodation, the dimension specification, services provided to the property and the interest to be let or sold. In most cases these brochures require outside designers to ensure effective use of colour, shape, layout, etc. in the brochures. A tenant's guide to the building could be drawn up which details the building, construction and specification and can also provide information on maintenance and energy saving data. Sometimes, videos are used in these situations.

Site boards and site hoardings

The use of site boards and site hoardings can be very effective for advertising purposes. They can also provide good public relations for the company involved as well as concealing what might be ugly construction works from adjoining roads.

Launch ceremonies

These can be quite effective but it is important to invite local dignitaries as well as agents, potential occupiers and the press.

Show suites and offices

If the property being built is speculative, then the marketing campaign will need to be supplemented by plans and models. One approach is to fit out a show suite and this will give a good idea to potential occupiers and agents of what the space will look like when occupied.

The marketing campaign

The planning of a marketing campaign is the task of the project manager of the property development process. It is important for the project manager to ensure that the advertising and marketing campaign is well thought out, properly co-ordinated and phased in such a way that the property is placed before the target audience in an ordered and consistent manner. It is important that, as well as some initial launches of the proposal, there is a follow through and an updating through the development period to ensure that potential users and funders are kept aware of what is happening. It is important to agree the budget for the marketing campaign and to monitor the work of the professional team associated with the marketing. Some key aspects of the project management of the marketing stage of property development can be found in Ratcliffe's paper (Ratcliffe 1984a).

The marketing team

As well as the choice of the right agent, it is necessary to consider the appointment of other specialist services in the marketing of the development. The position of the agent is important in relation to the rest of the professional team.

Marketing and disposal

It is important to determine the point at which the marketing campaign is first started and how it should be conducted and by whom. The prime aim of any private sector development scheme should be to produce a marketable building. It is important that the project manager at the beginning of a scheme focuses the attention of all the contributors to the professional team on the marketing dimension of the project. In selecting an agent for the property, the project manager will have to discuss such elements as whether the agent should be a national agent or a local agent, small or large, a firm or an individual, a generalist or a specialist and whether instructions should be on a joint or sole instruction basis.

Product life cycle

The traditional product life cycle involves four stages – introduction, growth, maturity and decline. As is suggested by the titles of the phases, sales and profits will increase over time to maturity and then fall. Sales and profits can then be supported by promotional activity to lift the cycle again, Cleaveley calls this the 'cycle–recycle' pattern (Cleaveley 1984, p. 50). Cleaveley suggests that bespoke property will generate profit on this pattern; on the other hand speculative property, because of the possibility of voids in the earlier years, will generate profits more akin to the traditional pattern of the product life cycle. These cycles are shown in Figure 12.4.

12.4   THE MARKETING PLAN

The marketing plan will need to look at the type of property involved, if it is a product and not a service which is being sold. Bevan (1991, p. 214) gives an example of a marketing plan for a 5 hectare site which contained a derelict factory. Such a plan would need to consider aspects such as an analysis of the site to explore potential users and identify target markets. It would also need to consider an approach to pricing and method of sale. Finally on the basis of the other considerations mentioned, a promotional plan is evolved to ensure that the right purchasers are approached at the right time to maximum effect. The analysis for the marketing plan needs to be done in a systematic way, the plan being a selling document, an encapsulation of advice on products, markets, pricing and promotion.

The plan should cover aspects of the analysis, as indicated in the Introduction (see marketing plans in section 12.1). Bevan (1991, p. 217) suggests the following approach:

Sales/profits (£)

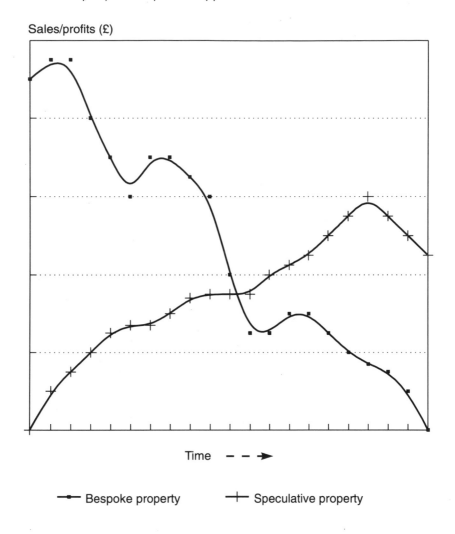

Source: Adapted from Cleavely (1984), p. 50.
Figure 12.4   *Product life-cycles: property patterns*

- *Product:*   What do you wish to sell; what needs does it meet?
- *Market:*   Who needs the product; why; how often; how many; how much will purchasers pay; what is its market worth; is there an identifiable segmentation of the market; what competition

exists; what is the summary of market opportunities?

- *Strategy:*   How can the market be developed; what are
                          the opportunities and pitfalls; how can com-
                          petitors and competing products be over-
                          come?
- *Tactical mix:*   Pricing; distribution; promotion.
- *Resource allocation:*   Tactical budgets; detailed plan; cost/benefit
                          summary.

12.5   DISPOSAL AND WARRANTIES

Warranties

The JCT forms of contract were discussed in Chapter 11 and it was noted that
provided the contractor executes the building work in good and workmanlike
manner and in accordance with the architect's drawings and the specification
in the bill of quantities provided by the quantity surveyor and with any subsequent instruction given to the contractor by the architect then the contractor would not normally have any responsibility if the building is not suited for
the purpose for which it has been designed. The developer will thus require the
design team, i.e. the architect, structural engineer, mechanical and electrical
engineer and sometimes the quantity surveyor, to enter into deeds of collateral
warranty for the benefit of their successors in title, financiers and tenants (Cadman and Austin Crowe 1991, p. 108). These warranties will extend the benefit of
the development contract with the professionals involved. Typically, arrangements of this type will require the professional practice or company to warrant
that all reasonable skill, care and attention has been exercised in their professional responsibility and they owe a duty of care. In addition the professionals
are required to warrant that they have not specified deleterious materials. It is
becoming increasingly difficult for developers to procure these warranties in a
form acceptable to both parties, as funding institutions (the insurance companies and pension funds) and banks require increased responsibility from the
professional design team. The professionals in turn are increasingly resisting
deeds of collateral warranty in the form required by funding institutions and
banks due to the possible risks to their professional indemnity insurance policies. This has become a major problem in the development sector with the
developer negotiating as a middleman between the designer and funder.

Experience suggests that professionals are unwilling to sign these agreements and will try to limit their liability in three ways:

- they will not sign under seal (which means that their liability may last
  six years not 12);

- they will wish to limit the assignability of their deeds of collateral warranty to the first purchaser and first tenant of the completed development;
- they will wish their liability to be restricted to remedial costs or defects, not consequential or economic loss.

Recently some developers have tried to provide insurance, in the form of latent defects insurance, particularly on large complex schemes. This form of insurance costs typically 1–2 per cent of the building contract sum but has the advantage that the insurer is responsible for pursuing remedies with the professional team. The insurer assumes responsibility for repairing the property should an inherent structural defect be discovered which renders the building unstable or threatens immediate collapse. The insurer usually agrees to cover a project for up to 10 years from completion provided that an insurance is in place before construction begins and an independent engineer's report is available on the design and cost of the building. The developer will have to pay for the fees of the independent engineer. This policy is totally assignable.

Management contracting

In this form of contract situation, the developer has no direct contractual relations with various contractors to carry out the works. The developer must enter into design warranties which are capable of being passed to successors in title and tenants.

Handover

A short time before the date of completion and handover of the buildings from the developer, the architect prepares a 'snagging' list indicating all the minor defects that must be remedied before handover takes place. At that time it is useful for the development surveyor and a representative of the intending occupier to accompany the architect to ensure that they are both satisfied with the snagging list prepared. At the outset of the project, the project manager will have confirmed that the building works are adequately protected by the contractor's own insurance arrangements. The contractor's insurance will no longer protect the building once it has been handed over, so one of the most important things is for the project manager to ensure that the developer has adequate insurance cover from handover until such time as the insurance cover provided by the occupier takes effect.

The JCT Contract (Cadman and Austin Crowe 1991, p. 127) will have provided for a certain percentage of the total cost to be retained by the building owner until the end of the defects liability period, often six months from the date of practical completion. Special maintenance periods may be agreed for particular parts of the works (e.g. landscaping). The contractor is responsible for remedying any defects (other than design) which have occurred during the defects liability period provided it has not been caused by the occupier. The buildings are inspected at the end of the liability period and any obvious defects at that time which the architect could not identify are assumed to be such that the architect would be prepared to accept the building subject to these defects.

The importance of the site and its environs on the handover date should not be overlooked. If during the building contract any damage is caused to adjoining property (damage to boundaries) the contractor must reinstate them. Inspection of roads, footpaths, etc. are carried out to ensure that the contractor remedies the damage, otherwise the highway authority might ask the developer to bear the cost of any remedial works. The architect should produce a building manual and maintenance schedule to assist the occupier by giving a comprehensive schedule and description of all components which might need replacing at some future date with recommendations for regular maintenance work to preserve the fabric.

REFERENCES

Ansoff, H. I. (1986) *Corporate Strategy*, Sidgwick & Jackson, London.

Bevan, O. A. (1991) *Marketing and Property People*, Macmillan Press, London.

Cadman, D. and Austin-Crowe, L.. (1991) *Property Development*, E. & F. N. Spon, London.

Cleaveley, E. S. (1984) *The Marketing of Industrial and Commercial Property*, Estates Gazette, London.

Etter, W. and Shaffer, S. (1987) 'Market Segmentation – applying a marketing concept to commercial real estate development', *Journal of Valuation*, vol. 6 no. 1, pp. 42–56.

Evans, J. R. and Berman, B. (1988) *Principles of Marketing*, St Martin's Press, New York.

Norton, M. D. (1988) 'Market Analysis and Project Evaluation' in C. Darlow (ed.) *Valuation and Development Appraisal*, Estates Gazette, London.

Ratcliffe, J. (1984) 'Marketing for Development', *Occasional Paper*, Polytechnic of the South Bank, Department of Estate Management.

Ratcliffe, J. and Butler, J. (1985) 'Marketing', *Estates Gazette*, 7 September.

Bibliography

Accounting Standards Committee (ASC) (1990) *Exposure Draft 51, Accounting for Fixed Assets and Revaluations*, ASC, May, London.

Albert, D. and Watson, J. (1990) 'An Approach to Property Joint Ventures' *Journal of Property Finance*, vol. 1, no. 2, pp. 89–95.

Ansoff, H. I. (1986) *Corporate Strategy*, Sidgwick & Jackson, London.

Aqua Group (1990) *Tenders and Contracts for Building*, Blackwell Scientific Publications, Oxford.

Armon-Jones, C. H. (1992) 'Underwriting Property Sales', *Journal of Property Finance*, vol. 2, no. 4 pp. 497–500.

Arnison, C. and Barrett, A. (1984) 'Valuations of Development Sites using the Stochastic Decision Tree Method' *Journal of Valuation*, vol. 3, no. 2, pp. 126–33.

Asch, D. and Kaye, G. R. (1989) *Financial Planning: modelling methods and techniques*, Kogan Paul, London.

Balchin, P. N. and Bull, G. H. (1987) *Regional and Urban Economics*, Harper & Row, London.

Balchin, P. N., Bull, G. H. and Kieve, J. L. (1995) *Urban Land Economics and Public Policy*, 5th edn. Macmillan Press, London.

Bank of England (1994a) *Quarterly Bulletin*, vol. 34, no. 3, August.

Bank of England (1994b) *Quarterly Bulletin*, vol. 34, no. 4, November.

Baring, Houston and Saunders (1991) *Property Report*, Baring, Houston and Saunders, London, November.

Barkham, R. J. and Purdy, D. E. (1992) 'Financial Company Reporting: Potential weaknesses', *Journal of Property Valuation and Investment*, vol. 11, no. 2, pp. 133–44.

Barkshire, R. (1986) *The Unitised Property Market*, Working Party of the Unitised Property Market, London, February.

Barter, S. L. (1988) 'Introduction' in S. L. Barter (ed.) *Real Estate Finance*, Butterworths, London.

Barter, S. and Sinclair, N. (1988) 'Securitisation' in S. L. Barter (ed.), *Real Estate Finance*, Butterworths, London.

Baum, A. (1987) 'An Approach to Risk Analysis', Henry Stewart Conference, *Property Investment Appraisal and Analysis*, Cafe Royal, London, 1 December.

Baum, A. and Crosby, N. (1988) *Property Investment Appraisal*, Routledge, London.

Baum, A. and Crosby, N. (1995) *Property Investment Appraisal*, Routledge, London.

Baum, A. E. and Schofield, A. (1991) 'Property as a Global Asset' in P Venmore-Rowland, P. Brandon and T. Mole (eds), *Investment, Procurement and Performance in Construction*, RICS, London.

Berkley, R. (1991) 'Raising Commercial Property Finance in a Difficult Market', *Journal of Property Finance*, vol. 1, no. 4, pp. 523–9.

Bevan, O. A. (1991) *Marketing and Property People*, Macmillan Press, London.

Beveridge, J. (1988) 'The Needs of the Property Company', in S. L. Barter (ed.) *Real Estate Finance*, Butterworths, London.

Beveridge, J. A. (1991) 'New Methods of Financing' in P. Venmore-Rowland, P. Brandon and T. Mole (eds), *Investment, Procurement and Performance in Construction*, RICS, London.

Bramson, D. (1988) 'The Mechanics of Joint Ventures', in S. L. Barter (ed.), *Real Estate Finance*, Butterworths, London.

Brett, M. (1983a) 'Growth of Financial Institutions' in C. Darlow (ed.) *Valuation and Investment Appraisal*, Estates Gazette, London.

Brett, M. (1983b) 'Indirect Investment in Property' in C. Darlow (ed.) *Valuation and Investment Appraisal*, Estates Gazette, London.

Brett, M. (1990a) *Property and Money*, Estates Gazette, London.

Brett, M. (1990b) *How to read the financial pages*, Hutchinson, London.

Brett, M. (1991a) 'How property futures work', *Estates Gazette*, 18 May, p. 71.

Brett, M. (1991b), 'Property and Money: Mortgages which convert into property', *Estates Gazette*, 17 August.

Briscoe, G. (1988) *The Economics of the Construction Industry*, Mitchell, London.

Britton, W., Davies, K. and Johnson, T. (1990) *Modern Methods of Valuation*, Estates Gazette, London.

Brown, G. (1986) 'A Certainty Equivalent Expectations Model for Estimating the Systematic Risk of Property Investments', *Journal of Valuation*, vol. 6, no. 1, pp. 17–41.

Brown, G. R. (1991) *Property Investment and the Capital Markets*, E. & F. N. Spon, London.

Building Cost Information Service (BCIS) (1994) *Quarterly Review of Building Prices*, BCIS, issue no. 55, September.

Building Engineer (1994), Sir Michael's Cure for Construction Conflict, *Building Engineer*, October, pp. 10–11.

Burgess R. and White G. (1979) *Building Production and Project Management*, The Construction Press, London.

Burke, R. (1993) *Project Management: Planning and Control*, John Wiley, Chichester.

Butler, D. and Richmond, D. (1990) *Advanced Valuation*, Macmillan, London.

Byrne, P. and Cadman, D. (1984) *Risk, Uncertainty and Decision Making in Property Development*, E. & F. N. Spon, London.

Cadman, D. and Austin-Crowe, L. (1978) *Property Development*, E. & F. N. Spon, London.

Cadman, D. and Austin-Crowe, L. (1991) *Property Development*, E. & F. N. Spon, London.

Cadman, D. and Catalano, A. (1983) *Property Development in the UK – Evolution and Change*, College of Estate Management, Reading,

Calachi, R. and Rosenburg, S. (eds) (1992) *Property Finance: An International Perspective*, Euromoney Books, London.

Central Statistical Office (CSO) (1992) *Financial Statistics: Explanatory Handbook*, CSO, London, December.

Central Statistical Office (CSO) (1993a) *Financial Statistics*, CSO, London, September.

Central Statistical Office (CSO) (1993b) *Housing and Construction Statistics*, CSO, London, September.

Central Statistical Office (CSO) (1994a) *Financial Statistics*, CSO, London, November.

Central Statistical Office (CSO) (1994b) *Economic Trends*, HMSO, London.

Central Statistical Office (CSO) (1995) *UK Economic Accounts*, no 8, HMSO, London, January.

Chapman, C. B. (1991) 'Risk' in P. Venmore-Rowland, P. Brandon and T. Mole (eds), *Investment, Procurement and Performance in Construction*, RICS, London.

Chartered Institute of Building (CIOB) (1982) *Project Management in Building*, Occasional Paper no. 20, CIOB, London.

Chesterton Financial (n.d.), *Internal uncirculated reports*, Chesterton Financial, London.

Chesterton Financial (1991) *Property Lending Survey*, Chesterton Financial, London, February.

Chesterton Financial (1992) *Property Lending Survey*, Chesterton Financial, London, February.

Chesterton Financial (1993) *Property Lending Survey*, Chesterton Financial, London, February.

Chesterton Financial (1994) *Property Lending Survey*, Chesterton Financial, London, February.

Chesterton Financial (1995) *Property Lending Survey*, Chesterton Financial, London, February.

Chesterton Financial/CSW (1993) *Property Confidence Barometer*, Chesterton Financial, London, July.

Clarke, R. J. (1990) 'Refinancing', *Journal of Property Finance*, vol. 1, no. 3, pp. 435–9.

Cleaveley, E. S. (1984) *The Marketing of Industrial and Commercial Property*, Estates Gazette, London.

Cohen, P. (1992) 'Non-recourse Property Funding' *Journal of Property Finance*, vol. 3, no. 3, pp. 319–24.

Colliers (1987) 'Unitisation: elaborate experiment or worthwhile and much needed solution?' *International Review* no. 20, Colliers International Property Consultants.

D. J. Freeman (1994) *The Language of Property Finance*, D. J. Freeman, London.

Darlow, C. (1988a) 'Corporate and Share Capital Funding' in C. Darlow (ed.) *Valuation and Development Appraisal*, Estates Gazette, London.

Darlow, C. (1988b) 'Direct Project Funding' in C. Darlow (ed.) *Valuation and Development Appraisal*, Estates Gazette, London.

Darlow, C. (1988c) 'The Supply and Sources of Finance' in C. Darlow (ed.) *Valuation and Development Appraisal*, Estates Gazette, London.

Darlow, C. (ed.) (1988) *Valuation and Development Appraisal*, Estates Gazette, London.

Darlow, C. (ed.) (1983) *Valuation and Investment Appraisal*, Estates Gazette, London.

Davidson, A.W. (1990) 'Parry's Valuation and Investment Tables', Estates Gazette, London.

Dawson, A. (1995) 'Finance: Picking a path through the hedges', *Estates Gazette*, 11 March, pp. 46–7.

Day, D.W. J. (1994) *Project Management and Control*, Macmillan Press, London.

Debenham, Tewson and Chinnocks (1984) *Property Investment in Britain*, Debenham, Tewson and Chinnocks, London.

Design and Construction Safety Ltd (1995) 'Construction (Design and Management) Regulations 1994', *DCS News*, issue 1, March.

Dixon, T. J., Hargitay, S. E. and Bevan, O. A. (1991) *Microcomputers in Property*, E. & F. N. Spon, London.

Department of the Environment (DoE) (1994a) *Housing and Construction Statistics 1982–1993 (Great Britain)*, HMSO, London.

Department of the Environment (DoE) (1994b) *Housing and Construction Statistics (Great Britain)*, June quarter 1994, part 2, HMSO, London.

DTZ Debenham Thorpe (1993) *Money into Property*, DTZ Debenham Thorpe, London, August.

Dubben, N. and Sayce, S. (1991) *Property Portfolio Management: An Introduction*, Routledge, London.

Duckworth, W. E., Gear, A. E. and Lockett, A. G. (1977) *A Guide to Operational Research*, Chapman & Hall, London.

Enever, N. and Isaac, D. (1995) *The Valuation of Property Investments*, Estates Gazette, London.

Estates Gazette (1994), 'Street Trees Threatened by Cable TV – Call for Review of Utility Rights', *Estates Gazette*, 24 September, p. 82.

Estates Gazette (1995), 'Mainly for students: Spreadsheets and Valuations', *Estates Gazette*, 21 January, pp. 116–19.

Etter, W. and Shaffer, S. (1987) 'Market Segmentation – Applying a marketing concept to commercial real estate development', *Journal of Valuation*, vol. 6, no. 1, pp. 42–56.

Evans, J. R. and Berman, B. (1988) *Principles of Marketing*, St Martin's Press, New York.

Evans, P. H. (1992) 'Statistical Review' *Journal of Property Finance*, vol. 3, no. 1, pp. 115–20.

Evans, P. H. (1993) 'Statistical Review', *Journal of Property Finance*, vol. 4, no. 2, pp. 75–82.

Fielding, M. and Besser, A. (1991) 'Syndicated Loans – *caveat* Borrower', *Estates Gazette*, 15 June, pp. 78 and 103.

Flanagan, R. and Norman, G. (1993) *Risk Management and Construction*, Blackwell, Oxford.

Fothergill, S., Monk, S. and Perry, M. (1987) *Property and Industrial Development*, Hutchinson, London.

Fox, J.W.W. (1993) 'Sale and Leasebacks: A Case Study', *Journal of Property Finance*, vol. 4, no. 1, pp. 9–12.

Franks, J. (1984a) *Building Procurement Systems*, Chartered Institute of Building, London.

Franks, J. (1984b) 'Building Procurement Systems', Royal Institution of Chartered Surveyors seminar, *Project Management – prospects, procedures and pitfalls*, November.

Franks, J. (1989) *Building Procurement Systems*, Chartered Institute of Building, London.

Franks, J. (1991) *Building Contract Administration and Practice*, Batsford/Chartered Institute of Building, London.

Franks, J. (1993) 'The Design-and-Build Approach to Procurement', *Construction Papers*, no 27, Chartered Institute of Building, London,

Fraser, W. D. (1993) *Principles of Property Investment and Pricing*, 2nd edn, Macmillan Press, London.

Freed, N. (1992) 'Bridging Finance', *Journal of Property Finance*, vol. 3, no. 2, pp. 187–90.

Freedman, P. and Ward, H.   (1993), 'The Environmental Factor', *Estates Gazette*, 27 November, pp. 132–3.

French, N. (1994) Editorial: 'Market Values and DCF', *Journal of Property Valuation and Investment*, vol. 12, no. 1, pp. 4–6.

Gibbs, R. (1987) 'Raising Finance for New Development', *Journal of Valuation*, vol. 5, no. 4, pp. 343–53.

Goldsmith, G. C. (1992) 'Sterling Interest Swaptions' *Journal of Property Finance*, vol. 3, no. 3, pp. 315–318.

Graham, J. (1985) 'New Sources of Finance for the Property Industry', *Estates Gazette*, 6 July.

Guy, G. (1994), *The Retail Development Process: Location, Property and Planning*, Routledge, London.

Hancock, P. (1984) *Building Costs and Contracts*, Centre of Advanced Land Use Studies, College of Estate Management, Reading.

Hargitay, S. E. and Yu, S- M., (1993) *Property Investment Decisions*, E. & F. N. Spon, London.

Harvey, R. C. and Ashworth, A. (1993) *The Construction Industry of Great Britain*, Newnes, Oxford.

Hillebrandt, P. M. (1985) *Economic Theory and the Construction Industry*, Macmillan Press, London.

Hillebrandt, P. M. and Cannon, J. (1990) *The Modern Construction Firm*, Macmillan Press, London.

Howarth, A. (1995), 'EU Funding: learning how to play the game', *Estates Gazette*, 4 March, pp. 53–5.

Investment Property Databank (1992) *Annual Review 1993*, IPD, London, December.

Isaac, D. (1986) *Corporate Finance and Property Development Funding: An analysis of property companies' capital structures with special reference to the relationship between asset value and share price*, unpublished thesis, Faculty of the Built Environment, South Bank Polytechnic, London.

Isaac, D. (1988) 'Property and Industrial Development', a review of *Property and Industrial Development* by S. Fothergill, S. Monk and M. Perry, *Journal of Local Economy*, vol. 3, no. 1, pp. 56–8.

Isaac, D. (1994) *Property Finance*, Macmillan, London.

Isaac, D. and Dalton, P. (1994) 'Education in the Built Environment: Experiences of a Modular Scheme', *Project*, July, pp. 8–9.

Isaac, D. and O'Grady, M. (1993) 'Thorough Approach the Key to Development Funding', *Property Valuer*, Dublin, Winter.

Isaac, D. and Steley, T. (1991) *Property Valuation Techniques*, Macmillan Press, London.

Isaac, D. and Woodroffe, N. (1987) 'Are Property Company Assets Undervalued?', *Estates Gazette*, 5 September, pp. 1024–6.

Isaac, D. and Woodroffe, N. (1995) *Property Companies: Share Price and Net Asset Value*, Greenwich University Press, London.

Jennings, R. B. (1993) 'The Resurgence of Real Estate Investment Trusts (REITs)' *Journal of Property Finance*, vol. 4, no. 1, pp. 13–19.

Jones Lang Wootton (1989) *The glossary of property terms*, Estates Gazette, London.

Jones, T. and Isaac, D. (1994) 'Finance for the Smaller Building Company and Contractor' *Chartered Institute of Building Directory*, CIOB/Macmillan, London.

Journal of Valuation (1989) 'Market Data' *Journal of Valuation*, vol. 8, no. 1, pp. 87–9.

Keogh, G. (1994) 'Use and Investment Markets in UK Real Estate' *Journal of Property Valuation and Investment*, vol. 12, no. 4.

Latham, M. (1994) *Constructing the Team*, HMSO, London.

Lock, D. (ed.) (1987) *Project Management Handbook*, Gower, Aldershot.

Lumby, S. (1991) *Investment Appraisal and Financing Decisions*, Chapman & Hall, London.

Mackmin, D. (1994) *The Valuation and Sale of Residential Property*, Routledge, London.

MacLeary, A. R. (1991) *National Taxation for Property Management and Valuation*, E. & F. N. Spon, London.

Mallinson, M. (1988) 'Equity Finance' in S. L. Barter (ed.) *Real Estate Finance*, Butterworths, London.

Marriott, O. (1967) *The Property Boom*, Pan Piper, London.

Marshall, P. (1991) 'Development Valuation Techniques', *Research Technical Paper*, RICS, London.

Marshall, P. and Kennedy, C. (1992) 'Development Valuation Techniques' *Journal of Property Valuation and Investment*, vol. 11, no. 1, pp. 57–66.

Masterman, J.W. E. (1992) *An Introduction to Building Procurement Systems*, E. & F . N. Spon, London.

Maxted, B. (1988) *Unitisation of Property*, College of Estate Management, Reading.

McClenaghan, T. (1990) 'The Expert Series: VAT and Property: A Practical Guide' *Journal of Valuation*, vol. 8, no. 4, pp. 394–402.

McIntosh A. and Sykes S. (1985) *A Guide to Institutional Property Investment*, Macmillan Press, London.

McKinney, J. (1982) *Management Contracting*, Chartered Institute of Building *Occasional Paper*, no 30, CIOB, London.

Millman, S. (1988) Property, Property Companies and Public Securities in S. L. Barter (ed.) *Real Estate Finance*, Butterworths, London.

Millman, S. (1993) 'Property, Property Companies and Public Securities', in S. L. Barter (ed.), *Real Estate Finance*, Butterworths, London.

Mitchell, C. and Peake, J. H. (1991) 'The Management of Interest Rate Exposure' *Journal of Property Finance*, vol. 1, no. 4, pp. 530–38.

Mollart, R. (1988) 'Computer briefing: Monte Carlo simulation using Lotus 1-2-3', *Journal of Valuation*, vol. 6, no. 4, pp. 419–33.

Mollart, R. (1994) 'Software Review: Using @Risk for Risk Analysis' *Journal of Property Valuation and Investment*, vol. 12, no. 3, pp. 89–94.

Morgan, P. and Walker, A. (1988) *Retail Development*, Estates Gazette, London.

Morley, S. (1988a) 'Financial Appraisal – Cashflow Approach' in C. Darlow (ed.) *Valuation and Development Appraisal*, Estates Gazette, London.

Morley, S. (1988b) 'Financial Appraisal – Sensitivity and Probability' in C. Darlow (ed.) *Valuation and Development Appraisal*, Estates Gazette, London.

Morley, S. (1988c) 'Partnership Schemes and Ground Rent Calculations' in C. Darlow (ed.) *Valuation and Development Appraisal*, Estates Gazette, London.

Morley, S. (1988d) 'The Residual Method of Valuation' in C. Darlow (ed.) *Valuation and Development Appraisal*, Estates Gazette, London.

Naylor, T. (1994) 'Aspects of Senior Debt Used by and Available to Property Development Companies' *Journal of Property Finance*, vol. 5, no. 1, pp. 23–28.

New Builder (1990) 'Growing Status of Project Managers', *New Builder*, 6 December, pp. 18–19.

Newall, M. (1989) 'Development Appraisals', *Journal of Valuation*, vol. 7, no. 2, pp. 123–33.

Norton, M. D. (1988) 'Market Analysis and Project Evaluation' in C. Darlow (ed.) *Valuation and Development Appraisal*, Estates Gazette, London.

Orchard-Lisle, P. (1987) 'Financing Property Development' *Journal of Valuation*, vol. 5, no. 4, pp. 343–53.

O'Shea, D. (1986) *Investment for Beginners, Financial Times* Business Information, London.

Oxley, J. (1995) 'Enterprise Zones: The Way Forward', *Estates Gazette*, 11 March, pp.120–1.

Paribas Capital Markets (1993) *Monthly Property Share Statistics*, Banque Paribas, November.

Paribas Capital Markets (1995a) *Prospects for the Property Sector*, Banque Paribas, January.

Paribas Capital Markets (1995b) *UK Property Sector Review 1*, Banque Paribas, March.

Pearce, B. (1989) 'Forecasting: An Overview', paper in seminar: *Application of Forecasting Techniques to the Property Market*, RICS/SPR Seminars, Spring 1989.

Peat, M. (1988) 'The Accounting Issues' in S. L. Barter (ed.) *Real Estate Finance*, Butterworths, London.

Pike, R. and Neale, B (1993) *Corporate Finance and Investment*, Prentice-Hall, London.

Project (1994) 'The Association of Project Managers' feedback to the Latham Review', *Project*, July, p. 22.

Project (1995) 'Case Study: Keeping Hong Kong on Target', *Project*, March, pp. 7–8.

Purdy, D. E. (1992) 'Provoking Awareness Through the Provision of Relevant Information in Property Company Accounts', *Journal of Property Finance*, vol. 3, no. 3, pp. 337–46.

Raftery, J. (1991) *Principles of Building Economics*, BSP Professional Books, Oxford.

Raftery, J. (1994) *Risk Analysis in Project Management*, E. & F. N. Spon, London.

Ratcliffe, J. (1978) *An Introduction to Urban Land Administration*, Estates Gazette, London.

Ratcliffe, J. (1983) 'The Valuation of Development Properties' *Journal of Valuation*, vol. 1, no. 1, pp. 24–31, no. 2, pp. 142–52, no. 3 pp. 268–74.

Ratcliffe, J. (1984a) 'Development Financing: Drawing up the Agreement', *Architects Journal*, 22 and 29 August p. 63.

Ratcliffe, J. (1984b) Project Management for Property Development, *Occasional Paper*, Polytechnic of the South Bank, Department of Estate Management, London.

Ratcliffe, J. (1984c) 'Marketing for Development', *Occasional Paper*, Polytechnic of the South Bank, Department of Estate Management, London.

Ratcliffe, J. (1985) ' "Total" Project Management', *Estates Gazette*, 17 August.

Ratcliffe, J. and Butler, J. (1985) 'Marketing', *Estates Gazette*, 7 September.

Ratcliffe, J. and Rapley, N. (1984) 'Development Properties' in W. H. Rees (ed.) *Principles into Practice*, Estates Gazette, London.

Ratcliffe, J. and Scott, G. (1985) 'Funding', *Estates Gazette*, 24 August.

Rees, W. H. (ed.) (1984) *Principles into Practice*, Estates Gazette, London.

Richard Ellis (1986) 'Development Finance', *Property Investment Quarterly Bulletin*, Richard Ellis, London, April.

Riley, M. and Isaac, D. (1991) 'Property Lending Survey 1991' *Journal of Property Finance*, vol. 2, no. 1, pp. 74–7.

Riley, M. and Isaac, D. (1992) 'Property Lending Survey 1992' *Journal of Property Finance*, vol. 2, no. 4, pp. 38–41.

Riley, M. and Isaac, D. (1993a) 'Property Lending Survey 1993' *Journal of Property Finance*, vol. 4, no. 1, pp. 43–8.

Riley, M. and Isaac, D. (1993b) 'Commercial Property Lending: Confidence Survey' *Journal of Property Finance*, vol. 4, no. 3.

Riley, M. and Isaac, D. (1994) 'Property Lending Survey 1994' *Journal of Property Finance*, vol. 5, no. 1, pp. 45–51.

Rogers Chapman *Project Management: a client's guide*, Rogers Chapman, London.

Ross, S. A., Westerfield, R. W. and Jaffe, J. F. (1993) *Corporate Finance*, Irwin, Boston.

Rougvie, A. (1987) *Project Evaluation and Development*, Mitchell, London.

Royal Institution of Chartered Surveyors (RICS) (1985) *The Unitisation of Real Property*, RICS, London.

Royal Institution of Chartered Surveyors (RICS) (1995) *Valuation of Development Land, Draft Consultation Paper,* RICS, London, January.

Rydin, Y., Rodney, W. and Orr, C. (1990) 'Why Do Institutions Invest in Property', *Journal of Property Finance,* vol. 1, no. 2, pp. 250–8.

Ryland, D. (1991) 'Authorised Property Unit Trusts', *Estates Gazette,* 9 November, pp. 163–4.

Ryland, D. S. (1992) 'Changes in accounting rules' *Journal of Property Finance,* vol. 3, no. 1, pp. 28–37.

Savills (1989) *Financing Property 1989,* Savills, London.

Savills (1993a) *Financing Property 1993,* Savills, London.

Savills (1993b) *Investment and Economic Outlook,* Savills, London, issue 3, October.

Schiller, R. (1994) 'Comment: The Interface between Valuation and Forecasting', *Journal of Property Valuation and Investment,* vol. 12, no. 4, pp. 3–6.

Scott, I. P. (1992) 'Debt, Liquidity and Secondary Trading in Property Debt' *Journal of Property Finance,* vol. 3, no. 3, pp. 347–55.

Scrimgeor Vickers & Co. (1986) *United Kingdom Research, Annual Property Report,* Scrimgeor Vickers & Co. London.

Seeley, I. H. (1984) *Quantity Surveying Practice,* Macmillan Press, London.

Seeley, I. H. (1995) *Building Economics,* Macmillan Press, London.

Sexton, P. and Laxton, C. (1992) 'Authorised Property Unit Trusts' *Journal of Property Finance,* vol. 2, no. 4, pp. 468–75

S. G. Warburg Securities (1993) *UK Property: Review of 1992 and Prospects for 1993,* S. G. Warburg, London.

S. G. Warburg Research (1993) *U.K. Property: Monthly Review,* S. G. Warburg, London, November.

Shale, A. (1991) 'The Use of Deep Discount and Zero Coupon Bonds in the UK Property Market' *Journal of Property Finance,* vol. 2, no. 1, pp. 11–17.

Sieracki, K. (1993) 'U.K. Institutional Requirements for European Property', *Estates Gazette,* July 17, p. 116.

Smee, R. (1992) 'Capitalisation of Interest for Property Companies' *Journal of Property Finance,* vol. 3, no. 1, pp. 13–22.

Smith, R. (1988) *Development Construction Costs* in C Darlow (ed.) *Valuation and Development Appraisal,* Estates Gazette, London.

Taylor, N. P. (1991), *Development Site Evaluation,* Macmillan Press, London.

Temple, P. (1992) 'How to Beat a Hostile Takeover' *Journal of Property Finance,* vol. 2, no. 4, pp. 476–83.

Turner, A. (1990) *Building Procurement,* Macmillan Press, London.

Turner, R., McLauchin, J. J., Thomas, R. D. and Hastings, C. (1994) 'A Vision of Project Management in 2020', *Project Management Yearbook,* Association of Project Managers, pp. 30–1.

UBS Global Research (1993) *UK Equities: Property Perspective,* UBS Ltd, January.

UBS Global Research (1995) *UK Property Service: Company ranking by market capitalisation,* UBS, London, January.

Venmore-Rowland, P. (1991) '*Vehicles for Property'* Investment in P. Venmore-Rowland, P. Brandon and T. Mole (eds), *Investment, Procurement and Performance in Construction,* RICS, London.

Walker, A. (1989) *Project Management in Construction,* BSP Professional Books, Oxford.

Westcott, D. J. (1988) *Tax and Property Development* in C. Darlow (ed.) *Valuation and Development Appraisal,* Estates Gazette, London.

Westwick, C. A. (1980) *Property Valuation and Accounts,* Institute of Chartered Accountants in England and Wales, London.

Whipple, R.T. M. (1988) 'Evaluating Development Projects', *Journal of Valuation,* vol. 6, no. 3, pp. 253–86.

Williams, R. H. and Wood, B. (1994) *Urban Land and Property Market in the United Kingdom,* UCL Press, London.

Willis, C. J. and Ashworth, A. (1987) *Practice and Procedures for the Quantity Surveyor,* BSP Professional Books, Oxford.

Wright, K. (1994) 'Company profitability and finance' *Bank of England: Quarterly Bulletin,* vol. 34 no. 3, August.

Wolfe, R. (1988) *'Debt Finance'* in S. L. Barter (ed.) *Real Estate Finance,* Butterworths, London.

Woodroffe, N. and Isaac, D. (1987) 'Corporate Finance and Property Development Funding', *Working Paper* of the School of Applied Economics and Social Studies, Faculty of the Built Environment, South Bank Polytechnic, London.

Wyles, M. (1990) 'Mortgage Indemnity – A Risk/Reward Arbitrage' *Journal of Property Finance,* vol. 1 no. 3 pp. 378–86.

Yates, A. (1991) *'Procurement and Construction Management'* in P. Venmore-Rowland, P. Brandon and T. Mole (eds), *Investment, Procurement and Performance in Construction,* RICS, London.

Yuen Ka Yin, McKinnell, K. and Isaac, D. (1988) *The Unitisation of Real Property in Hong Kong* unpublished research paper, Hong Kong University and University of Greenwich.

Index